JESUS

AN ILLUSTRATED LIFE

JEAN-PIERRE ISBOUTS
BEST-SELLING AUTHOR OF *In the Footsteps of Jesus*

NATIONAL GEOGRAPHIC

WASHINGTON, D.C.

CONTENTS

Page 1: A remnant of the Oxyrhynchus Papyri, probably dating to the third century C.E., includes a fragment from the Gospel of Matthew.
Pages 2–3: The Judean Wilderness evokes the serenity of the desert where Jesus prepared for his ministry.
Opposite: This 12th-century Byzantine mosaic of Jesus was created for Hagia Sophia in Constantinople, now Istanbul.

Introduction

According to a recent study by Pew Research Center, some 70 percent of American adults identify themselves as Christian. But *how* these Christians practice their faith is another matter. As I described in my 2014 book, *The Story of Christianity,* Christendom has always suffered from schisms and conflicting traditions, but never more so than in our modern times. Today, the Christian world is split across a wide spectrum of confessions: Protestant, Catholic, Mormon, Orthodox, Evangelical, Pentecostal, Fundamentalist, and other, more discrete movements around the globe.

This begs the question: What does it mean to be a Christian today? Could we identify some form of consensus among today's denominations, given their widely different views on faith, doctrine, and social issues? Is there a place where Christians can find common ground?

I wrote this book in an effort to answer at least part of that question. While it is certainly difficult to agree on all matters of faith and doctrine, one thing must surely be true: If we profess ourselves to be followers of Jesus, then the story of his life should serve as an inspiration to us all. Indeed, it is this story, as documented in the Gospels, that forms the very foundation of the Christian experience. It is also the subject of this book.

Of course, scores of books have been written about Jesus. But the idea of creating a new, illustrated story of his life, as seen through the Gospels, is certainly appropriate. New archaeological discoveries in the Holy Land continue to yield fascinating insights into the way people lived in the Galilee of Jesus' time. In addition, multidisciplinary research has

produced a better grasp of the unique social and economic fabric of Galilean society under the autocratic rule of the Herodians. Other modern research helps us to understand the uniquely Jewish framework of Jesus' teachings, as well as the allegorical meaning of biblical citations in the Gospel stories.

In some ways, then, this book is an ideal complement to National Geographic's 2012 publication of *In the Footsteps of Jesus*. In that book, I told the story of Jesus through the historical lens of two of the most important events in Antiquity: the rise of the Roman Empire and the growth of Roman Christianity. In this book, by contrast, we will not follow Jesus from the perspective of history, but try to *live in his world*. As we move from one Gospel event to the next, we will imagine what it was like to sit in the synagogue of Capernaum as Jesus read from the scrolls; or to feel the breeze from the Sea of Galilee while standing on the mountain, listening to his sermons; or to walk with him along the Jordan River, under the burning sun, on our way up to Jerusalem.

ABOVE: *The city of Scythopolis, the biblical Beth She'an, was a member of the Decapolis and the most Romanized city west of the Jordan River.*

OPPOSITE: *A coin, struck in Caesarea during the reign of Emperor Hadrian (r. 117–138), shows a man with a yoke of oxen, illustrating the rural character of Roman Palestine.*

TENSIONS IN GALILEE

Along the way, we will discover that Jesus' ministry coincided with many transformative changes in Judea and Galilee. Judea, previously the core of an autonomous kingdom ruled by Herod, was now a Roman province, governed by a Roman official or prefect. In Galilee, the ruthless Herodian tax regime had pushed thousands of farmers and their families from their ancestral lands. And Galilee's mostly rural Jewish character was increasingly threatened by the encroachment of Greco-Roman urban culture, as illustrated by the construction of two large cities, Sepphoris and Tiberias.

All of these developments led many people to conclude that their lives, and indeed their identity as observant Jews, were under threat. There was a palpable sense that the nation was sliding into a moral abyss—a feeling that was already expressed in the apocalyptic Book of Daniel, written in the second century B.C.E. This produced a deep yearning for deliverance, not only in a political but also a spiritual sense. Many believed that this redemption would be realized with the coming of the Messiah, a descendant from the line of David, who would restore the nation of Israel as a kingdom of God. How this Messiah would accomplish this restoration was not always clear; some believed he would evict the Romans and all other enemies by military means, while others thought his coming would be heralded by cataclysmic disasters. But all believed that in the end, the Messiah would once again establish a sovereign nation governed by the covenant made between God and Moses on Mount Sinai.

The primary purpose of the Gospel stories is to show that Jesus *was* that Messiah—but with an important qualification. Rather than a restoration of Israel by military means or as a new political entity, Jesus saw the Kingdom of God in very different terms, as this book illustrates.

THE FOUR GOSPELS

In following the life of Jesus, we will be guided primarily by the Gospels of Matthew, Mark, Luke, and John. Although Matthew's Gospel appears in first place in most Christian Bibles, the oldest Gospel is actually that of Mark. Many scholars agree that Mark's Gospel was probably written between 66 and 73 C.E., during or shortly after the First Jewish Revolt in Roman-occupied Judea. It is likely (though not certain) that Mark wrote his Gospel for a Christian congregation in Rome, at a time when the Jewish community in Rome would have fallen under intense suspicion. This was also a time when Roman sons went off to fight in faraway Judea to try to suppress the Jewish rebellion.

Emperor Augustus, here seen as Pontifex Maximus, *or chief priest (ca 12 B.C.E.), created an Imperial administrative system that remained valid for more than two centuries.*

In writing his Gospel, Mark probably relied on oral traditions about Jesus that had been circulating among Christian communities for several decades. Whether any of these traditions were available in written form is not known. Some scholars have speculated on the presence of so-called sayings documents, essentially records of citations and statements by Jesus. The so-called Gospel of Thomas, a Gospel text not included in the New Testament canon, is a remarkable example of such a possible sayings document about Jesus, but the version that has come down to us appears to be much later than the original Gospels.

Mark's Gospel formed the basis for the next two Gospels, those of Matthew and Luke, probably written between the 70s and 80s. Some believe that around 600 verses from Mark's text were incorporated by the two evangelists. But both authors also had access to other oral or written traditions about Jesus, including a putative source referred to as "Q." That is why the work of Matthew and Luke includes stories that do not appear in Mark.

There are, of course, other subtle differences. Whereas Mark's Gospel is a straightforward account of Jesus' life and ministry, written in rather basic Greek, Luke's version is remarkable for its great imagination and literary skill. Several

This detail of a third-century mosaic, known as the "Mona Lisa from Galilee," was discovered in a Roman villa of Sepphoris in the 1980s.

A first-century Roman fresco of fishermen surrounded by exotic fish species is testimony to the high realism of art from the Imperial era.

scholars have suggested that Luke was an educated author who cast his Gospel in the template of Greek history writing used throughout the Greco-Roman world. In following this format, Luke was careful to frame the narrative with both historical and symbolic references: the first to bolster the authenticity of the story and the second to explain its meaning. A key example of such a symbolism, widely used in Hebrew Scripture, was to herald the birth of a principal protagonist with angelic prophecies or miraculous portents. This signaled to readers that the child was meant to play a highly significant role as part of God's plan for humanity. Luke's great skill, and the key to his Gospel's popularity, is the way in which he was able to blend the Greek literary genre with the style and poetry of Hebrew Scripture. Because of their similarity, the three Gospels of Mark, Matthew, and Luke are sometimes called the synoptic Gospels (from the Greek *synoptikos*, literally "viewed together").

The Gospel of John, written near the end of the first century, develops a different emphasis. Written for a Gentile audience—to the extent that John must explain certain Jewish terms, such as Passover—this Gospel presents Jesus not only as the Jewish Messiah, but also first and foremost as the Son of God (John 1:18). John's Gospel, rather light on biographical details, instead focuses on developing Jesus' ideas as part of a highly articulate theology. He presents these ideas in the form of long monologues of great oratorical power that do not appear in the other Gospels. This is why some scholars have questioned the value of John's Gospel as a source for the historical Jesus. New research, however, has shown that this Gospel does have important historical roots that, as its prologue states, could be traced to an eyewitness account by a man named "John"—quite possibly a disciple of Jesus (John 1:19).

WHAT IF THE GOSPELS WERE WRITTEN TODAY?

We should also recognize that if the Gospels were written today, they would probably be very different. For example, there would be a much better sense of time, of the chronology of the story. In our modern world, everything is governed by time. When something happens, we want to know *when* it happened. For us, a biography can give an accurate portrait of a person's life only if we see the story in its correct sequence, so we can understand the psychological evolution of a person's identity, as well as his motives and actions. We are creatures of the 21st century, used to seeing narratives compressed in a linear arc in media such as television, motion pictures, and fiction.

But in Antiquity, people experienced stories very differently. Media, of any kind, did not exist. Time was measured mainly by the movement of the sun and the cycle of seasons and religious festivals. As a result, people were less interested in the dating and sequencing of events than in their meaning, their *purpose*. This explains why people in Jesus' time did not distinguish as clearly between *factual* truth and *moral* truth, as we would today. For us, something is of significance only if it actually happened. That's because newspapers, other media, and the Internet keep us informed about what's going on almost on a minute-by-minute basis. But people in first-century Galilee experienced truth very differently. They had no means to determine whether a story was factually true, and as a result they didn't particularly care. They were more interested in what a story meant for them individually, and if it could communicate something of value for their own welfare and that of their families. That is why *signs*, such as miracles, visions, or dreams, were far more important in authenticating a story than its historical context.

In response, the evangelists wrote their stories on two levels. On one level, they report the life and teachings of Jesus in a way that made sense to them— by organizing them thematically. And on the other, they try to explain to their mostly illiterate audience what these stories mean, why they are important, and why they should be cherished. The evangelists do so in the form of allegory—by invoking symbolic motifs and parallel stories from the only literary work that

A Torah scroll of wood and parchment, made in Northern Europe, is believed to date from the 15th century.

almost everyone was familiar with: Hebrew Scripture, the Old Testament.

In other words, if we tried to interpret these stories in a purely literal sense, we would be missing much of their implicit meaning. To truly understand this rich tapestry of story and symbolism, we must read the Gospels with new eyes: through the eyes of the first-century believers for whom these stories were written.

THE JEWISH LAW

We must also try to grasp the unique role that Jewish Law played in virtually every aspect of a person's life. In our modern world, we tend to separate work and faith. We isolate the office and the church as two distinct spheres of our lives. But in the Jewish-observant villages of Galilee, there was no distinction among faith, work, and home life, for all were governed by the precepts of the Torah, the Jewish Law, as described in great detail in the first five books of Hebrew Scripture.

This separation is not always understood. In the past few decades, several authors have tried to interpret Jesus' teachings from a single perspective, using a social, political, or religious focus, such as the recent attempt to

The Jerusalem Citadel, dating from the Mamluk and Ottoman periods, was originally built on the remains of a Herodian fortress from the time of Jesus.

portray Jesus as a Zealot. This approach is fundamentally flawed. The truth is that Jesus' teachings touched on all three domains, for in his world, they were inseparable.

As a Jewish rabbi, a "teacher," Jesus urged his listeners to abide by the Law, since the Torah lay at the core of what it meant to be Jewish—especially when that identity was under threat from other cultures and ideas. "Truly I tell you," Jesus says in the Gospel of Matthew, "until heaven and earth pass away, not one letter, not one stroke of a letter, will pass from the law until all is accomplished" (Matthew 5:18).

But in the same breath, Jesus argued for a compassionate *interpretation* of the Law rather than mindless obedience. More than any other Jewish preacher of his time, Jesus was deeply concerned with the social injustices of Lower Galilee, particularly the rampant hunger, poverty, and displacement among the Galilean peasantry (Luke 6:20-23) and the growing gap between the poor and the elites who "stored their wealth in barns" (Luke 12:13-21). He believed that the spirit, rather than the letter, of the Torah should be followed. Or as he puts it in the Gospel of Mark, "The Sabbath was made for man, not man for the Sabbath" (Mark 2:27). This may surprise some readers, but in trying to adapt the ancient rules of the Torah to the changing needs of the Jewish people during the Roman Era, Jesus was much closer to the Pharisees than we might think.

Explaining and debating the daily application of the Law was a central preoccupation of the Pharisaic community. Their debates were preserved in a collection known as the "Oral Law," which around 200 C.E. produced a book known as the Mishnah.

Jesus: An Illustrated Life is deliberately written from a nondenominational perspective. As has become common practice in National Geographic publications, this book uses the temporal indicators of B.C.E. (Before the Common Era) instead of the traditional B.C. (Before Christ) and C.E. (Common Era) rather than A.D. (*Anno Domini* or Year of the Lord) to identify key dates in history.

Finally, some of the most exciting new sources about the time of Jesus are the discoveries that archaeologists continue to make in the Holy Land, particularly at recent digs in Sepphoris, Magdala, and Bethsaida in Israel, as well as the East Bank of the Jordan River in the Kingdom of Jordan. By illustrating this story with the tangible products of this forensic quest, including pottery, textiles, utensils, inscriptions, and artifacts, I hope to truly transport readers to the Lower Galilee of the early first century and imagine what it was like to live in the time of Jesus. ■

A Roman glass pitcher, perhaps used for pouring wine, has a delicate luster glaze attesting to the sophistication of first-century glassblowing techniques.

CHAPTER ONE

THE PROPHECY OF JOHN'S BIRTH

In the days of King Herod of Judea, there was a priest named Zechariah, who belonged to the priestly order of Abijah.

LUKE 1:5

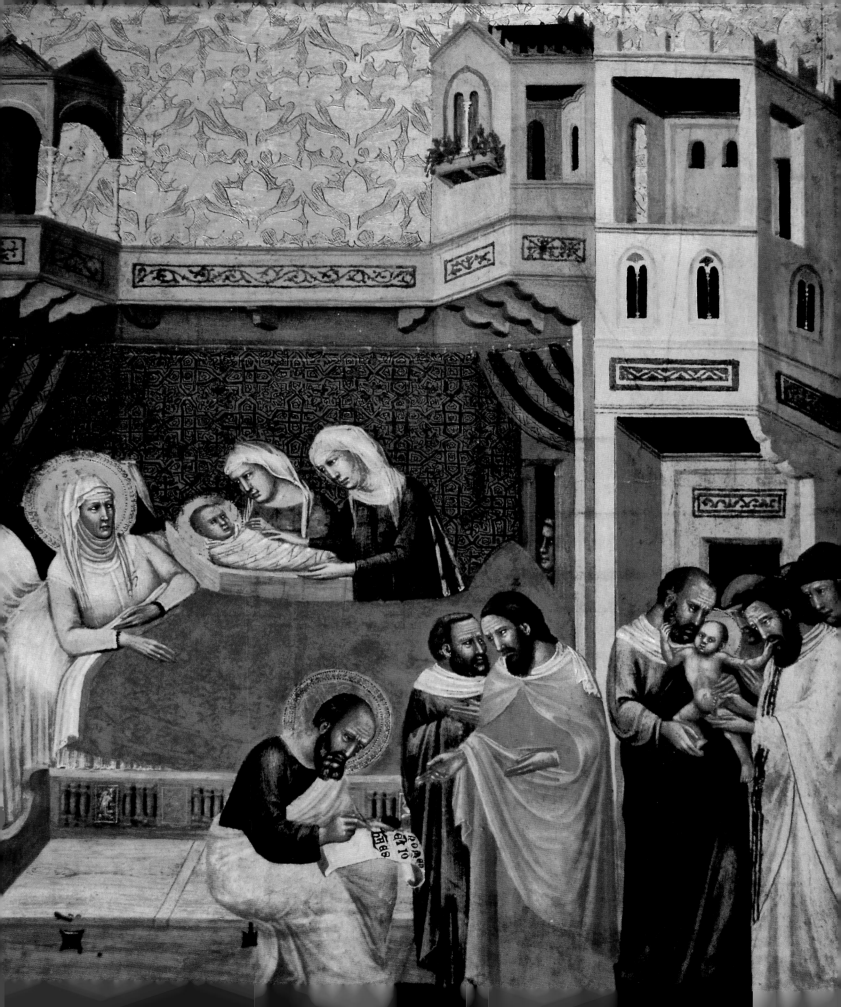

The Story of Zechariah in the Temple

In the year 5 B.C.E., King Herod the Great had been on his throne for more than 30 years. From his palace in Jerusalem, he ruled over a land whose borders evoked the legendary kingdom of David, comprising not only Galilee, Samaria, and the heartland of Judea, but also large regions east of the Sea of Galilee, such as Gaulanitis and Batanea, as well as the territory to the south known as Idumea, which pushed deep into the Negev desert. Although he governed these lands as a vassal prince of Rome, Herod behaved for all the world as an autonomous king, maintaining a sumptuous court while building cities and monuments with the trappings of pagan Roman culture. This may have pleased his Roman masters, but it infuriated his Jewish subjects.

As a conciliatory gesture to Jewish sensibilities, Herod decided to vastly expand the Temple in Jerusalem. This great Jewish sanctuary, which would play such an important role in the Gospel stories, had originally been built by King Solomon, only to be destroyed by the Neo-Babylonian king Nebuchadnezzar in 586 B.C.E. Seventy years later, as described in the books of Haggai and Zechariah, it was rebuilt with the support of the Persian king Cyrus the Great. This is why historians refer to the period between 515 B.C.E. and C.E. 70, including the life and times of Jesus, as the Second Temple period.

Even Roman Emperor Augustus recognized the unique role the sacrificial rites at the Temple played for Judaism. In an

unprecedented decree, he exempted the Jews of Judea from the duty, enforced throughout the rest of the empire, of offering sacrifices to statues of the reigning emperor. He even authorized the collection of Temple taxes throughout his realm, warning Roman governors "that their sacred offerings shall be inviolable," and therefore exempt from Roman taxation.

Around 22 B.C.E., Herod's architects set to work. Their task was to turn the modest Second Temple into one of the largest sanctuaries of the ancient world. To do so, they designed a vast forecourt around the Temple, ringed by a double colonnade, which would feature numerous facilities such as a large stoa or basilica along its southern perimeter. Since the Temple was built on the summit of a hill, the builders created a vast platform supporting the forecourt, supported by massive arches and retaining walls that towered high above the Lower City of Jerusalem. It is in this vast Temple complex, the largest structure in all of Roman Judea and Syria, that Luke placed the beginning of the story of Jesus.

ABOVE: *A view of a model of the Second Temple in Jerusalem shows the large Court of Women, looking toward the Nicanor Gate and the Temple proper.*

OPPOSITE: *An eighth-century fresco fragment from the Church of Santa Sofia in Benevento, Italy, represents the angel's announcement to Zechariah.*

PRECEDING PAGES: *"The Birth of John the Baptist" was painted by the Master of the Life of St. John the Baptist (active second quarter, 14th century) between 1330 and 1340 in Rimini, Italy.*

A PRIEST NAMED ZECHARIAH

Unlike a synagogue, the primary purpose of the Temple was not to serve as a communal space for liturgy or scripture readings, but rather as the focal point for the sacrificial rites prescribed in the Torah, the Jewish Law, as well as for prayer and collecting tithes and other offerings. This sacrificial cult, which involved the slaughter and sacrifice of various animals "without blemish," was supervised by a priestly community. By the time Jesus was born, this community was dominated by a highly conservative priestly aristocracy known as the Sadducees. Much of their wealth derived from the fact that the Temple treasury, or *korbanas,* containing tithes from Jewish communities throughout the empire, also served as a central bank of sorts. As Jerusalem's elite, the Sadducees occupied the finest mansions in the Upper City; one of these palatial residences, belonging to the high priest Caiaphas, would later serve as the location of Jesus' indictment after his arrest.

"Overview of the Temple Complex in Jerusalem" is a colored engraving by Charles Mottram (1807–1876), inspired by the works of the first-century historian Josephus.

The Sadducees were assisted by hundreds of priestly officials, including 24 divisions of Levites, each scheduled to serve in the Temple twice a year. One of these Levites opens Luke's Gospel. "In the days of King Herod of Judea," the evangelist says, using the usual formula of marking a date in ancient times, "there was a priest named Zechariah, who belonged to the priestly order of Abijah"—the

The Western Wall in Jerusalem is one of the original supporting walls of the Second Temple and the most important religious site in modern Judaism.

eighth of the 24 Levite divisions serving in the Temple on a rota system. Such Levites usually chose their wives from within the priestly community. Indeed, Luke introduces Zechariah's wife as "a descendant of Aaron, and her name was Elizabeth" (Luke 1:5). Aaron was the brother of Moses, the first high priest and the ancestor of the priestly line; thus, both Zechariah and Elizabeth had an impeccable pedigree, deeply rooted in Jewish liturgical life. But tragedy had befallen the couple; they were childless, so Zechariah's line was doomed to end.

Luke then moves the story inside the Temple proper. "Once when he was serving as priest before God," he writes, Zechariah was prompted to "enter the sanctuary of the Lord and offer incense" on the golden altar, just outside the Holy of Holies, a very great honor. He was chosen to do so by lot, Luke explains for his audience, which included Gentile Christians, "according to the custom of the priesthood."

A delicate glass bottle, used for precious perfumes or ointments, reveals the artistry of Roman glassblowing techniques developed in the first century C.E.

> *When [Zechariah] did come out, he could not speak to them, and they realized that he had seen a vision in the sanctuary.*
>
> LUKE 1:22

We should remember, however, that when Luke wrote these lines, somewhere between 75 and 85 C.E., the Temple no longer existed. The entire sanctuary complex was destroyed by Roman forces in 70 C.E. after a long and bloody siege. It would be difficult to overstate the trauma of this event for the Jews and Jewish Christians of Luke's time; perhaps it is comparable to the collective shock Americans experienced in the wake of the September 11 attacks. At one stroke, the center of ancient Judaism, and indeed its raison d'être as a sacrificial cult, had been wiped from the Earth.

And so Luke's decision to set the beginning of his Gospel on this hallowed ground, this beautiful sanctuary now tragically lost, must have served a very specific purpose—although at this early stage, that meaning is still a mystery. For as we will see, the Temple plays a crucial role in Luke's narrative—not only as one of its principal locations but also as a vivid symbol of Jesus' ultimate mission on Earth.

THE ANGEL'S PROPHECY

Luke writes that as Zechariah stood inside the Temple, "at the right side

THE TEMPLE PRIESTHOOD

The Jerusalem Temple was traditionally managed by a dedicated priesthood, defined by genealogy, which included a large body of chief priests, priestly officials, and Levite assistants supervising the ritual sacrifices in the forecourt of the Temple. From the second century B.C.E., this priestly community became increasingly dominated by a group known as Sadducees (*Tzedoqim* in Hebrew), a wealthy and archconservative group that claimed its ancestry from the high priest Zadok. The members welcomed the advent of the Roman occupation in 63 B.C.E. and collaborated with the local Roman authorities when Judea became a Roman province in 6 C.E. Their principal opposition were the Pharisees, a coalition of priests and pious laymen who scrupulously observed Covenant Law. They distinguished themselves by their views on cultic purity (the Hebrew term *perushim* means "separated ones"). While the Sadducees believed that ritual sacrifice was the only way for a person to please God, the Pharisees sought to extend the holiness and purity of the Temple to the lives of ordinary people. ∎

A modern illustration shows the corner of the Second Temple complex with the so-called Robinson's Arch, the principal gateway from Jerusalem's Lower City.

of the altar of incense," an angel appeared. Zechariah was terrified. But the angel said, "Do not be afraid, Zechariah, for your prayer has been heard. Your wife Elizabeth will bear you a son, and you will name him John." Luke probably modeled this verse on the story of Abraham and Sarah in Genesis, in which God told Abraham that "Sarah your wife shall bear you a son, and you shall call him Isaac" (Genesis 17:19). Luke then added another narrative layer, inspired by the story of Hannah and Elkanah in the first Book of Samuel. Like Sarah, Hannah was unable to give her husband a child. She prayed to God and promised that if she bore a son, she would raise him to become a Nazirite, a person devoted to the service of God. "He shall drink neither wine nor intoxicants," Hannah pledged, "and no razor shall touch his head" (Samuel 1:11). In Luke's Gospel, the angel tells Zechariah, "He must never drink wine or strong drink; even before his birth he will be filled with the Holy Spirit" (Luke 1:12-15).

This lovely 16th-century stained-glass window from the Church of Sainte Madeleine in Troyes, France, depicts the Pharisees gathered in the synagogue.

The purpose of these subtle allusions is to create a parallel between Luke's Gospel and Hebrew Scripture. Just as Hannah, long barren, gave birth to the prophet Samuel, so too did Elizabeth miraculously give birth to John the Baptist. And just as Samuel once anointed David, the king of Israel, so too would John the Baptist baptize Jesus as the Davidic Messiah in the waters of the Jordan.

Zechariah could not believe the angel's words because he and his wife were already advanced in age. "How will I know that this is so?" he asked incredulously. In response, Gabriel struck him deaf and mute until the day that his son would be born. When Zechariah emerged from the Temple, he was unable to speak. But everything came to pass as the angel had foretold. "After those days," Luke continues, "his wife Elizabeth conceived, and for five months she remained in seclusion" (Luke 1:24).

According to a fifth-century tradition, Zechariah and Elizabeth lived in the picturesque village of Ein Kerem, set among terraced vineyards some 12 miles southwest of Jerusalem. In Byzantine times, a church was built on the reputed site of Elizabeth's house. It was destroyed and rebuilt several times, but a grotto underneath the current church is still believed by some to contain the remains of a first-century dwelling. ■

FOLLOWING PAGES: *Italian Renaissance artist Domenico Ghirlandaio (1449-1494) painted this fresco of the "Annunciation of the Angel to Zechariah" in the Santa Maria Novella in Florence.*

CHAPTER TWO

THE ANNUNCIATION

*In the sixth month
the angel Gabriel was sent
by God to a town in
Galilee called Nazareth,
to a virgin engaged
to a man whose name
was Joseph.*

LUKE 1:26-27

A Young Woman of Nazareth Receives Great News

Few other themes in the Gospels have so enthralled artists as that of the Annunciation, the moment the angel Gabriel appeared before Mary to tell her that she would conceive a child by the power of the Holy Spirit. From medieval times onward, Mary has been depicted as a well-dressed young woman, reclining comfortably in the bourgeois surroundings that reflected the taste of the artist's donors. In reality, however, Mary (Maryam in Aramaic) was probably a girl of barely 13, working tirelessly alongside her mother in their humble home in Nazareth, most likely a small stone dwelling with an improvised thatched roof.

Her tiny hands were already experienced at the spindle, since her mother had taught her from an early age how to roll strands of wool or flax into spinning yarn, just as she knew how to knead dough for bread and help crush the olives from her family's orchard. Like all other girls her age, not only in her village but also throughout Lower Galilee, she was quietly being groomed for marriage, for her menses had started and the day of her wedding was nigh. That meant she had to learn to bake bread in the morning and cook stew with bits of fish at night, while feeding the animals, washing clothes, bartering foodstuffs with neighbors and relatives, and working the loom in what little spare time was left, weaving garments for her family. In the early first century, the village of Nazareth was a small hamlet, located some 7 miles from the Sea of Galilee and just 12 miles southeast of the regional capital, the city of Sepphoris. On market days—Mondays and Thursdays—the farmers of Nazareth traveled

to Sepphoris to sell their olives and olive oil, as well as their wheat, barley, and dates. Mary's parents were probably subsistence farmers as well. During excavations underneath the current Basilica of the Annunciation, traditionally believed to be the site of Mary's home, Franciscan archaeologist Bellarmino Bagatti found granaries, olive presses, and wells that he dated to the first or second century C.E.

As the daughter of a farmer's family, eking out a living from small ancestral plots, Mary would have been dressed like most other Galilean girls. A simple linen undergarment, which she also wore when she slept, was covered with a sleeveless garment, made from two strips of cloth, as wide as the loom allowed. As a concession to her budding femininity, this simple tunic was equipped with fringes on the bottom and tightened around her waist with a ribbon. Many centuries later, during the Renaissance, Mary would invariably be depicted in a flowing garment of aquamarine blue (the richest and most expensive color available), but such was far from the truth. As the Gospels clearly show, Mary and Joseph were poor, and luxuries were well beyond their reach.

ABOVE: *The rolling fields of the Beit Netofa Valley near Nazareth, Israel, have not changed much from the days of Mary and Joseph in the early first century B.C.E.*

OPPOSITE: *This woven shirt of a young woman was found in the Cave of Letters in the Judean Desert, which housed refugees from the Second Jewish War (ca 132–135 C.E.).*

PRECEDING PAGES: *Italian Renaissance artist Filippo Lippi (ca 1406–1469), a Carmelite friar, painted this panel of the Annunciation of the angel Gabriel to Mary.*

This detail of the angel Gabriel is taken from a fresco by Italian Renaissance artist Sandro Botticelli (ca 1445–1510), painted around 1481 in San Martino della Scala.

GABRIEL'S MESSAGE

And then, one day, this heavenly apparition arrived, this messenger named Gabriel, who entered Mary's home unannounced and startled the girl with the words, "Greetings, favored one! The Lord is with you" (Luke 1:28). Mary was taken aback. In first-century Galilee, grown men usually ignored pubescent girls who were not part of their immediate family. A more likely greeting would have been, "Is your mother home?" But this stranger clearly wanted to speak to Mary, even though he saw the evident distress on her young face.

"Do not be afraid, Mary," he said, "for you have found favor with God." Pausing a moment, he added the words that would change Mary's life, and indeed the world, forever: "And now, you will conceive in your womb and bear a son, and you will name him Jesus" (Luke 1:31).

Mary was stunned. She knew that her parents had betrothed her to a man named Joseph, whose family originally hailed from Judea, from the house of David in Bethlehem. That meant that a wedding contract, or *ketubah*, had already been executed between the two families, but the wedding itself had not yet taken place. Mary's response was therefore perfectly logical. "How can this be," she asked, "since I am a virgin?" In Luke's original Greek, her response is "since I do not know a man," meaning that she hasn't had marital relations yet. But the meaning is the same: Luke wants to emphasize Mary's status as a virgin (*parthenos* in Greek), untouched by man, so as to stress the divine nature of what is about to happen.

Gabriel then explained, "The Holy Spirit will come upon you, and the power of the Most High will overshadow you; therefore the child to be born will be holy;

> *[Mary] will bear a son, and you are to name him Jesus, for he will save his people from their sins.*

MATTHEW 1:21

he will be called Son of God." This rush of information, so filled with emotional and theological meaning, must have overwhelmed the poor girl. Perhaps seeing the stricken look on Mary's face, Gabriel moved to reassure her, saying that "nothing will be impossible with God." After all, he continued, "your relative Elizabeth in her old age has also conceived a son" even though she was said to be barren (Luke 1:36-37).

JOSEPH'S RESPONSE

The Gospel of Matthew also describes the virginal conception, albeit in more laconic terms. "When his mother Mary had been engaged to Joseph, but before they lived together," Matthew writes, "she was found to be with child from the Holy Spirit" (Matthew 1:18). The phrase "lived together" is important, because under Jewish Law, a couple was considered to be married as soon as their union was consummated. A premarital pregnancy involving a man other than the future groom would therefore invalidate the wedding contract, and it put Mary at risk of being ostracized in her village community. It would have exposed her—and her future child—to condemnation and shame. According to Deuteronomy, a woman who was engaged to be married but found to have lost her virginity could be stoned to death on the steps of her father's house (Deuteronomy 22:20-21). Even Paul, who makes no reference to Mary's virgin birth in his letters, extols virginity as a woman's perfect condition (I Corinthians 7).

We can imagine Joseph's reaction when he heard the news that Mary, his fiancée, was pregnant. Matthew says that "her husband Joseph, being a righteous man and unwilling to expose her to public disgrace, planned to

These bundles of wool belonged to women who fled with their families into the Cave of Letters, in the Judean Desert, during the Second Jewish War (ca 132–135 C.E.).

dismiss her quietly." It is only after "an angel of the Lord" appeared to him in a dream to explain that "the child conceived in her is from the Holy Spirit" that Joseph agreed to take Mary as his wife after all (Matthew 1:19-20).

As a midrash, a Jewish exegetical story, the Annunciation narratives in both Matthew and Luke follow the literary tradition of Hebrew Scripture. The miraculous power of God to create life where none was expected, and the device of angels to announce such news to unsuspecting women, are motifs found throughout the Bible. Thus, it was that Abraham's wife, Sarah, conceived, even though she was already of an advanced age, and that Jacob's beloved wife, Rachel, gave birth to Joseph even though her womb was closed.

> *In those days Mary set out and went with haste to a Judean town in the hill country, where she entered the house of Zechariah.*
>
> **LUKE 1:39**

But the second part of Gabriel's message, telling Mary that her child will be holy and be called a Son of God, also followed biblical precedent. The appellation "Son of God" is used in Hebrew Scripture to denote David and all of his royal descendants. In Psalm 2, God says to his "anointed" (*Mashiach* in Hebrew, meaning "Messiah"), "You are my son; today I have begotten you" (Psalms 2:7). The second Book of Samuel, moreover, describes God's promise to David as follows: "I will raise up *your* offspring after you, *who shall come forth from your body,* and I will establish his kingdom . . . I will be *a* father to him, and he shall be *a* son to me" (II Samuel 7:12-14).

Luke's passage therefore presents the birth of Jesus as the fulfillment of biblical prophecy in Hebrew Scripture—both as the future Messiah, the "anointed one," as well as the man who will be called Son of God. These ideas are succinctly combined in Gabriel's statement that "he will be great, and will be called the Son of the Most High, and the Lord God will give him the throne of his ancestor David" (Luke 1:32).

In Matthew's Gospel, the Annunciation story is also linked to biblical prophecy. Matthew, however, draws inspiration from a verse by Isaiah, which he

This elaborate glass bottle with attached handles, found near Jerusalem, probably dates from the early Roman period of the first to second century C.E.

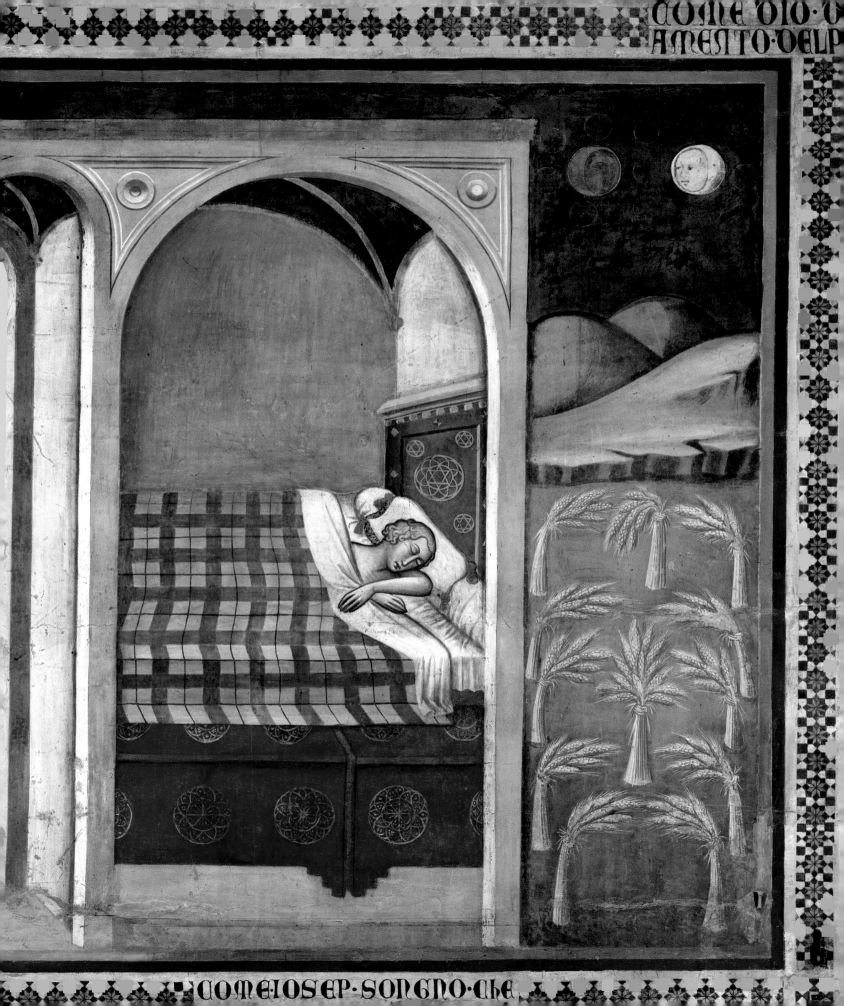

quotes verbatim: "Look, the virgin shall conceive and bear a son, and they shall name him Emmanuel," which means "God is with us" (Matthew 1:23; Isaiah 7:14). Like Luke, Matthew spoke and wrote in Greek. He therefore quoted not only from Scripture in Hebrew, but also from a Greek translation of the Bible then current in the Diaspora known as the Septuagint. And while the Septuagint uses the word *parthenos,* which can mean both "virgin" and "young woman of nubile age," the original Hebrew text uses the word *'almah.* In the Hebrew Bible, this word appears several times (notably in Genesis, Exodus, and Psalms) to describe a "young woman." And while this issue is hotly debated, many scholars believe that the point of Isaiah's verse was not to foretell the coming of a future Redeemer, but to describe the length of time—the period required for a baby to be weaned—in which Israel would be saved from its foreign enemies.

THE NAME OF JESUS

In Luke's Gospel, Gabriel completes the prophecy by naming the child that Mary will carry in her womb: "And now, you will conceive in your womb and bear a son, and you will name him Jesus" (Luke 1:31). Jesus was a very common name in ancient Judaism, in both Judea and Galilee. It is a contraction of Yehoshuah, meaning "YHWH is salvation" or "God saves." Similar diminutives are Joshua and Hosea. In Aramaic, Jesus would have been called Yeshua.

By naming a child, usually after *berit,* or ritual circumcision, a father conferred legitimacy on his child by openly proclaiming the boy as his offspring. Gabriel thus confirms the divine origin of Jesus' birth by explicitly telling Mary what she should name her son. Luke's model for

THE ANNUNCIATION IN NAZARETH

As early as the third century C.E., pilgrims to the Holy Land visited a grotto in the soft chalk hills of Nazareth, believed to be the place of the Annunciation. In the fourth century, after Christianity was officially recognized in the Roman Empire, the mother of Constantine the Great, Empress Helena, ordered a church to be built on the site. It was torn down during the Persian invasion of 614 but rebuilt several times. The largest was a 12th-century Crusader basilica, destroyed in 1263. In 1730, the Franciscans obtained permission from Ottoman rulers to build yet another church, which was demolished in 1955 to make room for the current structure, the most modern church building in Israel today. Designed by the Italian Giovanni Muzio, it was inaugurated by Pope Paul VI in 1964 and completed in 1969. Based on the original Crusader church plan, its lower floor gives access to the grotto. ■

The Basilica of the Annunciation in Nazareth, completed in 1969, marks the location where tradition holds that the angel Gabriel visited Mary in her home.

NORTHERN KINGDOM OF HEROD THE GREAT

MAP KEY

- ·········· District or region boundary
- Herod's Kingdom
- Roman province of Syria
- Nabataean Kingdom
- ● / ○ City of the Decapolis / location uncertain
- ○ Location uncertain
- ○ Herodian fortress

Expanded by Herod the Great and named in honor of his patron, Caesar Augustus, this city was known for its splendid buildings. It would become a Roman administrative center.

Herod the Great built a large acropolis on the ancient location of Samaria and renamed the city Sebaste, the Greek version of "Augustus."

THE GREAT SEA
(MEDITERRANEAN SEA)

| 0 | 20 | 40 kilometers |
| 0 | 20 | 40 miles |

Present-day drainage, coastlines, and country boundaries are represented. Modern names appear in parentheses.

The Decapolis was a commercial league whose member cities enjoyed a measure of autonomy within the Roman province.

this verse is God's declaration to Abraham that his wife, Sarah, would conceive: "Your wife Sarah shall bear you a son, and you shall call him Isaac." In the same breath, God revealed his plan for the newborn child: "I will establish my covenant with him as an everlasting covenant for his offspring after him" (Genesis 17:19). Luke does the same by having Gabriel spell out Jesus' destiny: "He will reign over the house of Jacob forever, and of his kingdom there will be no end."

Mary then submits. "Here I am, the servant of the Lord," she says, echoing the words of Hannah in the first Book of Samuel; "let it be with me according to your word" (Luke 1:38).

MARY'S MAGNIFICAT

Eager to share the good news, Mary soon traveled south to Judea to visit the house of Zechariah and Elizabeth (Luke 1:39-56). As soon as Elizabeth heard Mary's greeting, says Luke, her child leaped in her womb—an anticipation of the

A precious French 14th-century brooch with rubies, diamonds, emeralds, and pearls depicts the Annunciation of the angel Gabriel to Mary.

A lily is one of Mary's attributes in art as a symbol of her perpetual virginity.

This grotto on the lower level of the Basilica of the Annunciation in Nazareth has been revered as the place of the Annunciation since the third century C.E.

important role that John the Baptist would play in the next chapter of Jesus' life. Filled with rapture, Mary then sang one of the most beautiful poems in the New Testament: a hymn of praise that later would become known as the *Song of Mary* or the *Magnificat,* the first word of the hymn in the Latin version of the New Testament. It is actually one of four such hymns or canticles in Luke's Gospel, patterned on the Psalms as well as the *Song of Hannah,* which also strengthens the ties between the Annunciation and the Book of Samuel. The other three canticles are Zechariah's *Benedictus Deus* ("Blessed be the Lord God," Luke 1:67-79), the *Gloria in Excelsis Deo* ("Glory to God in the highest") sung by the angels at Jesus' birth (Luke 2:13-14), and Simeon's *Nunc Dimittis* ("Now you dismiss . . .") at the Presentation in the Temple (Luke 2:28-32). Beginning in the Renaissance, the *Magnificat* was set to music by composers such as Claudio Monteverdi and Antonio Vivaldi, but the most famous musical version is undoubtedly the one that Johann Sebastian Bach composed for the Christmas Vespers of 1723.

The Annunciation would also become one of the most popular themes in Christian art. Its earliest depiction is a fresco in the Priscilla catacombs in

BETROTHAL AND MARRIAGE

Marriage was a cornerstone of Jewish community life in Galilee, and indeed in the Greco-Roman world altogether. Unlike our modern times, marriage was prompted not by romantic interests but more by economic and family needs. It was a transaction between two families—usually within the same community or clan—that ensured the continued ownership of property and the production of offspring to tend to that property. Love had little or nothing to do with it, particularly since the pairing of a daughter or son with a suitable spouse was a matter for the heads of family to decide. Most Jewish adolescents were betrothed early—a young man when he was 18, a girl usually around 12 or 13. To seal the match, the families

"The Marriage of the Virgin" by Italian Renaissance artist Raphael (1483–1520) was completed in 1504 for the Church of San Francesco in Città di Castello.

would negotiate the *ketubah,* or marriage contract, which specified the type of dowry that the bride's family would contribute. This was meant to compensate the groom's family, because the bride's cost of living was now their responsibility. A dowry usually consisted of personal items such as clothing or simple jewelry, as well as parcels of land or animals such as sheep and goats. In return, the groom's family could offer the bride a pension, known as bride price, to be released in the event that her husband divorced her or died prematurely, leaving her a widow and their children fatherless. In practice, however, the relative ease by which a Jewish man could divorce his wife caused a great many single women, often elderly, to live in penury. ■

Rome, dating from the second century. As the veneration of Mary steadily gained prominence in the emerging Church, the popularity of the Annunciation became widespread—not only in Western Christianity but also in the East, where the pregnant Mary is known as Theotokos, God-bearer. During the Middle Ages, as apocryphal texts about Mary began to proliferate, the depiction of the Annunciation gained a number of allegorical attributes. Gabriel was shown with an olive branch, symbol of Jesus as the "Prince of Peace," while Mary was invariably accompanied by a bouquet of lilies, symbol of her purity and chastity. During the Counter-Reformation, the lily also evoked the doctrine of the Immaculate Conception—the idea that Mary herself was conceived in her mother's womb without sin. ■

FOLLOWING PAGES: *Italian artist Fra Angelico (ca 1387–1455) painted this panel of "The Visitation of Mary and Elizabeth" for the Annunciation Altarpiece, completed around 1432.*

CHAPTER THREE

JESUS IS BORN

Joseph also went from the town of Nazareth in Galilee to Judea, to the city of David called Bethlehem.

LUKE 2:4

LETI SVNT DIES VT PARERET ⁊ PEPERIT FILIVM SVVM PRIMOGENITVM. LVCE. II. C.

IM VENIET AD ẽHPLŨ SÃCTŨ SVṼ DOMINATOR DÑS ⁊ANGEL͂ ESTAMẽTI QVᷠE VOS VVLTIS. MAIACHI. II. C.

A Magical Night in Bethlehem

In Luke's Gospel, the next scene unfolds with an important political development. "In those days," he writes, "a decree went out from Emperor Augustus that all the world should be registered" (Luke 2:1). The purpose of such a census was not to determine the demographic makeup of a particular region, as we would expect today, but to establish a detailed inventory of individual owners and their property in areas under Roman control. Over the past decades, the Roman Empire had grown at an astonishing rate, vastly extending Rome's reach while placing a severe strain on its governmental apparatus and treasury.

In order to maintain this vast new commonwealth, with the attendant need to build new roads and garrison new legions in strategic places, Rome urgently needed new sources of revenue. The most obvious way to raise such funds was to charge its conquered lands with annual tribute—in essence, forcing the occupied population to pay for the occupation themselves.

At this early stage of the empire, however, Rome did not yet have the administrative system in place to collect such tribute in overseas possessions by itself. It therefore *outsourced* tax collection to free agents—the hated *telones,* or publicans as the Gospels call them. And in order to vouchsafe that these publicans indeed delivered the taxes that each province was worth without skimming a portion for themselves, Rome periodically conducted audits of the people

and property under its sway. One such audit was conducted by Gaius Pub-
lius Sulpicius Quirinius, a longtime friend of Julius Caesar, whom Augustus
appointed as the new governor of Roman Syria, a Roman dependency since
64 B.C.E. Around the same time, the emperor dismissed Archelaus, a son of
Herod the Great who had ruled over Judea and Samaria as ethnarch, because
of his gross incompetence. Rather than handing over the territory to another
of Herod's tiresome sons, Augustus decided to annex Judea as a Roman province and integrate it with Roman Syria. That is the reason that, when Quirinius
called for a tax audit in the lands under his control, the people of Judea were
made subject to this assessment as well. Luke confirms these developments
when he writes that "this was the first registration"—meaning, in Judea—"and
[it] was taken while Quirinius was governor of Syria" (Luke 2:1-2). Historians
have pointed out that Luke's dates are off a bit—the Quirinius census was held
in 6 C.E., some ten years after the putative birth date of Jesus—but we should
remember that the Gospels are documents of faith, not history books. Furthermore, it is doubtful that in the latter part of the first century, Luke would
have been able to consult Roman state documents about an event that was
already 70 years in the past.

ABOVE: *A view of Bethlehem,
on the West Bank in the
Palestinian Territories,
shows several lit church
spires piercing a dark
winter's night.*

OPPOSITE: *A leading artist
of the Italian trecento,
or 13th century, Duccio
di Buoninsegna (ca 1255/
1260–ca 1318/1319) painted
"The Nativity with the
Prophets Isaiah and
Ezekiel" around 1311.*

PRECEDING PAGES: *This image
of the Nativity was painted
by Italian artist Fra Angelico
(ca 1387–1455), a Dominican
friar who was beatified by
Pope John Paul II in 1982.*

The cultivation of grapes was very prominent in Gali-lee. Grapes usually ripened in early spring and produced the first wine some seven weeks after Pentecost.

What is important for his story is that when Mary was in her final trimester, the Quirinius census compelled her and Joseph to travel from Galilee to the village of Bethlehem in Judea, where Joseph's family presumably had some holdings. Such a journey, some 85 miles over hilly terrain, would undoubtedly have caused great hardship for the young woman, not only because of the distance but also because roads were scarce and often infested with bandits. Worse, when the couple arrived in Bethlehem, "there was no place for them in the inn." Bethlehem was a relatively small place, at a distance of some six miles from Jerusalem, so it could not have offered many alternative lodgings for weary travelers.

But as it happened, this was the moment when Mary's birth pangs came. Fortunately, Joseph found refuge in a cave or a stable, for Luke writes that after Mary "gave birth to her firstborn son," she "wrapped him in bands of cloth, and laid him in a manger"—a trough, in other words, used for feeding livestock

(Luke 2:7). A firstborn son held a special place in the Jewish tradition. "I consecrated for my own all the firstborn in Israel," says God in the Book of Numbers (Numbers 3:13). Later in the story, when Jesus is presented in the Temple, Luke cites from the Book of Exodus that "every firstborn male shall be designated as holy to the Lord" (Luke 2:23; Exodus 13:2). Not surprisingly, the firstborn son was the principal heir of his father's estate. In Luke's elegant allegory, Jesus, as God's firstborn son, will become the heir to the Lord's estate, namely, the "throne of his ancestor David" (Luke 1:32).

To reinforce this notion, Luke adds the poignant scene of Mary, Joseph, and their newborn son being visited by shepherds who were "living in the fields, keeping watch over their flock by night." An angel appeared to them and said, "To you is born this day in the city of David a Savior, who is the Messiah, the Lord." And suddenly, says Luke, there came "a multitude of the heavenly host" singing "Glory to God in the Highest." The symbolism of this scene would not have escaped Luke's Jewish listeners, for David himself had been a shepherd before he was anointed (I Samuel 17:15).

There is one other interesting detail that has escaped some historians, and perhaps Luke as well. When the evangelist writes that Mary placed her newborn in a manger since the inn was full, he may actually be referring to the established practice in other parts of the Roman Empire. Around the second century (the record is uncertain), a Greek physician named Soranus of Ephesus gained considerable fame as the author of a number of authoritative works on the medical practice of his time, including a four-volume treatise on gynecology. Among others, Soranus counseled midwives to disinfect a newborn baby with powdered salt and to rinse the nose, mouth, ears, and anus with warm water. The child should then be tightly swaddled with woolen or linen strips, and placed in an upright cradle in order to lift the baby's head, as in a "feeding trough" or manger—exactly as Luke describes.

One church tradition claims that Luke was a physician himself—not an unreasonable assumption, given these interesting details. It is traditionally assumed that Luke accompanied Paul during his journey in Greece, and near the end of Paul's letter to the Colossians, at a point where Paul often exchanges greetings, there is a tantalizing verse that reads, "Luke, the beloved physician, and Demas

An early 12th-century Romanesque ivory depicts Mary and Joseph's journey to Bethlehem, against the backdrop of a Byzantine church, possibly the Church of the Nativity.

OPPOSITE: *The Church of the Nativity in Bethlehem, begun by Byzantine Emperor Justinian in 565 C.E., is one of the oldest continuously operating churches in the world.*

greet you" (Colossians 4:14). Some historians question that suggestion, however. First, Luke (Loukas in Greek) was not an uncommon name. And second, other than the Nativity scene, Luke's Gospel does not reveal any particular interest in medical issues, particularly when it comes to scenes of Jesus' healing.

THE BIRTH IN MATTHEW'S GOSPEL

Just as Matthew provides a different perspective on the Annunciation, taking Joseph as his main protagonist, so too does his Gospel portray the Nativity from a rather unique vantage point: the court of King Herod in Jerusalem.

THE VILLAGE OF BETHLEHEM

The name Bethlehem, literally *Bet Lehem* or the "House of Bread," is attested very early in Israel's history and could refer to several villages. It appears as "Bit-Lahmi" in the so-called Amarna Letters, a collection of diplomatic correspondence between Pharaoh and the Egyptian governor of Canaan around the middle of the 14th century B.C.E. In Hebrew Scripture, it is identified as the place where Rachel died while giving birth to her second son, Benjamin, for she was buried "on the way to Ephrath, which is Bethlehem" (Genesis 35:19). Several centuries later, the widow Ruth returned to Bethlehem, her hometown, and sustained herself by gleaning kernels from the barley harvest from a nearby field. Eventually she met the owner of the field, named Boaz, and agreed to become his wife (Ruth 3:11). She then gave birth to Obed, the future father of Jesse, and grandfather of a young man named David, who was anointed by Samuel as king of Israel (I Samuel 16:13). ∎

Today Bethlehem is a town of some 25,000 people, including both Muslim and Christian Palestinians, located about six miles from Jerusalem.

"After Jesus was born in Bethlehem," Matthew writes, "wise men from the East came to Jerusalem, asking, 'Where is the child who has been born king of the Jews'?" The Greek word that Matthew employs for wise men is *magoi,* often translated as "magi." And indeed, at many courts in the East, including Persia, learned astrologers and scientists served as advisers to the king on a variety of matters. The astrology connection is further strengthened by the fact that the three distinguished visitors observed "his star at its rising" and have therefore "come to pay him homage." In ancient times, an unusual astronomical event was often interpreted as the harbinger of great social or political change. Thus, the interest of the three magi may have been piqued by the anticipation of an important development. Then again, Matthew may also be alluding to Balaam's oracle in the Book of Numbers, which states that "a star shall come out of Jacob, and a scepter shall rise out of Israel" (Numbers 24:17).

The news that "a child has been born king" soon reached King Herod,

> *And you, Bethlehem, in the land of Judah . . . from you shall come a ruler who is to shepherd my people Israel.*
>
> MATTHEW 2:6

who was immediately struck with fear. In this, Matthew was probably on solid historical ground. Throughout his reign, Herod treated almost everyone with deep distrust, suspecting a conspiracy at every turn. This is one of the reasons that the king surrounded his kingdom with a string of fortresses at a monumental cost, including the famed stronghold of Masada on the Dead Sea and the equally impressive redoubt of Machareus, where John the Baptist would eventually be incarcerated. As Herod's reign dragged on, his paranoia turned the kingdom into a police state where, as Jewish historian Josephus tells us, citizens were encouraged to inform on one another. Dissidents, political or

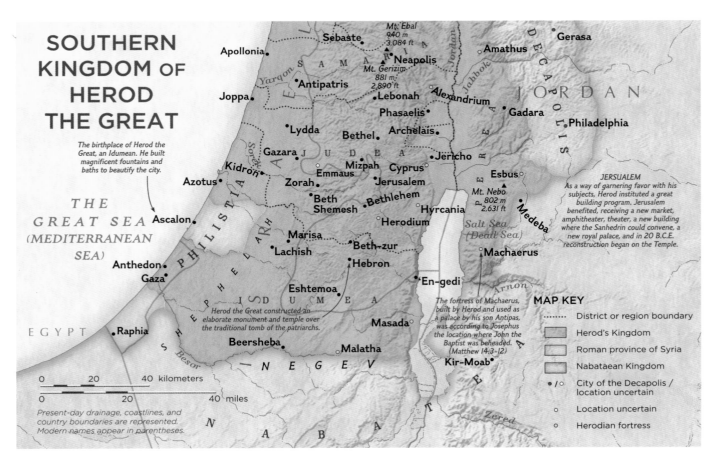

SOUTHERN KINGDOM OF HEROD THE GREAT

The birthplace of Herod the Great, an Idumean. He built magnificent fountains and baths to beautify the city.

THE GREAT SEA (MEDITERRANEAN SEA)

Herod the Great constructed an elaborate monument and temple over the traditional tomb of the patriarchs.

The fortress of Machaerus, built by Herod and used as a palace by his son Antipas, was according to Josephus the location where John the Baptist was beheaded. (Matthew 14:3-12)

JERSUALEM
As a way of garnering favor with his subjects, Herod instituted a great building program. Jerusalem benefited, receiving a new market, amphitheater, theater, a new building where the Sanhedrin could convene, a new royal palace, and in 20 B.C.E. reconstruction began on the Temple.

MAP KEY

- .... District or region boundary
- Herod's Kingdom
- Roman province of Syria
- Nabataean Kingdom
- • / ○ City of the Decapolis / location uncertain
- ○ Location uncertain
- ○ Herodian fortress

Present-day drainage, coastlines, and country boundaries are represented. Modern names appear in parentheses.

0   20   40 kilometers
0   20   40 miles

otherwise, were arrested and sent to one of Herod's fortresses for execution. Herod's suspicions even fell on his wife, the Hasmonean princess Mariamne, who bore him five children and with whom the king was genuinely in love. Nonetheless, when one day she refused to come to his bed, Herod's suspicions were instantly aroused. She was put on trial for conspiracy, and even her own mother was forced to appear as a witness for the prosecution. It did not help either of them, for both Mariamne and her mother were put to the sword.

> *Go and search diligently for the child; and when you have found him, bring me word so that I may also go and pay him homage.*

MATTHEW 2:8

Frankincense, an aromatic resin that the three magi in the Gospel of Matthew presented to the newborn Jesus, was harvested in southern Arabia for use as incense and perfume.

The suggestion that such a deeply deranged character could be frightened by the news that a "new king" had been born must surely have rung true for Matthew's audience.

Matthew continues that Herod then summoned "all the chief priests and scribes of the people" and asked them "where the Messiah was to be born" (Matthew 2:4). This is a most revealing passage, because it clearly indicates that Herod himself had little understanding of Jewish matters, particularly as they related to the royal line of Jewish kings. Perhaps Matthew was aware that Herod, who was appointed king of the Jews by Rome, was not a native Jew himself. He was an Idumean, a member of a people who lived in today's Negev and southern Jordan. In 125 B.C.E., they had been conquered by John Hyrcanus, the Hasmonean king, and forced to convert to Judaism. Herod's elevation to the throne of Judea therefore violated the kingly rule in Deuteronomy that only "one from among your brethren shall you set as king over you; you may not put a foreigner over you" (Deuteronomy 17:15), but of course the Romans would not have bothered with such details. While Herod's family outwardly pretended to be Jewish so as to secure high appointments in Jerusalem, in temperament

This Roman terra-cotta statuette of a young mother and her newborn child probably dates from the early Roman period, first to second century C.E.

An aerial view reveals the strategic location of Herod's Masada stronghold near the Dead Sea, later used by the Zealots during the First Jewish War (66–73 C.E.).

they remained Arab, and they probably continued their pagan cults in private. Indeed, throughout his life, Herod indulged in the construction of Roman-style theaters and gymnasia (sport venues where men exercised in the nude) as well as temples dedicated to Roman gods, which shocked and disgusted his Jewish subjects.

THE MAGI IN BETHLEHEM

So where would the Messiah be born? Herod's Jewish advisers had the answer. They told him that the child must be in Bethlehem of Judea, for it was there that according to the prophet Micah, "a ruler who is to shepherd my people Israel" would be born (Micah 5:2). Herod then summoned the wise men from the East and implored them to search diligently for the child, and "when you have found him, bring me word so that I may also go and pay him homage." The three magi, obviously pleased with the interest shown by the king, set out and followed the star "until it stopped over the place where the child was." They were "overwhelmed with joy," and on "entering the house, they saw the child with Mary, his mother," and paid him homage with rich gifts of "gold, frankincense, and myrrh" (Matthew 2:11). Here again, Matthew may be seeking a parallel with Scripture, particularly Isaiah's vision of nations rendering tribute to Jerusalem: "A multitude of camels shall cover you . . . they shall bring gold and frankincense, and proclaim the praise of the Lord" (Isaiah 60:6). The reference

THE STAR FROM THE EAST

Is the star in Matthew's Gospel a literary symbol or an actual astronomical phenomenon? This question has occupied astronomers since the invention of modern astronomy in the late Renaissance. On December 17, 1603, German astronomer Johannes Kepler observed a conjunction of the planets Jupiter and Saturn in the constellation of Pisces, which caused them to appear as a single bright star. Working backward, he postulated that a similar conjunction would have occurred in 7 B.C.E. Modern scientists question whether the two stars would actually have been close enough to appear as "conjoined." Some believe that Kepler was inspired by the 15th-century rabbinical sage Isaac Abravanel, who prophesied that the conjunction of Saturn and Jupiter in Pisces would herald the coming of the Messiah.

A dramatic infrared image, captured by the Hubble Space Telescope, shows the birth of stars in a haze of gases and dust.

Another possibility is Halley's comet, which was observed in 12 B.C.E. throughout the Roman Empire. Unlike planets, Halley's comet had a tail, visible to the eye, which could conceivably have served as an arrow pointing to Bethlehem. Halley's comet visits the Earth every 74 to 79 years. Jewish historian Josephus observed the return of the comet over Judean skies in 66 C.E.; it may also have been seen by Matthew himself, either in Judea or elsewhere in the empire. Some scholars, however, suggest that the star in Matthew's Gospel is a literary device, since in Antiquity, the life of each person was thought to be linked to a particular star. According to Roman historian Suetonius, the birth of Octavian, later Emperor Augustus, was also attended by a major celestial phenomenon. ■

to myrrh is particularly significant. This precious aromatic resin, harvested in southern Arabia, was commonly used for both anointing and embalming, foreshadowing two cardinal events in the story of Jesus.

But when did all this take place? Traditionally our modern calendar has been pegged to the year 1 as the year of Jesus' birth. However, it is clear from both the Gospels of Luke and Matthew that Jesus was born during the reign of King Herod. Herod, who was born around 73 B.C.E., assumed his reign after the overthrow of the Hasmonean king Antigonus in 37 B.C.E., and died in 4 B.C.E. Furthermore, as we shall see shortly, the birth in Bethlehem took place near the end of Herod's life. We should therefore accept the possibility that Jesus was born around 5 or 4 B.C.E. ■

FOLLOWING PAGES: *This panel of "The Adoration of the Magi with Saint Anthony Abbot" was painted around 1400 by a French or Flemish artist in Burgundy, France.*

CHAPTER FOUR

HEROD'S REVENGE

*Then Herod secretly called
for the wise men and learned
from them the exact time when
the star had appeared.*

MATTHEW 2:7

A Terrible Massacre in Bethlehem

Having discovered the place of Jesus' birth, the magi would probably have returned to Herod's court to tell the king exactly where the child could be found. However, says Matthew, they were "warned in a dream not to return to Herod" and left for their country by another road (Matthew 2:12). As soon as word reached Herod that the magi had "tricked" him, he exploded in fury. Determined to kill the child, wherever he might be, he ordered that "all the children in and around Bethlehem who were two years old or under" be murdered forthwith. Fortunately, says Matthew, an angel of the

Lord appeared to Joseph in a dream and warned him to "take the child and his mother, and flee to Egypt, and remain there until I tell you." Thus, Joseph got up and led his young family to Egypt, where they stayed until Herod died and the danger had passed.

As we saw earlier, the principal purpose of the Gospels is not only to tell the story of Jesus' life and death, but also to explain their meaning. In doing so, the evangelists availed themselves of both *factual* and *symbolic* material, since their audience did not distinguish as clearly between actual fact and literary allegory as we would today. In ancient times, both genres were considered valid containers of truth, because in a world that believed deeply in supernatural phenomena and magic, truth was not judged solely on the basis of its actual occurrence. Both Jews and Gentiles believed that the divine—whomever they held that to be—often communicated in other ways, such as dreams, signs, or visions.

We should therefore probe Matthew's coda to the Nativity story for its figurative meaning rather than read it as literal truth. From a strictly practical point of view, a voyage to Egypt would have been daunting. The distance from Bethlehem to the borders of Egypt at Pelesium (now Tell el-Farama) is about 250 miles. In Herodian times, it was a long and arduous journey fraught with risk, particularly from marauding bands of raiders and thieves. The route ran partly along the Mediterranean Sea with few watering holes and was used only by caravans, which traveled in groups for mutual protection. To compel a young family to undertake such a dangerous journey would have exposed them to far greater risk than if Joseph had simply tried to evade Herod's militia, perhaps by fleeing across the Jordan to areas outside the king's jurisdiction.

Instead, Matthew's deliberate coupling of Herod's Massacre of the Innocents with the journey to and from Egypt is probably meant to communicate something else, namely, another parallel with Hebrew Scripture—in this case, the Book of Exodus. This book opens with the news that after many centuries, a new pharaoh had risen in Egypt (quite possibly King Seti I) "who did not know Joseph"—in other words, who did not recognize the special privileges that a previous pharaoh had granted to Joseph and the family of his father, Jacob. "Look," said this new pharaoh, "the Israelite people are more numerous

ABOVE: *The sun rises over a palm grove in the Nile Delta, which would have been the presumed destination of Mary and Joseph on their flight to Egypt.*

OPPOSITE: *"The Dream of St. Joseph" is the work of Spanish Renaissance artist Juan de Borgona (ca 1470–ca 1535), painted around 1535.*

PRECEDING PAGES: *German artist Bertram of Minden (ca 1345–ca 1415) painted "The Massacre of the Innocents" as part of the Grabow Altarpiece, completed in 1383.*

and more powerful than we" (Exodus 1:8-9). In response, he condemned the Hebrews to slave labor and "set taskmasters over them" (Exodus 1:8-11). But the more they were oppressed, says the Bible, "the more they multiplied and spread," notwithstanding the "hard service of mortar and brick."

In the end, the pharaoh decided on a more drastic measure to curtail the growth of the Hebrew community. He issued a decree to his people that "every boy that is born to the Hebrews you shall throw into the Nile." One young Hebrew woman named Jochebed saved her newborn boy by placing him in a papyrus basket, plastered with bitumen and pitch. She cast the baby adrift on the river, where he was soon spotted by Pharaoh's daughter. Overcome with pity, the princess took the baby in and raised him at Pharaoh's court. Thus begins the story of Moses, the man who many years later freed his people from the clutches of Pharaoh and led them out of Egypt to the borders of the Promised Land.

In Matthew's coda, therefore, Herod's massacre of the newborn of Bethlehem is a perfect parallel to the pharaoh's equally cruel order to throw all of the Israelite male babies into the Nile, just as Joseph's and Mary's return from Egypt retraces the route of the Exodus to the Promised Land. The purpose of this poetic vision is to reveal Jesus as the new Moses, the man who has come to renew God's covenant with his people by creating a new covenant, a new *testament,* that will redeem not only the Jewish people but all of humanity.

A restored oil press, used to crush olives to make olive oil, was excavated near a house in Hazor in northern Galilee.

WHERE DID MARY AND JOSEPH LIVE?

Matthew is the only evangelist who implies that Mary and Joseph were not Galileans by birth. Whereas Luke tells us that the angel Gabriel appeared before Mary in "a town in Galilee called Nazareth," Matthew, by contrast, has the magi following the star to Bethlehem, to "the place where the child was," and where they entered a "house" *(oikian).* Furthermore, after the death of Herod, the angel warns Joseph not to *return* to Judea but to move to Galilee instead. This suggests that in Matthew's Gospel, Bethlehem was actually Joseph and Mary's residence. For Matthew, the need to abide by the prophecy of the eighth-century prophet Micah, that "a ruler who is to shepherd my people Israel" would come from Bethlehem, was of paramount importance—so important, in fact, that he does not let Jesus be born in Bethlehem accidentally, as Luke does, but as a legitimate resident of the city, in the house of his parents. ■

THE DEATH OF HEROD

And then at last Herod died, unloved and unmourned. The last months of his reign were particularly oppressive.

Herod . . . appointed Antipas, to whom he had before left the kingdom, to be tetrarch of Galilee and Perea, and granted the kingdom to Archelaus.

JOSEPHUS, *ANTIQUITIES OF THE JEWS*

Even as Herod lay on his deathbed, fully expecting the news of his passing to prompt wild celebrations among his populace, he ordered that all the "principal men" of Judea be rounded up and held in the stadium of Jericho as hostages. As soon as he died, he told his military commanders that all of these dignitaries were to be killed, so as to force the population into a state of mourning, one way or another.

Fortunately, Herod's son Archelaus and his sister Salome, who were widely expected to inherit the kingdom, persuaded the military not to implement this insane order, perhaps because they did not relish the idea of taking the reins of a nation in uproar. In this context, it is not difficult to imagine that a man as pathologically insane as Herod was capable of ordering the deaths of innocent

This coin, which features a helmet surmounted by a star and the inscription "Of King Herod," is among the largest-denomination coins issued during the reign of King Herod.

A reconstruction of the bathhouse at Herod's palace of Machaerus, created by the Hungarian Academy of Arts, shows that the lower portions of the columns were painted red.

This ostracon, or potsherd, was taken from the fortified palace of the Herodion, the resting place of King Herod the Great.

King Herod and his guests enjoyed stunning views of the Judean Desert from this peristyle court, part of the Suspended Palace of the fortress of Masada.

children in Bethlehem. Even though historically this slaughter may not have come to pass, Matthew's audience would have had no problem accepting the idea that Herod was capable of such an act.

After the king had been laid to rest in his tomb, his will was read. It transpired that, uncharacteristically, Herod had ordered a breakup of his vaunted kingdom. Archelaus, the son by his Samaritan wife, Malthace, was to rule over the largest territory: that of Judea, Idumea, and Samaria. The second portion, that of Galilee, was combined with Perea (the Transjordan) and given to Antipas, the younger brother of Archelaus, also by Malthace. The third segment, consisting of the largely Gentile territory northeast of the Sea of Galilee including the Gaulanitis (today's Golan region), was to be ruled by Philip, whose mother was called "Cleopatra of Jerusalem." Salome received the crumbs left on the table: the coastal strip around Azotus, today's Ashdod, as well as the region around Jabneh and Phaesalis. In sum, after nearly two centuries of Hasmonean and Herodian rule, Israel's southern heartland of Judea was once again to be separated from the northern regions, including Galilee.

The Gospel of Matthew confirms this arrangement. After an angel had appeared to Joseph in a dream to tell him to "go to the land of Israel, for

those who were seeking the child's life are dead," Joseph obeyed and began the long journey back. "But," says Matthew, "when he heard that Archelaus was ruling over Judea in place of his father Herod, he was afraid to go there" (Matthew 2:19-22). Why Joseph would have reason to be afraid of Archelaus is not explained. Historically, we know that Archelaus's elevation led to riots in Jerusalem during Passover when it became clear that Archelaus planned to continue the crushing taxes his father had imposed on the nation, as well as the cronyism that had developed around his court. These disturbances caused the governor of Syria, Quinctilius Varus, to order an inquiry led by a Roman legate named Sabinus. But upon his arrival in Jerusalem, Sabinus was more interested in investigating the extent of Herod's wealth and possessions. This soon prompted rumors that Sabinus was not trying to calm the tempers in Jerusalem but laying the groundwork for a complete Roman takeover of Judea. When, during the subsequent festival of Shavuot, or "Weeks" (Pentecost in Greek), news spread that Sabinus had broken into the Temple treasury and absconded with "400 talents"—some four million dollars in modern currency—the riots spread to an all-out rebellion. This revolt was suppressed only by the deployment of several Roman legions, as well as additional auxiliary forces from surrounding regions.

In May 2007, a team of archaeologists uncovered this pink sarcophagus on the slopes of the Herodion; it may have contained the body of Herod the Great.

It doesn't seem that Matthew is referring to these hostilities because his Gospel tells us that "after being warned in a dream, [Joseph] went away to the district in Galilee. There he made his home in a town called Nazareth" (Matthew 2:22-23). As it happened, some of the fiercest fighting in this rebellion, led by a man named "Judas of Galilee," took place in and around Sepphoris, the provincial capital located a mere seven miles away from Nazareth. Rather, Matthew's roundabout way of taking the story into the tiny hamlet of Nazareth is necessitated by a simple fact: That's where Jesus grew up, as attested by all Gospels.

In the end, however, these discrepancies in the Nativity stories of Luke and Matthew are of less importance. What both narratives agree on is that Jesus was born in Bethlehem in fulfillment of Hebrew Scripture, and that the years of his youth took place far up north, in the soft, rolling hills of Lower Galilee. ∎

FOLLOWING PAGES: *"The Flight to Egypt," painted by Venetian Renaissance artist Vittore Carpaccio (ca 1465–1525/1526), betrays the influence of Carpaccio's master, Giovanni Bellini.*

CHAPTER FIVE

YOUNG JESUS IN NAZARETH

When the time came for their purification according to the law of Moses, they brought him up to Jerusalem to present him to the Lord.

LUKE 2:22

Jesus Grows Up in Galilee

Luke's Gospel then picks up the thread of the story. "After eight days had passed," he writes, "it was time to circumcise the child." This ritual of the *brit milah* was done in accordance with God's decree to Abraham that "throughout your generations every male among you shall be circumcised when he is eight days old," as physical evidence of God's covenant with his people. Circumcision was (and is) an important event because it identifies the child as a full member within the covenantal community of Judaism. Joseph named the child Jesus, using the name that the angel had given him (Luke 2:21). The ceremony probably took place in a prominent spot in the village, near the well or threshing floor, with the elders present.

THE PURIFICATION CEREMONY

Luke writes that the family then "brought him up to Jerusalem to present him to the Lord" when the "time came for their purification according to the law of Moses" (Luke 2:22). This reference is somewhat confusing. According to the Torah, the Jewish Law, only Mary, not Joseph or Jesus, was considered ritually impure after childbirth. As Leviticus states, she was considered "ceremonially unclean" for seven days after the birth because of her postpartum blood flow. During this first or "major" phase of impurity, she was not allowed to touch any person or any commonly used objects for fear of contaminating her relatives through simple contact. This first phase was then followed by a lesser period of "uncleanliness" that lasted 33 days and restrained her only from touching anything holy, such as entering the sanctuary in Jerusalem. As the mother of a newborn son, the total period of Mary's ritual impurity was therefore 40 days,

a common number in the Bible when signifying a period of completion. If she had borne a daughter, both periods would have lasted twice as long: 14 days and 66 days, respectively.

The period of impurity prescribed in Leviticus may also have served to allow a new mother to recover from the strain of birth while the women in her village helped her cope with the joys and chores of new motherhood. Then after the "minor" phase of 33 days was fulfilled, Mary was expected to go to "the priest at the entrance of the tent," meaning the tabernacle or the Temple, and offer "a lamb in its first year for a burnt offering, and a pigeon or a turtledove for a sin offering" (Leviticus 12:2-7).

SIMEON BLESSES JESUS

A "burnt offering" was usually a sacrificial animal without blemish, such as live-stock, of which certain parts were burned on the altar in front of the Temple

ABOVE: *The beautiful northern shore of the Sea of Galilee, near the township of Capernaum, evokes the setting of Jesus calling his disciples.*

OPPOSITE: *This first-century bronze* patera, *or shallow dish, was possibly used as a bath scoop by the more affluent families in the region.*

PRECEDING PAGES: *Melchior Broederlam (ca 1355–1411) painted this panel of "The Circumcision of Jesus," which forms part of the Champmol Altarpiece completed in 1399.*

*Now there was a man in Jerusalem
whose name was Simeon; this man was
righteous and devout, looking forward
to the consolation of Israel.*

LUKE 2:25

as an offering to the Lord (Leviticus 1:1-4) and the edible parts were eaten by worshippers. A "sin offering," by contrast, did not imply atonement for sinful behavior but the need for blood purification. In Judaism, no form of sin (such as the later Christian concept of "original sin") was attached to a young mother who gave birth to a child as the result of conjugal activity with her hus-

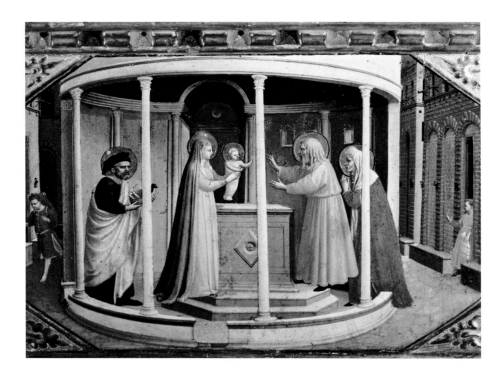

Italian artist Fra Angelico (ca 1387–1455) painted this panel of "The Presentation in the Temple" from the predella of the Annunciation Altarpiece.

band. The purpose of the sin offering was instead to atone for her state of impurity and restore her as a full member of her community, "clean from the flow of blood." But the price of an unblemished lamb, used for the burnt offering, was clearly beyond Mary's means. Fortunately, there was a special provision in Leviticus for families who were poor. "If she cannot afford a sheep," the text states, "she shall take two turtledoves or two pigeons, one for a burnt offering and the other for a sin offering" (Leviticus 12:6-8). As Luke writes, that is exactly what Mary did, thus proving that she and her husband were indeed poor folk (Luke 2:22-24).

Luke also implies that it was the custom to present every firstborn male to the Temple in Jerusalem, quoting the reference in Exodus that "every firstborn male shall be designated as holy to the Lord" (Exodus 13:2), but in reality there is no such requirement in the Torah. Aberrations such as these have led some scholars to conclude that Luke himself was not raised as a Jew. A more plausible explanation may be that Luke was a Diaspora Jew, a member of any of the Greek-speaking Jewish communities in the Mediterranean that the Book of Acts refers to as "Hellenists," who observed the Torah but did not generally recognize the importance of Temple ritual.

The purpose of Luke's story is to set the stage for Jesus' Presentation in the Temple, in the presence of a man named Simeon. A devout Jew, Simeon had been told "by the Holy Spirit" that he would not die without seeing "the Lord's Messiah." When he saw Mary and her baby entering the Temple, Simeon took the child in his arms, saying, "Master, now you are dismissing your servant in peace, according to your word; for my eyes have seen your salvation, which you have prepared in the presence of all peoples, a light for revelation to the Gentiles and for glory to your people Israel" (Luke 2:29-32). This fourth canticle in Luke's narrative, *Nunc dimittis,* summarizes what will become the key motif of his Gospel: that Jesus came to Earth as the Messiah to redeem not only the people

A large grinding wheel discovered near the village of Bethany in Judea was used for grinding large quantities of wheat kernels into flour.

THE BREAD OF LIFE

Bread was the principal staple of a Galilean's diet, as reflected in the prayer that Jesus taught his disciples: "Give us today our daily bread" (Matthew 6:11). To feed the five thousand, Jesus multiplied five loaves of bread. And in the Gospel of John, Jesus declares, "I am the bread of life; whoever comes to me will never go hungry" (John 6:35). In most villages, women baked fresh bread every day at dawn, to sustain their families for the rest of the day. First, they poured a measure of grain into a grain mill, which consisted of two round stones anchored on a wooden spike. By rotating the upper stone, they crushed the kernels and ground them into fine flour. They mixed this with water, salt, and oil, as well as a bit of yeast to make the bread rise. The resulting dough was rolled out in thin cakes and baked in the oven. ■

of Israel but *all* of humankind, Jew and Gentile, and that this is the reason that he would ultimately be condemned by his Jewish compatriots. Or as Simeon explains to Mary: "This child is destined for the falling and the rising of many in Israel, and to be a sign that will be opposed so that the inner thoughts of many will be revealed—and a sword will pierce your own soul too" (Luke 2:34-35).

JESUS GROWS UP IN NAZARETH

And then, says Luke, "the child grew and became strong, filled with wisdom; and the favor of God was upon him" (Luke 2:40). As a member of a poor family,

Jesus would have been raised in a humble home, built of the local basalt stone and mortared with mud. The roof was probably made from a latticework of thin beams and branches, covered with palm fronds or leaves, and packed with mud. A reconstruction of such a first-century hamlet was recently built near Qasrin in Upper Galilee, close to the Golan. Among these homes is a simple single-family dwelling, built of rough stone, with small rugs offering a measure of comfort on the hard-packed earth. It was in a home such as this that Mary and Joseph ate, played with their son, kept their stores, slept, and shared their dreams about the future, as any newlywed couple would.

A reconstruction of a family dwelling from the first century shows the stable where stores and farming implements were kept and animals found shelter in winter.

OPPOSITE: *This canvas of "St. Joseph, the Carpenter" was painted by French artist Georges de la Tour (1593–1652) under influence from the Italian artist Michelangelo Caravaggio.*

Quite often such dwellings were grouped around a common courtyard, housing several married couples within the family. The courtyard was the place where animals were kept and the women had their "kitchen appliances," usually a stone mill and an oven made of clay or brick. Living together allowed an extended family to share in the cooking, cleaning, weaving, and watering of animals, while also enabling married men and women to live in close proximity to their parents and siblings.

There may also have been a defensive motive for such residential clusters. As we saw, Jesus' early years coincided with much political instability, punctuated by two peasant revolts: one in 4 B.C.E. after the death of King Herod and one in 6 C.E., after the ill-fated Roman census. Both rebellions led to bloody reprisals throughout the Galilean countryside. In addition, many of Herod's soldiers had refused to give up their arms after the king's death, and they formed roving bands that terrorized the peasantry. A community of family units, grouped around a common courtyard, was more easily defended against such dangers. Remains of these multifamily units have been excavated throughout Galilee by Ze'ev Safrai and other archaeologists. The concept became so common that

This red earthenware jug with tapering neck and loop handle, used for water or wine, was excavated in southern Israel and probably dates to the late first century C.E.

in later centuries, Talmudic literature would refer to residential groupings as simply "a courtyard."

We should remember that the services and protections that modern states offer their citizens did not exist in Jesus' time. Although the Herodians taxed the Galilean peasantry mercilessly, both to raise the tribute to Rome and support their own lavish courts, none of these taxes translated into tangible benefits for the population. Hence, everything from the upkeep of wells to the protection of property and the construction of country roads, to take the harvest to market, was the responsibility of the village community. While the family provided a shared resource for food, clothing, companionship, and love, the village offered economic assistance, mutual protection against thieves and gangs, and the sharing of ceremonial rituals. Wells, cisterns,

Herod also built a wall about Sepphoris . . . and made it the metropolis of the country.

JOSEPHUS, *ANTIQUITIES OF THE JEWS*

A simple stone mill, equipped with wooden handles, would have been used on a daily basis to make fresh flour from crushed wheat kernels.

farming tools, draft animals, and a common winnowing area were all carefully maintained for collective use. To be ostracized from such a community, as we will see in chapter 13, was a terrible sentence that condemned a villager to misery, hunger, and death.

FARMING IN GALILEE

In Jesus' time, the vast majority of Galileans sustained themselves by cultivating their ancestral plots, which had been passed down from generation to generation. "We don't have a maritime tradition, nor do we excel in trade," Josephus noted, "but we do have a fruitful country for our sustenance, and we take pains in cultivating it."

The secret of Galilee's agricultural bounty was its soil and its access to water. Its bedrock of porous limestone was covered with fertile terra rossa topsoil in the western part and volcanic soil in the eastern region, suitable for growing a variety of crops. These were watered by a number

of underground aquifers; in his 1992 study, archaeologist Zvi Gal identified no fewer than 25 springs between the Nazareth Ridge and Geba'ot Allonim.

Traditionally Galilean farmers practiced subsistence farming, which means that they sustained their families by planting a broad spectrum of produce in small quantities. Separate patches of land were set aside to cultivate cereals such as wheat and barley, as well as garden vegetables such as onions, squash, radishes, beets, and leeks. Many farmers also had small orchards for olives, figs, grapes, and dates. The Talmudic literature lists more than 500 types of produce grown in Galilee, including 8 types of grain, 24 types of vegetables, and 30 types of fruits.

This prompts the question: If as Josephus says, virtually everyone in Galilee was involved with agriculture, would that have applied to Joseph as well? At first glance, the answer would be no. According to the Gospel of

THE CONSTRUCTION OF SEPPHORIS

Shortly after his brother Archelaus was removed as ruler of Judea and Samaria by Emperor Augustus, Herod Antipas, the tetrarch of Galilee, decided to rebuild the provincial capital of Sepphoris, which had been destroyed during the first peasant revolt of 4 B.C.E. Some historians have argued that up to this point, Antipas may have nurtured the hope of replacing his brother Archelaus in Jerusalem and of becoming a true heir to his father, King Herod. When that hope was dashed by Augustus's decision to turn Judea into a Roman province, Antipas realized he needed to content himself with what he had, and he decided to turn Sepphoris into "the ornament of all Galilee," as Josephus writes. The result was a stupendous construction project, unprecedented in the

The Roman theater of Sepphoris, built by Herod Antipas, was partly carved from the natural rock of a local hill and enlarged to a 4,000-seat capacity in the third to fourth centuries C.E.

history of Galilee. Up to this point, few rulers had bothered to build anything of note in a region that was primarily known for its fecund valleys.

Several scholars have recently argued that this building project would have had a deep impact on the family of Mary and Joseph. Construction workers were usually recruited—by force, if necessary—from surrounding villages and townships. Nazareth was only seven miles away. What's more, if Joseph was indeed a *tekton* or craftsman, as Mark calls him, he would have been in great demand for such a project. Since sons usually followed in the trade of their fathers, Jesus may also have been recruited to work in Sepphoris. This might be one reason that the Gospels are silent about Jesus' adulthood until age 30. ■

Mark (which sets the precedent followed by other Gospels), Joseph was a carpenter. Mark tells us that when Jesus returned to his native Nazareth after the launch of his ministry, the people of his hometown were astonished by his words. "Is this not the carpenter [*tekton*], the son of Mary and brother of James?" they asked (Mark 6:3). The Greek word *tekton,* which traditionally has been translated as "carpenter," actually means craftsman in a variety of trades. Carpentry as we understand it—the crafting of tables, chairs, and cabinets—would not be one of them, since workable wood was very scarce in Galilee and well beyond the budget of the average Galilean. The form of timber that did exist, such as olive wood, was suitable only for small implements, like the handle of a knife, scythe, or other farming tools. It is quite possible that Joseph was skilled in crafting these items. But that alone would not have sustained his family.

A view of the rolling hills of Galilee near the western shore of the Sea of Galilee reveals the diversity of Galilean cultivation to this day.

An orchard in the vicinity of Sepphoris in Galilee has olives ripe for the plucking.

Surprisingly, the answer to this dilemma may lie in the Gospels themselves. One of the most beloved devices of Jesus' ministry is the so-called parable, a pithy story that illustrates a point in the cultural vernacular of the time. The Gospels feature no parables that are in some way or form related to carpentry. But a great many relate to agriculture, such as the parable of the sower, the mustard seed, the budding fig tree, the "tares" or weeds, the workers on the vineyard, or the unjust steward. These parables betray a close familiarity with the annual cycle of cultivation in Galilee, such as the parable in which a gardener diagnoses a fig tree that has not borne fruit for three years. "Leave it alone for one more year," he counsels the owner, "until I dig around it and put manure on it. If it bears fruit next year, well and good; but if not, you can cut it down" (Luke 13:8-9). This sounds not like a man who grew up in a carpenter's workshop but who accompanied his father to the field and watched Joseph sow his plots and nurture the budding fruit until harvesttime. ■

Figs are often mentioned in the Bible, such as in the parable of the budding fig tree (Matthew 24:32) and the barren fig tree (Luke 13:6).

FOLLOWING PAGES: *Venetian artist Giovanni Bellini (ca 1430–1516) painted this depiction, "The Presentation of Jesus in the Temple," around 1490 to 1500.*

CHAPTER SIX

THE VISIT TO THE TEMPLE

*The child grew and became
strong, filled with wisdom;
and the favor of God
was upon him.*

LUKE 2:40

Jesus Debates the Doctors of the Law

Now every year his parents went to Jerusalem for the festival of the Passover," Luke writes, "and when he was twelve years old, they went up as usual for the festival" (Luke 2:41-42). Passover, or Pesach, was one of three Jewish festivals, the others being Weeks or Pentecost (Shavuot) and Booths (Sukkot). Whereas Passover commemorates the release from bondage in Egypt, the Shavuot festival celebrates the day God presented the Torah to the nation of Israel at Mount Sinai. The seven-day autumn festival of Sukkot reminds worshippers of the tents in which the Israelites lived during their long journey from Egypt to the Promised Land (Leviticus 23:42-43).

After the completion of the Temple in Jerusalem, these three feasts became pilgrimage festivals, when worshippers from around Israel and the Diaspora converged on Jerusalem.

There is no reason to think that Mary and Joseph, poor though they may have been, would not have made the arduous journey to Jerusalem at least once a year, and particularly for Passover, the most important of the three festivals. The Passover feast was traditionally set according to a lunar calendar, which specifies that the 14th day of the month of Nisan must coincide with the first full moon of the first month of spring (Exodus 12:2-6). Passover therefore did not conflict with the cycle of Galilean agriculture, for barley was

typically harvested in April (Nisan/Iyyar), and wheat a month later. To protect themselves from the ever present danger of bandits, as well as wild animals at night, Mary and Joseph traveled in a large group (Luke 2:44). Many of their companions would have been relatives of Jesus, as well as other members of the village community.

As soon as the pilgrims arrived in Jerusalem, they would have looked for a place to stay. An inn in Jerusalem was probably out of the question, since such accommodations were often not only crowded and unsafe but also expensive, particularly during the high season of religious festivals. Instead, most pilgrims settled in improvised camps on the Mount of Olives, just beyond the Kidron Valley, where they could observe the magnificent Temple complex, the extension of which was then still under construction. If my calculation is correct, this journey would have taken place in the year 7 or 8 C.E., 12 years after Jesus' putative birth in either 5 or 4 B.C.E.

ABOVE: *A view of Jerusalem shows the Zion Gate and the Hagia Maria Sion Abbey, formerly known as Dormition Abbey, close to the location of the Hall of the Last Supper.*

OPPOSITE: *A limestone ossuary, dated to the first decades of the first century C.E., features a colonnade possibly inspired by the Temple in Jerusalem.*

PRECEDING PAGES: *Italian artist Duccio di Buoninsegna (ca 1255/1260–ca 1318/1319) painted this panel of "The Disputation with the Doctors" around 1311.*

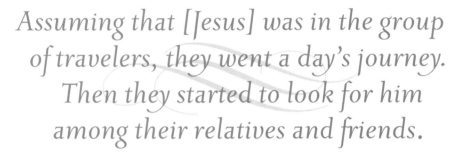

Assuming that [Jesus] was in the group of travelers, they went a day's journey. Then they started to look for him among their relatives and friends.

LUKE 2:44

JESUS IS MISSING

"When the festival was ended and they started to return," Luke continues, "the boy Jesus stayed behind in Jerusalem, but his parents did not know it" (Luke 2:43). Since they were traveling in a large group, Mary and Joseph must have assumed that Jesus was walking with cousins or friends under the watchful eye of their relatives. Only after they had walked "for a day's journey" did they get concerned, particularly when it transpired that none of their kinsmen knew where Jesus was. Mary then realized that she hadn't seen her son since the moment they left Jerusalem. There was no alternative but to hurry back the way they had come and retrace their steps into the city.

For three days, Joseph and Mary searched high and low for Jesus throughout Jerusalem, their fears growing by the minute. So we can imagine Mary's feelings of intense relief, mixed with some chagrin, when she found her son sitting quietly in the Temple, immersed in a learned debate with "the teachers." These were arguably rabbis who were in the Temple to advise visitors about any topic related to Jewish Law. But now the roles were reversed: Instead of the rabbis, it was Jesus who was doing all of the talking. "And all who heard him," Luke says, "were amazed at his understanding and his answers" (Luke 2:47).

The theme of a great sage whose wisdom is revealed at a precociously young age is a popular motif in the writings of this period. In Josephus's *History of the Jews,* young Moses is credited with a "quickness of apprehension unusual for his age," while the historian claims that when he himself was a child, "high priests and principal men of the city frequently came to hear of my opinion about points of the law." But in Luke's narrative, this meeting with the "teachers of the Law" has a specific meaning. We hear that the rabbis were "amazed at his understanding," but it is not clear if Jesus' remarks actually met with their approval. In fact, this encounter between learned scholars and the humble son of a craftsman is actually a foreshadowing of the future conflict between the Sadducees and the Pharisees, the Jewish authority figures of the time, and Jesus, the rabbi from Galilee. Continuing the motif that began with the story of Zechariah, Luke places the event in the Temple, the "ground zero" of his Gospel.

THE *BEIT MIDRASH*

How did Jesus, the son of a poor farmer/worker in rural Galilee, become so knowledgeable about the Torah that he could lecture the teachers of the Temple? This is a cardinal question that has confounded scholars for many years. Significantly, the story states that Jesus was 12 years old—not yet the age of bar mitzvah, when a boy was considered an adult, ready to begin work alongside his father. Even then, we must ask what opportunities existed in a small hamlet like Nazareth for a young boy to be educated—other than perhaps the learning of the Torah from elders by rote. Rabbinic sources from the third century C.E. suggest that larger villages and townships typically maintained a *beit midrash,* a school where young boys received some schooling starting at age six; however, it is very unlikely that such facilities existed in rural Galilee at the time. But Jesus may have been taught by his parents and elders in his greater family. ∎

This detail from a fourth-century ivory reliquary from Brescia, Italy, shows Jesus in dispute with doctors in the Temple.

THE TEMPLE

Of course, Jesus and the teachers were not actually sitting *in* the Temple. As we saw, the Temple itself was not a place of communal prayer or worship, but a House of the Lord accessible only to priests. This sanctuary was surrounded by three separate courts, each with a specific function.

The large outer court, built by Herod, was a vast esplanade accessible to all visitors, Jewish and Gentile. Passing the *soreg,* the boundary beyond which no Gentile was allowed to pass, Jewish visitors then climbed 15 unevenly raised stairs to the Court of Women. This was the most public of the inner courts,

OPPOSITE TOP: *The drawing on these plaster fragments, dating to the time of King Herod, shows the menorah, the large seven-branched lamp stand that stood in the Temple.*

OPPOSITE BOTTOM: *"Jesus Found in the Temple" was painted by French artist James Jacques Joseph Tissot (1836–1902).*

accessible to both Jewish men and women, although women were probably restricted to an upper gallery that ran around the enclosed area. Around this court stood 13 trumpet-shaped depositories *(shoparoth)* into which visitors dropped a variety of tithes and other offerings. Only men were allowed to proceed to the next area directly facing the Temple: the Court of the Israelites, the Court of the Priests, and the Temple Court, including the area where animal sacrifice took place.

Mary probably found her son in an area known as the Royal Porch, or Stoa, a basilica-type structure located near the main entrance to the outer court. The Stoa gallery featured a colonnade of 162 pillars, lined up in four rows, and thus it offered plenty of shaded space to scribes, teachers, and other officials who made themselves available for consultation.

Under any other circumstance, Mary might have felt a deep pride at the sight of her young son lecturing these doctors, but the anxiety of the past three days was too much for her. "Child, why have you treated us like this!" she cried, relieved and upset in equal measure; "look, your father and I have been searching for you in great anxiety."

A reconstruction of the Second Temple in Jerusalem shows a view of the colonnade of the Royal Stoa, the large open area where Jesus could have met with the doctors of the Law.

At this point, we would expect Jesus to make some gesture of contrition. But that is not the answer we get. In fact, it almost sounds as if Jesus is rebuking his mother: "Why were you searching for me?" he says. "Did you not know that I must be in my Father's house?" (Luke 2:48-49) The reply is doubly injurious: first, because Jesus doesn't acknowledge the obvious heartbreak he has caused his parents, and second, because the reference to "my Father's house" is a slight against Joseph as his nominal father and head of the household. But as we will see in the unfolding Gospel drama, Jesus is an uncompromising figure; his commitment to his mission is such that he cannot allow himself to be waylaid by the feelings of others. "Whoever loves [his] father or mother more than me is not worthy of me," he tells his followers in Matthew's Gospel—words sure to wound a mother's heart (Matthew 10:37).

But here too, the point is that in the pursuit of his destiny, Jesus must place all other considerations aside. That is the purpose of his reference to "my Father's house." It is not his intent to hurt Joseph's feelings; rather, he wants to stress that his destiny lies not in a farmer's cottage but in the Temple, the crucible of the great crisis looming in Judaism. That is why he would ultimately leave Nazareth to begin his ministry.

His parents, as Luke tells us, "did not understand what he said to them," but in a poignant reference to things to come, Luke adds that "his mother treasured all these things in her heart." And without demur, Jesus then followed them out of the Temple and "came to Nazareth, and was obedient to them" (Luke 2:51).

This is where Luke's infancy narrative ends. When we next meet Jesus, he is around 32 years old and on his way to meet the most charismatic preacher of his time: a man named John the Baptist. ■

Screens separate male and female worshippers at the Western Wall, one of the retaining walls of the Second Temple and today the holiest site in modern Judaism.

FOLLOWING PAGES: *"Jesus with the Doctors" is a detail from a fresco series by Barna da Siena (active 1330–1350) in the Collegiata Church of San Gimignano, Italy.*

CHAPTER SEVEN

A DISCIPLE OF JOHN THE BAPTIST

He went into all the region
around the Jordan,
proclaiming a baptism
of repentance for
the forgiveness of sins.

LUKE 3:3

Jesus Is Baptized in the Jordan

"I n the fifteenth year of the reign of Emperor Tiberius," Luke writes, "when Pontius Pilate was governor of Judea, and Herod was ruler of Galilee . . . the word of God came to John son of Zechariah in the wilderness" (Luke 3:1-2). With these words, Luke sets the stage for the ministry of John the Baptist in the wilderness of the Jordan. Following the convention of Greek history writing, Luke dates this event to the rule of prominent leaders in the region. We know that Tiberius succeeded

Augustus in 14 C.E., and that Pontius Pilate assumed his office as Roman Prefect in Judea in 26 C.E. This would indicate that Luke is talking about the year 28 C.E., which also dovetails with the rule of Herod Antipas, the tetrarch of Galilee and Perea, who reigned from 4 B.C.E. to 39 C.E.

The evangelists are not the only ones who tell us about John the Baptist. Jewish historian Josephus also has much to say about him in his book *History of the Jews,* published near the end of the first century C.E. John, says Josephus, "was a good man, who urged the Jews to exercise virtue, both in terms of righteousness toward one another and piety toward God, and so come to baptism." That baptism was intended for "the purification of the body, since he believed that the soul was thoroughly cleansed by righteous conduct."

The idea of submersion as an act of ritual cleansing was a core element of ancient Judaism. Before entering the Temple, for example, every Jewish pilgrim was expected to enter a *mikveh,* a ritual bath replenished by a natural source of water, in order to become ritually pure. Similar ritual ablutions were required for other events, such as conjugal activity after a woman's menstrual flow had passed. Many affluent homes in Jerusalem even had their own private *mikva'ot* for this purpose.

John, however, practiced immersion with a different idea in mind. His baptism was meant to affect the soul, not the body. It was a symbolic gesture that signified a resolute break with immoral living. Perhaps he was inspired by the words of Ezekiel: "I will sprinkle clean water on you, and you will be clean; I will cleanse you from all your impurities and from your idols" (Ezekiel 36:25).

What "impurities and idols" could John be thinking of, and why would the Jews of his time need to repent? For one, the pagan Greco-Roman culture so wholeheartedly embraced by Herod the Great was still present, particularly in the cities. In many townships, as the work of Richard Horsley and Mark Chancey has shown, devout and observant Jewish communities lived in an uneasy coexistence with people enjoying a Roman lifestyle. Worse, Judea itself, the land that God had given to Israel, was occupied by Roman forces, as a crown province of Emperor Augustus. Once again, the Hebrew nation was suffering under the boot of a foreign potentate, as it had in centuries past during the occupation of

ABOVE: *A branch of the Jordan River flows near one of the places identified with Jesus' baptism by John the Baptist, close to the Greco-Roman city of Scythopolis.*

OPPOSITE: *The Roman gladius, or sword, equipped with a 20-inch iron blade and razor-sharp edge, was the principal weapon of Roman occupying forces in Judea.*

PRECEDING PAGES: *"The Baptism of Christ," a fresco from around 1305, is the work of Italian artist Giotto di Bondone (1266–1337).*

> *Whoever has two coats must share with anyone who has none; and whoever has food must do likewise.*

LUKE 3:11

A panel by 14th-century artist Ugolino di Nerio (active 1317–1327) depicts John the Baptist with a scroll taken from the Gospel of John: "Behold the Lamb of God" (John 1:29).

Assyrian, Neo-Babylonian, Persian, and Greek overlords. Once again, many Jews, including the Sadducees, were openly collaborating with the Roman enemy for either political influence or profit. And just as former prophets had warned that the Lord would save Israel only if the nation repented and returned to its covenant with God, so too did John warn that a major reckoning was at hand. "May God cleanse Israel against the day of mercy and blessing," says the Book of the Psalms of Solomon, written some 50 years before the birth of Jesus, "against the day of choice when He brings back His Anointed" (*Mashiach* in Hebrew, or Messiah).

Who was this Messiah, this redeemer? He appears in several other Jewish apocalyptic writings of the period, where invariably his coming is attended by cataclysmic events that literally wipe the slate clean, before a new Davidic state can be established. This is echoed in the words of John the Baptist. "You brood of vipers!" he cries when spotting a group of Pharisees and Sadducees in the crowd. "Who warned you to flee from the wrath to come? Bear fruit worthy of repentance" (Matthew 3:7-8). "Even now the ax is lying at the root of the trees," he excoriates his audience in Luke; "every tree therefore that does not bear good fruit is cut down and thrown into the fire" (Luke 3:9).

But Jewish writings did not always agree on the identity of this redeemer. Many saw him as a warrior-king in the mold of King David; others saw him as a supernatural being, as an angel like Michael, or "one like a son of man" (Daniel 7:13). The Dead Sea Scrolls speak of *two* messiahs: a warrior king from the "branch of David" and a priest named the "Messiah of Aaron."

The Gospels, however, leave no doubt about the identity of the Messiah in John's sermons. It is Jesus. John's role is that of a prophet who prepares his way. To make this case, all Gospels invoke the words of the prophet Isaiah: "The voice of one crying out in the wilderness: Prepare the way of the Lord, make his path straight" (Matthew 3:2; Mark 1:2-3; Luke 3:4; John 1:23).

JOHN'S BAPTISM

Unlike the ritual immersion in a mikveh, which a Jew was expected to practice often, John's immersion was a special event, a physical seal on a person's resolve to repent. That is how Josephus interpreted John's baptism. "John," he writes, "exhorted the Jews to join in baptism, practicing virtue and treating their fellows with righteousness and God with piety. In this way, [John] said, baptism would indeed be acceptable to God: not by using it to gain remission for some sins, but for the purification of the body."

The evangelists see this differently. For them, John's baptism is a rite of forgiveness, a pardon of sins committed by an individual during his past immoral life. Much later, under Paul, the role of Christian baptism would change again, to one of initiation, of a welcome into the Christian community, based on a pledge of faith. "When you were stripped," Cyril of Jerusalem would write in the fourth century, "you were anointed with exorcised oil, from the very hairs of your head to your feet, and were made partakers of the good olive-tree, Jesus Christ." As such, the Christian ritual would once again move closer to its Jewish precedent, for a convert to Judaism is fully immersed in the natural waters of a mikveh.

This ambiguity in the allegorical meaning of Luke's story is also present in John's vision of Jesus as the Messiah. On the one hand, John presents him as a powerful spiritual force. "I baptize you with water," he tells his followers, "but one who is more powerful than I is coming . . . He will baptize you with the Holy Spirit and fire." The symbolic imagery of Spirit and fire would later return in the story of Pentecost in the Acts of the Apostles, when tongues of fire energize the disciples to go out and preach the word of Jesus. But in other passages, John's idea of Jesus as the Messiah is closer to the Jewish model of warrior-king. "His winnowing fork is in his hand, to clear his threshing floor and to gather the wheat into his granary," the Baptist says sternly in the Gospel of Luke; "but the chaff he will burn with unquenchable fire" (Luke 3:17).

This belt, made from woven flax, was found among other belongings of a family who had found refuge in the Cave of Letters during the Second Jewish War (132–135 c.e.).

JESUS JOINS THE BAPTIST

And then, just as John had prophesied, Jesus did join the Baptist's movement in the wilderness of the Jordan. This is where all four Gospels converge; in fact, both Mark's and John's stories of Jesus' ministry begin with the moment that "Jesus came from Nazareth of Galilee and was baptized by John in the Jordan" (Mark 1:9).

But why did Jesus decide to leave his native home in Galilee for the Jordan wilderness? What drew him to John's movement? This question is not explored in any of the Gospel stories, though the answer may be found in Josephus's *History of the Jews.* "Crowds flocked to [John]," Josephus claims, "and they were greatly moved by his words." This is echoed in the Gospel of Matthew, which tells us that "the people of Jerusalem and all Judea were going out to him, and all the region along the Jordan" (Matthew 3:5). Simply put, John was a celebrity preacher who attracted many young men and women filled with idealistic fervor to build a better future.

According to Josephus, John's popularity became so widespread that it roused the suspicions of Herod Antipas, who, as we saw, was the ruling authority in both Galilee and Perea, the region on the eastern bank of the Jordan where John presumably had established his camp. When told that John's followers "seemed prepared to do whatever he would tell them," Antipas immediately feared "the specter of a revolt," as no doubt his father would have.

John certainly looked the part of a dissident, a first-century hippie. "John wore clothing of camel's hair with a leather belt around his waist, and his

THE COMMUNITY OF QUMRAN

Qumran is a place of many steep cliffs near the Dead Sea, where in the winter of 1947, a Bedouin shepherd named Muhammad el-Hamed found several jars containing ancient scrolls. Soon scores of other ancient "Dead Sea Scrolls" were found here, spread over some 40 caves. Samples from the scrolls, mostly written in Hebrew, have been carbon-dated to between 200 B.C.E. and 60 C.E., including the time of Jesus. They thus offer a fascinating window into the Hebrew Scripture that Jesus would have been familiar with. Nearby, excavators found the remains of a religious community that, scholars believe, was responsible for producing the scrolls. The complex featured an elaborate system of stepped cisterns that could have been used for ablutions or water storage. Several scholars have sought to link John the Baptist with this community. Some of the Qumran texts bear similarity with John's sermons, such as the need to share one's possessions. ■

Among these remains of the Qumran settlement, archaeologists found potsherds and other artifacts dated between 150 B.C.E. and 70 C.E.

Herod feared John, knowing that he was a righteous and holy man, and he protected him.

MARK 6:20

food was locusts and wild honey," says Matthew, perhaps inspired by the image of Elijah, who was also described as "a hairy man, with a leather belt around his waist" (Matthew 3:4, II Kings 8). The reference to Elijah is important, for it reminded Matthew's audience of God's promise that "I will send you the prophet Elijah before the great and terrible day of the Lord comes" (Malachi 4:5).

Jesus' desire to be baptized as well, however, posed a dilemma for John the Baptist. His baptismal rite was designed for *sinners,* for people who needed to make a radical break with their sinful way of life. Why would Jesus have to undergo such a ritual? Wouldn't this imply that Jesus had lived a sinful life as well? The Gospel of Matthew is keenly aware of the rather thorny theological questions involved. In Matthew's version, John tries to prevent Jesus from being immersed, saying, "I need to be baptized by *you,* and [yet] you come to me?" But Jesus answers him, "Let it be so now; for it is proper for us in this way to fulfill all righteousness"—meaning, to fulfill all that God had planned for him (Matthew 3:14-15).

As Jesus emerged from the flowing waters of the Jordan, something miraculous happened that is reported with remarkable unanimity across all four Gospels: The heavens split, and the Holy Spirit descended on Jesus in the shape of a dove. A voice from heaven then spoke: "You are my Son, the beloved; with you I am well pleased" (Mark 1:10-11). This verse, which combines the verse "You are my Son" from Psalms 2:7 with Isaiah ("My chosen, in whom my soul delights," Isaiah 42:1), is described almost verbatim in the other Gospels (Matthew 3:17; Luke 3:22; and John 1:32-33).

In the Middle Ages, the unique heart-shaped petals of the Caltha flower, either marigold or mayflower, would become associated with the cult of Mary.

This large Roman vessel from the first century was reused in the 13th-century Crusader fortress of Monfort as a baptismal font.

The purpose of this symbolic vision is to allay any lingering doubt about the reason that Jesus is being baptized. This immersion has nothing to do with the remission of sins, for Jesus doesn't have any. Instead, it is the first of several supernatural events whereby God clearly shows to the world that Jesus' arrival on the scene is by divine fiat, as part of God's plan. The baptism is not a

OPPOSITE: *A sixth-century Byzantine mosaic from the Baptistery of Ariani in Ravenna, Italy, depicts the baptism of Christ, surrounded by images of the Twelve Apostles.*

cleansing act by the hand of John, but rather an anointing ritual by the power of the Holy Spirit, which establishes Jesus as the Anointed One, the Messiah (Christos in Greek).

The Jordan River winds its way through a bend in the lush landscape of Galilee on its way to the Dead Sea, located 1,300 feet below sea level.

JOHN'S ARREST

At some point after Jesus joined the Baptist in the Jordan, Herod Antipas decided to act. He sent his soldiers to arrest John and take him to one of his father's fortresses, the citadel of Machaerus. The Gospel of Mark adds some interesting details about the circumstances of John's execution. Mark writes

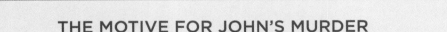

THE MOTIVE FOR JOHN'S MURDER

The Gospels and Josephus offer two different scenarios for the reason of John's arrest. Herod Antipas was married to the daughter of King Aretas IV Philopatris, the ruler of Nabataea. But after Antipas met Herodias, the wife of his half brother Philip, he decided to divorce his first wife and marry his sister-in-law instead. Herodias was also Antipas's niece, for she was the daughter of another half brother, Aristobulus (son of Herod the Great and Mariamne). John was incensed over the marriage. He warned Antipas that according to Jewish Law, "it is not lawful for you to have your brother's wife" (Mark 6:18), referring to the Book of Leviticus, which states that "you shall not uncover the nakedness of your brother's wife; it is your brother's nakedness" (Leviticus 18:16).

Josephus, however, sees things from a political angle. In his version, Antipas acted preemptively, before John could be tempted to exploit the tensions in the region and incite his followers to a rebellion. "[Antipas] thought that by putting [John] to death, he would prevent any mischief he might cause," Josephus adds. Such would suggest that John himself could be the instigator of a protest, as a Messiah who with his winnowing fork made ready to "clear his threshing floor." According to Matthew, this was not the case; John told his audience that "one who is more powerful than I is coming after me; I am not worthy to carry his sandals" (Matthew 3:11). But Matthew was well aware of John's popularity; "[Antipas] feared the multitude, because they counted [John the Baptist] as a prophet," he writes elsewhere (Matthew 14:5). ∎

A golden medallion from the late first century C.E. depicts a young, seminude woman dancing, evoking the story of Herod's stepdaughter Salome.

OPPOSITE: *Located close to the Sea of Galilee, Hammat Gader ("the hot springs of Gadara") was developed into a sprawling spa resort by the Romans in the second century C.E.*

FOLLOWING PAGES: *"The Feast of Herod and the Beheading of Saint John the Baptist" by Benozzo Gozzoli (ca 1421–1497) shows the lithe figure of Salome, dancing for her stepfather, Herod Antipas.*

that while Herod Antipas "feared John, knowing that he was a righteous and holy man," his new wife, Herodias, "had a grudge against him, and wanted to kill him" (Mark 6:19). Her motive was simple: John the Baptist had committed lèse-majesté by publicly agitating against her marriage. The reason was that Herodias had previously been married to Antipas's half brother; therefore, a marriage to Antipas was unlawful, against the Torah. Herodias had never forgiven him, but she was well aware that her husband, Herod, was rather fond of John and in no hurry to send the man to the scaffold. Mark tells us that while John's words often left Herod "perplexed," he still "liked to listen to him" (Mark 6:20). Herodias would therefore have to resort to some subterfuge to enact her revenge.

That opportunity came when the court celebrated Herod's birthday with a lavish banquet, which brought together "his courtiers and officers and . . . the leaders of Galilee." Herod's daughter, Salome, decided to mark the occasion with a dance. This she did with such alluring grace that Herod, greatly pleased, told her, "Ask me for whatever you wish, and I will give it." Flushed, she ran to Herodias for advice, who didn't think twice. Ask for "the head of John the baptizer," she replied. Salome did so. Hearing this, Herod was "deeply aggrieved," says Mark, but he could not renege on this promise in front of all the dignitaries who had gathered for the banquet. A guard was dispatched to go to John's cell and behead him (Mark 6:21-27). ∎

The Dead Sea Scrolls, including this fragment of the Psalms Scroll, were found in 1947 in a group of caves just outside the ancient settlement of Qumran, close to the Dead Sea.

CHAPTER EIGHT

A WEDDING
IN CANA

*We have found him about
whom Moses in the law and
also the prophets wrote,
Jesus son of Joseph
from Nazareth.*

JOHN 1:45

Jesus Performs His First Miracle

His sojourn with John the Baptist must have left a deep impression on Jesus. John had urged his audience to repent and to reject sinful living so as to prepare for a future kingdom of God, an idea that would become a key theme of Jesus' ministry. John drew large crowds with his sermons. He excoriated the elites, such as soldiers and tax collectors, for their exploitation of the poor. And John, like Jesus, was called "Teacher" by his disciples. So it is plausible to think that John became an important role model for Jesus when, in the months to come, he began to form his own movement in Galilee.

The Gospel of John suggests that the first seeds for Jesus' ministry were sown while he was still in the wilderness of the Jordan. One day John the Baptist pointed to Jesus and said to two of his followers, "Look, here is the Lamb of God!" The two disciples then decided to follow Jesus. When Jesus turned and saw them, he asked, "What are you looking for?" They replied, "Rabbi, where are you staying?" whereby John helpfully explained for his non-Jewish audience that *rabbi* means "teacher." As it happened, one of these followers was Andrew, the brother of another disciple, named Simon. Andrew went to see Simon and told him, "We have found the Messiah" (John 1:38-41). Thus, Jesus had formed his first group of disciples.

Jesus took a liking to Simon. "You are to be called Cephas," he said. The Greek word *kephas* is a transliteration of the Aramaic word *kêfa,* meaning "stone" or "rock." In other words, Jesus gave Simon a nickname, like "Rocky."

In Christian literature it would be translated into the more familiar Greek word for rock, namely *Petros,* or Peter.

THE TOWN OF BETHSAIDA

Andrew, Peter, and a disciple named Philip were natives of a town called Bethsaida, located on the shores of the Sea of Galilee. Since the evangelist identifies this place by name, some historians believe that this is where Jesus went after he left the Baptist's camp. It would have made a lot of sense. Perea, the eastern bank of the Jordan, and Galilee were part of the territory ruled by Herod Antipas. No one could know if Herod would be satisfied with John's arrest, or if he would try to go after his followers as well. As it happened, Bethsaida was located just across the border from Galilee in the Gaulanitis, the region governed by Antipas's half brother Philip. This was a largely Gentile region that had strong cultural and commercial ties with Greco-Roman cities throughout the Mediterranean. Its population was perfectly content to be ruled by the Pax Romana, the Roman peace, in stark contrast to the brewing tensions in Judea. Bethsaida would have been a good choice if Jesus and his new disciples wanted to lay low until things calmed down and Herod's intentions became

ABOVE: *A sunset scene of fishermen mending their nets on the shore of the Sea of Galilee is a timeless setting of many stories in the Gospels.*

OPPOSITE: *Oil lamps with scenes from Homer's Odyssey are typical of the type of terra-cotta lamps that were used throughout the Roman Empire.*

PREVIOUS PAGES: *Sienese artist Duccio di Buoninsegna (ca 1255/1260–ca 1318/1319) painted "The Calling of the Apostles Peter and Andrew" between 1308 and 1311.*

*Now Philip was from Bethsaida,
the city of Andrew and Peter.*

JOHN 1:44

clear. Matthew seems to suggest as much when he writes, "When Jesus heard that John had been arrested, he withdrew to Galilee" (Matthew 4:12).

The location of Bethsaida, which literally means "house of fishermen," has long been the subject of controversy. In 1987, archaeologist Rami Arav started to dig at a tell, or mound, about a mile or so inland from the Sea of Galilee, several hundred yards north of the Jordan River. This location corresponds to Josephus's comment that Bethsaida was located in the lower Gaulanitis, near the estuary of the Jordan River. According to Eusebius, an important church historian from the fourth century, Bethsaida was expanded under Philip and elevated to the status of a polis, a Greek city, under the name of Julias. The excavators were able to corroborate this. Among the dwellings built of the local, charcoal-colored basalt stone, they found a number of coins from 30 c.e., struck during the reign of Tiberius, whose mother's name was Julia,

Universities from the United States, Germany, and Poland excavated the ancient city gate of Bethsaida during a campaign starting in 1987.

a dating that brings us very close to the time of Jesus.

The excavation campaign, which is ongoing, has since revealed a fairly large settlement surrounded by city walls that date from both the Iron Age IIB (850–732 B.C.E.) and Roman periods. These walls are pierced to the southeast by an impressive city gate. From there, a beaten earth road led to what was probably an embankment on the Sea of Galilee. Although the site is now a mile removed from the sea because of earthquakes and the formation of silt beds along the banks of the Jordan, this was probably the road that Jesus and his three followers took when they returned from the Jordan wilderness, safe from Herod Antipas's militia.

THE TEMPTATION IN THE DESERT

The synoptic Gospels give a slightly different version of what happened after John's arrest. According to Mark, the oldest Gospel, Jesus was first driven into the wilderness by the same Spirit who had descended on him like a dove. "He was in the wilderness forty days," says Mark, "tempted by Satan; and he was with the wild beasts; and the angels waited on him." This passage, like many others in the Gospels, is imbued with allegorical meaning that Jewish listeners would readily recognize. As we saw in the Introduction, the evangelists often use such symbolic verses to enhance their narrative with a special significance, using the vocabulary of Hebrew Scripture. "Forty days in the wilderness" harks back to the forty years that the Israelites spent in the desert before their entry into the Promised Land. Similarly, the prophet Elijah went "forty days and forty nights to Horeb the mount of God" before the word of God found him (I Kings 19:8). Forty days, in biblical vernacular, is a time of preparation, punctuated by trial.

For Jesus, this trial takes the form of temptations from Satan, God's adversary; their purpose, as in the case of Job, is to verify a protagonist's faith and commitment. And finally, the "wild beasts" of this verse may refer to the

This 16th-century stained-glass window from the Church of Sainte Madeleine in Troyes, France, depicts Satan's temptation of Christ in the wilderness.

primordial state of the Earth before the Fall of Man, which Jesus has come to redeem. In sum, Mark's passage is meant to remind us that Jesus did not embark on his path to ministry without a period of profound preparation and reflection, guided by the hand of God—as illustrated by the angels who waited on him.

Both Matthew and Luke take the story of Satan's temptation and develop it further, once again using symbolic language from Hebrew Scripture. Their treatment is so similar that scholars are inclined to believe that this passage and other shared stories originated from a common source, a putative sayings document, now lost, known as "Q" for *Quelle* (or "source" in German). In their version, Jesus returned from his fast of "forty days and forty nights" to find he was famished. Satan, the "tempter," said, "If you are the Son of God, command these stones to become loaves of bread." This challenge evokes the story of the Hebrews in the desert, crying for bread, and God's miraculous gift of manna (Exodus 16:15). Jesus parried the devil by quoting from Deuteronomy: "One does not live by bread alone, but by every word that comes from the mouth of God" (Deuteronomy 8:3).

Next, Satan took Jesus to Jerusalem and placed him on the pinnacle of the Temple. "If you are the Son of God," he said, "throw yourself down," challenging Jesus with a biblical citation of his own, Psalm 91:11, 12: "For he will command his angels concerning you," and "On their hands they will bear you up." Jesus was having none of it. He replied, "Again it is written, 'Do not put the Lord your God to the test,'" quoting Deuteronomy once more (Deuteronomy 6:16).

LOCATING CANA

Cana appears several times in John's Gospel, notably as the birthplace of Nathanael (the Apostle known as Bartholomew in the synoptic Gospels), and later, as the location where Jesus will be asked to heal the son of a royal official. This suggests that Cana was a place of some consequence in Lower Galilee, and yet historians and archaeologists have been stymied in their attempts to identify it. One tradition places it in the Arab town of Kafr Kanna, located some four miles east of Nazareth. Another contender, Khirbet Kana, lies six miles north of the city. Of the two, Kafr Kanna has been the preferred choice for pilgrims going back to the Byzantine period, as evidenced by two churches. But other than a sixth-century church, no ancient remains have been found. Excavations at Khirbet Kana, however, show that the village was inhabited from the Hellenistic to the early Byzantine periods, roughly from the third century B.C.E. to the ninth century C.E. ■

The Franciscan church of Cana, completed in 1883, is built on the site where, according to tradition, the wedding of Cana took place as described in the Gospel of John.

This view of the Judean Desert was taken from the northern side of Herod's stronghold of Masada. The remains of a Roman legion's camp are still visible at left.

The devil then took Jesus for a third and final temptation. He placed him on a high mountain with a view of all the kingdoms of the world, arrayed in their splendor. This is a typical motif in Matthew's story; mountains often serve as the location of sacred or momentous events. Satan turned to Jesus and said, "All these I will give you, if you will fall down and worship me." With that, the ultimate

> *On the third day there was a wedding in Cana of Galilee, and the mother of Jesus was there.*
>
> **JOHN 2:1**

Soft leavened flatbread, baked from wheat flour, has been a mainstay of people's diet in the Near East since biblical times.

purpose of the devil's machinations was revealed: to derail Jesus from his divine mission by seducing him with earthly possessions and concerns. But Jesus resolutely rebuked him. "Away with you Satan!" he cried, "For it is written, 'Worship the Lord your God, and serve only him,'" quoting from Deuteronomy 6:13. Defeated, the devil left him, but not for long. Soon he would appear again, by possessing men, women, and even swine, challenging

OPPOSITE: *Italian artist Fra Angelico (ca 1387–1455) painted this panel of "The Marriage Feast of Cana" around 1450.*

This aureus, a gold coin that served as Rome's most valuable currency unit, was struck during the reign of Emperor Tiberius (r. 12–37 C.E.).

While affluent families drank wine from silver or glass cups, families in Galilee used a simple earthenware beaker.

Jesus to exorcise them and thus try to contest Satan's dominion in the Kingdom of God (Matthew 4:1-11; Luke 4:1-13).

It is interesting that Jesus, in all of his responses, relies on the Book of Deuteronomy, the fifth and last of the Five Books of Moses. Of all the writings of the Torah, this book is perhaps the most succinct in laying out the covenantal relationship between God and his people: their past, their present, and their future. It clearly specifies the conditions that Israel must meet to enjoy God's favor—conditions that in Jesus' time had once again been abandoned, as John the Baptist had so vividly argued. Traditionally Moses delivered the last of the book's three sermons on the eve of the entry into the Promised Land. By reminding their audience of the quintessential tenets of Deuteronomistic law, therefore, Matthew and Luke reiterate what is at stake: the final fulfillment of God's covenantal promise on the eve of the launch of the ministry that will make this promise a reality.

Mark then takes the story to the Sea of Galilee. Here, Jesus recruits Simon and his brother Andrew, both fishermen, by saying, "Follow me and I will make you fish for people." They are soon joined by two more followers, James and John, sons of Zebedee, who were in their boat mending their nets (Mark 1:16-19). Although Mark doesn't identify the location, it is possible that the story takes place in a port city like Bethsaida, as we surmised previously, for in the next paragraph, Mark says, "They went up to Capernaum," the town that from that point on would serve as the base of Jesus' ministry.

WATER IS CHANGED INTO WINE

Before that ministry could begin, however, John tells a story that appears only in his Gospel. Back in Galilee, Jesus and his disciples were invited to accompany Mary, Jesus' mother, to a wedding in a town called Cana. At one point during the celebration, however, the "wine gave out." This was not unusual, since wedding feasts in ancient times, even in Galilee, could often stretch over several days. Jesus' mother (curiously, John never refers to her by her name) then turned to him and said, "They have no wine," no doubt with a meaningful look in her eyes. And Jesus said, "Woman, what concern is that to me and to you? My hour has not yet come"—meaning the hour of his death. This response sounds a bit harsh in its English translation, but the original Greek word for "woman," *gunai* or *guné,* may have been used to address a woman with a measure of respect, perhaps similar to our use of "my lady," though the meaning is not always clear.

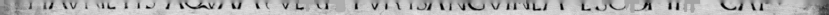

VOX DOMINI̅ TONVIT SVPER AQVAS · P̅S · XXVIII · C̊ ·

DE SC̅EDIT ꝫLAVIT SE PTIES INIORDANE · III · R̅ · V · C̊ ·

"The Marriage Feast of Cana" forms part of the Maestà Altarpiece, painted by Duccio di Buoninsegna (ca 1255/1260–ca 1318/1319) for the altar of the Siena Cathedral in 1308.

Mary, however, was undeterred by Jesus' response. She turned to the servants and said, "Do whatever he tells you," perhaps thinking that it would be more difficult for Jesus to deny others than his own mother. Her tactic worked. When Jesus spotted six stone water jars standing nearby, he told the servants to "fill them up to the brim." Stone vessels were often used for water storage, for unlike pottery made of clay, they were considered to be ritually clean. John confirms as much when he adds, for the benefit of his Gentile listeners, that the vessels were "for the Jewish rites of purification"—the cleansing of hands, plates, and implements used in a Jewish meal. The fact that each vessel held "twenty or thirty gallons," as John tells us, suggests that this was a very large wedding party indeed.

Jesus then instructed the servants to "draw some out, and take it to the chief steward," the man who, as master of ceremonies, would be responsible for the wine being served. When this steward tasted the water, it had become wine—and not just everyday table wine, but wine of an excellent vintage. The steward was so surprised that he called the bridegroom and said, "Everyone serves the good wine first, and then the inferior wine after the guests have become drunk. But you have kept the good wine until now" (John 2:1-10).

Jesus, John adds, "did this, the first of his signs in Cana of Galilee." Signs are important for this evangelist. According to Josephus, a prophet claiming to speak on God's behalf was expected to deliver a *semeion,* a miraculous, supernatural sign so as to authenticate himself. Miracles were seen as a seal of divine approval; for John, they justify a person's faith. Some scholars believe that John's Gospel is partly based on a document that records seven such signs by Jesus.

And then, says John, "he went down to Capernaum with his mother, his brothers, and his disciples." It is here that the ministry of Jesus would begin in earnest. ∎

FOLLOWING PAGES: "The Marriage Feast of Cana" is one of the frescoes painted by Giotto di Bondone (1266–1337) in the Scrovegni Chapel in Padua, Italy.

THE MYSTERIES OF CANA

The miracle at Cana may have multiple symbolic meanings. Theologian Rudolf Bultmann has argued that the early Church celebrated this miracle on January 6, the Feast of the Epiphany. In Antiquity, this date was associated with the feast of Dionysus, the Greco-Roman god of wine, when empty jars at every temple dedicated to the god would be filled with wine. Bultmann believes that the Cana story sent a message to John's Gentile audience that Dionysus had now been upstaged by a far more powerful deity in the form of Jesus, the Son of God.

Other historians have argued that the Cana story may have had a special significance for Jewish Christians. Throughout the Torah, water is associated with ritual purification. Jesus, however, changes this water into a new and vital component,

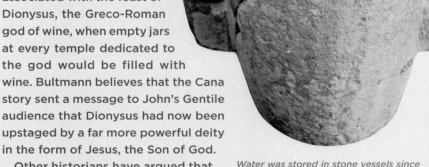

Water was stored in stone vessels since these were believed to be impervious to ritual impurity, as in the case of this stone measuring cup.

wine, symbol of life. The underlying message is that with Jesus, the Laws of Moses gain a whole new dimension. Such symbolic clues may be largely lost on modern readers, but for a first-century audience, they may have been readily recognizable.

Finally, the miracle has also been interpreted from a uniquely Christian perspective. Some scholars believe that Jesus' rebuke to his mother, "What concern is that to me and to you?" is a reproach to those whose faith relies on the strength of miracles they've witnessed, a theme that will run through this Gospel up to the story of the disbelieving Thomas (John 20:25). Others see the wine as a metaphor of the divine Spirit, which has chosen Jesus as the last and most eminent of Israel's prophets. ∎

CHAPTER NINE

THE MINISTRY BEGINS

*They went to Capernaum;
and when the Sabbath came,
he entered the synagogue
and taught.*

MARK 1:21

Jesus Teaches in the Synagogues

In the life of every judge, king, or prophet in Hebrew Scripture, there comes a time when the individual is called to his mission. Moses heard his calling in the burning bush in Sinai, and with his brother Aaron set out for the court of Pharaoh in Egypt. Samuel was serving at YHWH's shrine at Shiloh when the Philistine capture of the Ark prompted the Israelites to ask him to anoint a king. And Israel had suffered through a three-year famine when God called Elijah out of hiding in the Transjordan and ordered him to confront the Baal cult in Samaria once and for all.

According to Mark, the moment when Jesus formally embarked on his mission took place in Capernaum, a township near the Sea of Galilee. He entered the synagogue on the Sabbath, when all of the community was gathered inside to hear Scripture, and taught. "They were astounded at his teaching," says Mark (Mark 1:22).

Luke places this story in Nazareth. After Jesus returned to Galilee and "began to teach in their synagogues," he writes, "he went to the synagogue on the Sabbath day, as was his custom" (Luke 4:14-16). When Jesus stood up to read, he was handed the scroll of the prophet Isaiah. While Sabbath readings usually were texts from the Torah, some rabbinic texts suggest that these readings could be complemented with an excerpt from the collection of the *Nevi'im,* or Prophets. Jesus opened the scroll, found the passage he was looking for, and said, "The Spirit of the Lord is upon me, because he has anointed me to bring good news to the poor," quoting from Isaiah 61:1. And then he continued:

He has sent me to proclaim release to the captives
and recover of sight to the blind,
to let the oppressed go free,
to proclaim the year of the Lord's favor. (Luke 4:18-19)

With that, Jesus rolled up the scroll, gave it back to the attendant, and sat down. All eyes were fixed on Jesus as the congregation waited for his commentary, or the reason that he had chosen this passage. And then Jesus said in a voice filled with confidence, "Today this scripture has been fulfilled in your hearing."

Did his audience gasp? Chances are they did, for these were certainly audacious, if not presumptuous, words. What was the "good news" that he was supposedly bringing to the poor? And who were these captives and the oppressed? Was this some veiled reference to John the Baptist or any of the other political prisoners whom Herod Antipas had locked in his prisons? And how could this stranger, this Jesus, claim that he was the *anointed one,* the Messiah, as Isaiah prophesied?

In Mark's version, the people in the synagogue responded positively, for "he taught them as one having authority, and not as the scribes." This latter

ABOVE: *Most residential structures surrounding the ancient synagogue of Capernaum were built using basalt stones that were quarried locally.*

OPPOSITE: *Many Roman jewelry designs, such as these delicate golden earrings shaped in the form of seashells, were made by Greek artisans in the Greek style.*

PRECEDING PAGES: *This anonymous 14th-century fresco, "Jesus Preaching at the Nazareth Synagogue," is in the Basilica di Santa Caterina d'Alessandria in Galatina, Italy.*

part is a swipe at Mark's favorite target, the scribes: a group of professional "notaries" who catered to the vast majority of Galilee's illiterate peasantry in the preparation of all sorts of legal documents, including wedding contracts and wills. Given that observant Jews in Galilee followed the precepts of the Torah, the Jewish Law, such scribes needed to be experts in the application of Mosaic legislation as well. Mark, however, often grouped them together with the other intellectual elites of his time, the Pharisees and Sadducees, as the principal opposition to Jesus' ministry.

But in Luke's version of Jesus' synagogue presentation, set in Nazareth, the mood turned sour. While some "spoke well of him and were amazed at the gracious words that came from his mouth," others scratched their heads. "Is this not Joseph's son?" they asked incredulously. "Isn't this the boy that we saw growing up in our midst?" they might have added. How, then, can this man, a son of one of our villagers, suddenly proclaim himself as the Messiah?

Jesus sensed the shifting mood and confronted the murmuring crowd head-on. "Truly I tell you," he said, "no prophet is accepted in the prophet's home town." And to underscore his case, he told the story of the prophet Elijah, whom God had sent to the widow at Zarephath, a Gentile woman no less, while all of Israel was suffering from famine because they didn't deserve divine intervention. "There were also many lepers in Israel at the time of the prophet Elisha," Jesus continues in another stinging rebuke, "and none of them was cleansed except Naaman the Syrian"—another Gentile more worthy of God's favor than the Jews themselves. The subtext was unmistakable:

THE TWELVE APOSTLES

I n Antiquity, it was the disciple who was expected to approach a teacher with the hope of being accepted into his group of students. Jesus, however, went out to handpick his followers himself. One reason, perhaps, is that Jesus was a preacher on the move. He therefore needed assistants, or *delegates,* more than disciples in the traditional sense. As a delegate (*shaliach* in Hebrew and Aramaic, translated in the Gospels as *apostolos,* or Apostle), these followers served as his advance party, preparing a village for Jesus' impending arrival, while managing crowds during large public events. Jesus eventually recruited 12 Apostles, a number that is probably inspired by the 12 tribes of Israel. In addition to the first five— Simon Peter, Andrew, Philip, and James and John, the sons of Zebedee—he also took in "Bartholomew, and Matthew, and Thomas, and James son of Alphaeus, and Thaddaeus, and Simon the Cananaean, and Judas Iscariot, who betrayed him" (Mark 3:18-19). ∎

An anonymous Byzantine artist created this sixth-century ivory depicting Christ surrounded by the Twelve Apostles.

If Nazareth did not accept Jesus as the Messiah, then they would be less deserving of his Kingdom of God than any Gentile in Galilee.

For the synagogue congregation, this opprobrium was too much. "When they heard this," says Luke, "all in the synagogue were filled with rage." They took Jesus out of the synagogue and led him "to the brow of the hill on which their town was built"—a brow that is still visible to this day, overlooking the Beit Netofa Valley. For a moment, it looked as if they were going to hurl Jesus off the cliff to his death, but the threat was not acted on. Jesus, says Luke, "passed through the midst of them and went on his way" (Luke 4:20-30).

Why is this great coming-out moment, this wonderful declaration of Jesus' mission, marred by this sudden, almost murderous hostility? Why do the people in the synagogue community reject Jesus before he has even had the chance to explain himself? The answer, perhaps, lies in the pivotal dilemma that the evangelists, including Luke, confronted in writing their Gospels. It came down to this: If Jesus was indeed the Messiah foretold in Hebrew Scripture, then

TOP: *The synagogue of ancient Capernaum, built of blocks of white limestone, has been dated to the late third century c.e., although it may have been built on an older synagogue structure.*

BOTTOM: *Tilapia fish, also known as "St. Peter's fish," are one of three main species caught in the Sea of Galilee since biblical times.*

A first-century B.C.E. inscription refers to a synagogue "built by Theodotos, son of Vettenos" and shows that synagogues existed in the late Second Temple period.

why did so many Jews of Luke's time reject him? Why were many Christian Jews ostracized from synagogues throughout Judea and Galilee, as well as Asia Minor?

These were the urgent questions that the evangelists were forced to address, and they resolved them by suggesting that opposition to Jesus' mission had been present from the start. This conflict, as we saw, is an important theme in Mark, but nowhere more prominently than in the Gospel of Luke. In Luke's narrative, Jesus came to Galilee to lead humanity to a new covenant with God—but ironically, it was the Gentile community, not Jesus' own fellow Jews, who would embrace him and accept him.

> *[Jesus] made his home in Capernaum by the sea, in the territory of Zebulun and Naphtali, so that what had been spoken through the prophet Isaiah might be fulfilled.*
>
> MATTHEW 4:12-14

THE SYNAGOGUES OF GALILEE

The synagogue passage in Luke and Mark is revealing for other reasons as well. Both evangelists show that in the opening phase of his ministry, Jesus deliberately targeted Galilean synagogues as the place to launch his teachings. Until recently, however, it was a virtual maxim in the archaeological community that there were no purpose-built synagogues in Galilee before 70 C.E. and the fall of Jerusalem, because the principal center of Jewish worship before that year was the Temple. Sabbath functions such as communal worship, readings, and other community events were believed to have taken place in the home of elders, in the village courtyard, on the threshing floor, or at any other commons area. In fact, as many historians have pointed out, the word "synagogue" comes from the Greek *synagogē,* which doesn't mean a particular building at all but, rather, an "assembly" or "gathering." Further evidence is found in the Book of Acts of the Apostles, which describes how Paul and his companions "went [on the Sabbath day] outside the gate by the river, where we supposed there was a place of prayer" (Acts 16:13).

But recent discoveries have radically changed this assumption. In Galilee alone, seven synagogues from the pre-70 C.E. era have been excavated, including one at Magdala, which may date from the time of Jesus. Therefore, the suggestion in the Gospels that Jesus deliberately moved from synagogue to synagogue in announcing his mission seems more plausible, and less a projection from Luke's own time, as has sometimes been argued.

In Mark and Luke, Jesus' presentation in the synagogue is immediately followed by an exorcism. This was the sign, the *semeion,* that people of the time expected as evidence that Jesus' mission had indeed a divine sanction. Among the synagogue assembly, Mark writes, was a man "with an unclean spirit, and he cried out: 'What have you to do with us, Jesus of Nazareth? Have you come to destroy us?' " Jesus rebuked him sternly, saying, "Be silent, and come out of him!" In that moment, the "unclean spirit" left the man

According to the Gospel of Luke, Jesus read from the book of the prophet Isaiah, shown here in a sixth-century mosaic from Ravenna, Italy.

The fourth-century remains of this Byzantine octagonal church have traditionally been identified as the location of Peter's house in Capernaum.

(Mark 1:24-26). The exorcism had its intended effect, for "at once [Jesus'] fame began to spread throughout the surrounding region of Galilee."

From a Jewish perspective, the exorcism showed that Jesus had the power and authority to defeat Satan. When people suffered from a chronic illness, and particularly mental illness, they were believed to be possessed by demonic forces. Jesus' ability to exorcise such evil spirits thus sealed his status of the anointed one, the Messiah. It signaled to the people of Galilee that the power of Satan was beginning to wane and that the forces behind a new Kingdom of God—the primary focus of Jesus' mission—were beginning to emerge.

Significantly, the casting out of the demon—the first of five such exorcisms on the Sabbath in the Gospel of Luke—did not involve any physical contact or, indeed, any form of physical effort. This is surprising, because the act of exorcism, which (according to Josephus) was widely practiced at the time by so-called professional magicians, usually involved all sorts of elaborate spells, dances, or rituals. "The ability to [exorcise] remains very strong among us even to this day," Josephus writes in his *History of the Jews*. But in this exorcism, the demon left immediately simply because Jesus commanded him to do so. Thus, the healing did not violate any Sabbath commandment against physical effort. Later in the story, such would become an important issue of contention between Jesus and the Pharisees.

But the day wasn't over yet. After the presentation in the synagogue, Jesus and his followers withdrew to the house of Simon's mother-in-law,

The Great Isaiah Scroll, dated to 100 B.C.E., is one of the Dead Sea Scrolls recovered from Cave 1 in Qumran, near the Dead Sea.

OPPOSITE: *Italian artist Fra Angelico (ca 1387-1455) painted this panel of "St. Peter Dictating the Gospel of St. Mark" for the Linaiuoli Altarpiece, completed around 1435.*

> That evening, at sundown, they brought to him all who were sick or possessed with demons. And the whole city was gathered around the door.

MARK 1:32-33

presumably their home base, and found that she was in bed with a fever. Jesus "took her by the hand and lifted her up," and the fever left her.

Within hours, the news of these two miraculous events spread through the town and across the region. As evening fell, a long line of people began to form at the house—sick people, including "demoniacs, epileptics, and paralytics," who were all hoping to be cured (Matthew 4:24). And Jesus did not disappoint them. Since it was after sunset, marking the end of the Sabbath, Jesus was no longer restricted by Sabbath observance and could freely do all that was required to heal the many sick and disabled who were brought into his presence (Mark 1:32-34).

THE CITY OF CAPERNAUM

Jesus chose to become an itinerant preacher, and in that sense, the use of Capernaum as a base was an excellent choice. It had access to good roads, for the town had a tollbooth straddling one of the principal trade routes between the Decapolis, the League of Ten Cities, and Jerusalem. It also had a port for shipping traffic across the Sea of Galilee. This may be one reason that Jesus chose his disciples among the local community of fishermen, for they would have access to a large boat. Since Capernaum was built near an important crossroads, it even featured a modest military garrison; Jesus would later heal the sick slave of the Roman centurion. In the 1920s, archaeologists uncovered the remains of an octagonal structure, which may be the ancient Byzantine church built over the house

The city of Capernaum, literally "Nahum's Village," may have been the hometown of Peter's wife.

of Simon Peter's mother-in-law as described in early pilgrim records. Nearby are the remains of a beautiful ancient Jewish synagogue, a basilica supported by two rows of columns, with a two-column row in the back. Stone benches lined the walls of the prayer hall, while the exterior featured lovely ornamental details. Significantly, the synagogue was built of limestone, which in Galilee was a far more expensive material than the locally quarried basalt. Was this the synagogue in which Jesus declared his ministry? Modern historians now date the building to the late third century c.e., also given its similarity to the synagogue of Chorazin of 300 c.e. But the remains of a structure underneath the Capernaum synagogue could be the *proseuchè,* or prayer hall, where Jesus taught. ■

A NEW MISSION

One of the loveliest spots on the Sea of Galilee is the shoreline near Tabgha, just a few miles from the remains of Capernaum. According to Luke, Jesus was often drawn to such spots to pray and meditate in the stillness of the dawn. One day Simon Peter and the other disciples went looking for him. When they found him, they said, "Everyone is searching for you" (Mark 1:37). But Jesus hardly acknowledged them. He had been up for a long time, and had spent hours reflecting on his ministry. He had taught in the synagogues and healed all those who had been brought to him, including the sick, the lame, and the possessed. The great prophets of the past, such as Elijah and Elisha, had done the same.

OPPOSITE: Most Roman keys were made of bronze by fusing a mass-produced handle to a shank with custom-made pins.

A colorful sixth-century mosaic from the St. Apollinare Nuovo in Ravenna, Italy, depicts Jesus healing the demoniac of Gergesa.

But Jesus' mission was different. Unlike them, his purpose was not to persuade people to repent, but to go and *build,* to create a new society, a Kingdom of God, a Kingdom of Heaven on Earth. To accomplish this, he couldn't remain in one place, as John the Baptist had done, and wait for the people to come and listen to him. He would have to go out, and canvass *all* of Galilee: visit *all* of the hamlets, villages, and townships where Jewish men and women of goodwill could be found.

Jesus looked up at Simon Peter and said, "Let us go on to the neighboring towns, so that I may proclaim the message there also." He paused and added, "for that is what I came out to do" (Mark 1:35-38). ■

FOLLOWING PAGES: This anonymous Byzantine painting is a vivid illustration of Jesus reading from the Book of Isaiah in the synagogue of Nazareth.

CHAPTER TEN

THE SERMON ON THE MOUNT

*When Jesus saw the crowds,
he went up the mountain;
and after he sat down,
his disciples came to him.
Then he began to speak.*

MATTHEW 5:1-2

Jesus Presents His Program for a Kingdom of God

On the northwestern shore of the Sea of Galilee, roughly between Capernaum and Gennesaret, is a soft undulating hill known in Byzantine times as Mount Eremos. From its summit, a mere 100 feet above sea level, a visitor can enjoy a stunning view of the plain of Gennesaret, one of the most fertile fields bordering the Sea of Galilee. Tradition states that this is the spot where Jesus often "spent the night in prayer," and where he designated 12 followers to be his Apostles.

One day, "a great multitude of people from all Judea, Jerusalem, and the coast of Tyre and Sidon" converged on this mountain "to hear him and be healed of their diseases" (Luke 6:18). When Jesus saw the great crowd coming toward him, he stood up and taught his famous Sermon on the Mount. For the first time in the Gospel story, we hear Jesus teaching *in his own words;* we hear him talk about what he considers the essential purpose of his ministry: the creation of the Kingdom of God.

The concept of God's kingdom was a deeply rooted principle of post-Exilic Judaism, certainly in the growing eschatological yearning of the Second Temple period. From the very first, the 12 tribes that had settled in the Promised Land believed themselves to be a nation, or a *kingdom,* of God. The Books of the Prophets continued to breathe the fundamental principle that while kings may come and go, God is the ultimate ruler of Israel's destiny, just as the land on which the Israelites lived is God's land.

As Jesus saw it, this was the raison d'être of the Jewish commonwealth; without it, the nation had no moral compass, no manifest destiny. But Roman Judaea had strayed far from the ideals of its original founding. One reason was the seductive influence of Hellenistic civilization, a culture rooted in pagan motifs. Another was the growing schism between rich and poor, accelerated by the economic exploitation by the Romans and the collaborationist elites and exacerbated by a priesthood that was indifferent to the plight of the poor. All of these ideas would frame and inform Jesus' great sermon.

Its most detailed version appears in Matthew. Jesus opens with a rhetorical device known as blessings, or Beatitudes, a Latin translation of the Greek expression *makarioi,* which means "blessed are . . ." The expression also appears as *ashrei* ("Happy are . . . ") in the Hebrew Scriptures (Psalms 1:1; Job 5:17; Daniel 12:12). Usually these "blessings" appear in groups. In the book of the Wisdom of Sirach, for example, the teachings include nine Beatitudes; some believe that one of them, "Happy is he who lives with an intelligent life," may have had some influence on Matthew's structure of the Sermon (Sirach 25:7-10). Matthew's version opens as follows:

ABOVE: *The sun rises over the calm waters of the Sea of Galilee, also known as Lake Gennesaret, bathing the hills on the eastern shore in a golden glow.*

OPPOSITE: *Jesus' Sermon of the Beatitudes inspired the creation of these finely detailed ivory plaques on an 11th-century coffer, made in Spain.*

PRECEDING PAGES: *A sixth-century mosaic from the St. Apollinare Nuovo in Ravenna, Italy, shows Jesus delivering the Sermon on the Mount, surrounded by his Apostles.*

"The Sermon on the Mount," painted by Italian artist Fra Angelico (ca 1387–1455) around 1442, places this event on a barren rocky landscape.

Blessed are the poor in spirit, for theirs is the kingdom of heaven.

Blessed are those who mourn, for they will be comforted.

Blessed are the meek, for they will inherit the earth.

Blessed are those who hunger and thirst for righteousness, for they will be filled. (Matthew 5:3-6).

> *You are the salt of the earth; but if salt has lost its taste, how can its saltiness be restored? It is no longer good for anything, but is thrown out and trampled under foot.*

MATTHEW 5:13

It is obvious that the tone of Jesus' sermon is very different from that of his former teacher, John the Baptist, who took a more confrontational approach with his audience. John accused his listeners of laxity and moral abuse, while urging them to repent before it was too late. Jesus, by contrast, begins by acknowledging the suffering of the underclass, the downtrodden, the disenfranchised. He then presents the messianic promise not as a vengeful battle against Israel's foes or as a great natural cataclysm, but as a wondrous, brand-new world: a world of justice and tolerance, which his audience has in its power to establish if only they accept the stringent moral conditions on which this new society will be founded.

THE SERMON IN MATTHEW'S GOSPEL

In Matthew's version of the Beatitudes, the sermon then gradually assumes a more legalistic character. It describes in detail the moral code that all those who enter the Kingdom are expected to follow. In this, Jesus appears to go well beyond the ethical precepts found in the Torah, the Jewish Law. For example, while the ancient commandment against murder is obvious, Jesus also condemns those who want to hurt in more subtle ways, such as being angry with a sister or insulting a brother. Nor can these offenses be remedied by simply offering a gift at the Temple, as the sacrificial cult of ancient Judaism might suggest. "If you remember that your brother or sister has something against you," Jesus says, "leave your gift there before the altar and go; first be reconciled to your brother and sister, and then come and offer your gift " (Matthew 5:21-24).

A rare fourth-century Roman relief depicts the curing of the woman with continuous blood flow and scenes from the Sermon on the Mount.

Similarly, Jesus rejects the ancient maxim of an eye for an eye from Exodus (21:23) in favor of a policy of utter nonresistance: "If anyone strikes you on the right cheek, turn the other also." The commandment that "you shall not commit adultery" is also not sufficient, for just by looking at a woman with lust, Jesus says, one "has already committed adultery with her in his heart." Nor is the decree from Leviticus to "love your neighbor" (19:18) enough for those who wish to live in the Kingdom, for one must "love your enemies" as well and "pray for those who perse- cute you, so that you may be children of your Father in heaven" (Matthew 5:44-45). Even John the Baptist's call to share one's possessions is not satisfactory: "If anyone wants to sue you and take your coat," Jesus says, "give your cloak as well," thus leaving a person practically naked (Matthew 5:39-41).

Leather sandals, such as this pair from the Cave of Letters, were made with three layers of leather, secured with leather bindings.

"Do not worry about your life," he declares in a later passage, "what you will eat, or what you will drink. . . . Is not life more than food, and the body more than clothing?" The road to destruction is easy, Jesus says, and there are many who take it. But the road to life is hard, "and there are few who find it" (Matthew 7:13-14). Therefore, Jesus concludes, almost paraphrasing John the Baptist, "every tree that does not bear good fruit is cut down and thrown into the fire."

What is the point of these harsh, almost extreme commandments? Could anyone but the most self-ef- facing ascetic ever satisfy these conditions? Or is Jesus deliberately making his case in stark black-and-white terms so that his listeners will remember them, and perhaps adhere to them in some degree? Is this simply an instance of rhetorical hyperbole, a favorite device of many ancient sages? We are perhaps reminded of several other examples of Jesus' somewhat uncompromising stance, such as his rather shock- ing statement that "whoever loves father or mother more than me is not worthy of me" and "whoever loves son or daughter more than me is not worthy of me" (Matthew 10:37). What these expressions suggest is that Jesus required a total and unequivocal commitment from his audience if they were to be worthy of building his great Kingdom society. That is perhaps the reason that he sets the bar almost impossibly high: so that his followers will have a clear goal to strive for.

THE SERMON IN LUKE'S GOSPEL

In Luke's version of the Beatitudes, the terms are notably milder, and the emphasis is less on moral rectitude than on rectifying the great gap between rich and poor, between those who have possessions in abundance and those who suffer from poverty and hunger:

Blessed are you who are poor, for
* yours is the kingdom of God.*
Blessed are you who are hungry now,
* for you will be filled.*
Blessed are you who weep now, for
* you will laugh.*
Blessed are you when people hate you,
* and when they exclude you, revile*
* you, and defame you on account*
* of the Son of Man. (Luke 6:20-22)*

Luke then follows his four blessings with four denunciations. "But woe to you who are rich," he continues, "for you have received your compensation. Woe to you who are full now, for you will be hungry. Woe to you who are laughing now, for you will mourn and weep" (Luke 6:24-25). This almost sounds like a different Jesus: a Jesus who is more concerned with the social injustices suffered by the peasant population of Lower Galilee than the stringent spiritual and ethical strictures stipulated by Matthew. In these Beatitudes, Jesus seems to reach out to his audience in an effort to fundamentally change people's

THE BIBLE IN JESUS' TIME

Jesus spoke Aramaic, a Semitic language closely akin to Hebrew, but nowhere do the Gospels indicate that he also read Hebrew itself (a language that by the first century only educated scholars understood). Jesus probably took his Bible citations from so-called *targumim*, Aramaic translations paraphrasing the original Hebrew text. Jesus explicitly cites Psalm 22 in Aramaic during his final moments on the cross: *"Eloi, Eloi, lema sabachthani?—*My God, my God, why have you forsaken me?" The existence of such targumim is well attested. An Aramaic translation of Scripture was reportedly compiled by Jonathan ben Uzziel, a disciple of the great Jewish sage Hillel (active 30–10 B.C.E.), while an actual targum of Job was found in one of the caves in Qumran, dating to the first century B.C.E. The Dead Sea Scrolls, furthermore, indicate that our version of the Hebrew Bible is very close to the version that Jesus was familiar with. ∎

This first-century lidded jar is typical of the type of vessel that was used to store the Dead Sea Scrolls in the vicinity of Qumran, near the Dead Sea.

Affluent families used polished bronze plates as mirrors, as in the case of these two mirrors with handles from the late Second Temple period.

behavior toward each other by surrounding themselves with love. "Love your enemies," he says; "do good to those who hate you, bless those who curse you, pray for those who abuse you." After all, Jesus argues, "if you love those who love you, what credit is that to you? For even sinners love those who love them."

Therefore, to live in the Kingdom, one must "be merciful, just as your Father is merciful. Do not judge, and you will not be judged; do not condemn, and you will not be condemned" (Luke 6:36-37). These are magnificent words, and the intervening two millennia have done nothing to diminish their power. These are the words of a Jesus we recognize, words that would become the quintessential tenets of Christianity as later formulated by Paul. Certainly Luke's Beatitudes require no less of a commitment, no less of an effort, than the terms Matthew

specified. But they are more persuasive. These are words that one can strive to live by.

JESUS AS RABBI

Was Jesus defining new boundaries in formulating these conditions? Was he trying to establish an entirely new social compact in the way people should behave toward each other and toward God? Jesus would emphatically argue that he was not. "Do not think that I have come to abolish the law and the prophets," he warns in the Beatitudes, referring to the first two divisions—the Law (Torah) and the Prophets *(Nevi'im)*— that formed the canon of Hebrew Scripture in his time; "I have come not to abolish but to fulfill" (Matthew 5:17). For Jesus, moral behavior, social compassion, and faith in a merciful God had always been the fundamental pillars of Judaism, even as in the Galilee and Judea of his time, much of Jewish ritual practice was focused on sacrificial rites.

In this, he must surely have found inspiration in the eighth-century prophets of Hebrew Scripture. A wide gap between rich and poor had also fired the ministry of Amos and Micah, particularly the aggregation of land by wealthy speculators at the expense of local farmers, which threatened the social cohesion of the nation. "They covet fields and seize them," Micah writes in a striking parallel to what Galilee would experience under the confiscation policies of the Herodian regime; "they oppress householder and house, people and their inheritance" (Micah 2:2). Hosea too pleads with his audience to return to the social precepts of the Law: not by the mere observance of rituals but with a true faith in God, as captured in his famous words, "I desire mercy and not sacrifice, and the knowledge of God rather than burnt offerings" (Hosea 6:6).

Jesus' Sermon on the Mount not only reveals him as a passionate and skilled orator but also as a man deeply familiar with Hebrew Scripture. His knowledge extended not only to the canonical writings of the Law and the Prophets but also the Psalms. The Beatitude "Blessed are the meek, for they will inherit the earth" is most likely inspired by Psalm 37: "But the meek shall inherit the land" (Psalms 37:11). Jesus' obvious familiarity with scriptural references explains why his contemporaries called him Teacher, even though this honorific was usually reserved for members of the Jewish intellectual elite, including priests, scribes, and other experts of the Jewish Law. His knowledge is further revealed in the

A group of bronze cosmetic boxes once belonged to an upper-class family living in Jerusalem during the late Second Temple period (200 B.C.E.–70 C.E.).

OPPOSITE: *The Church of the Beatitudes, inspired by the Raphael painting shown on page 35, marks one of the locations associated with Jesus' Sermon on the Mount.*

midrashic debates with the Pharisees and the Sadducees in which he often challenged their traditional interpretation of the Law.

Most modern scholars have argued that both Luke's Sermon on the Plain and Matthew's Sermon on the Mount were derived from the older sayings document known as Q and that the differences between Luke and Matthew, including the biblical citations, are largely the work of the evangelists themselves. A few have argued that Luke's version was adapted from Matthew and subsequently enriched with this evangelist's superior talent for evocative and lyrical language. But this idea has not found broad support in biblical scholarship.

INTERPRETING THE LAW

In Jesus' lifetime, the Torah, or Jewish Law, was paramount in governing the lives of observant Jewish men and women. But not everyone interpreted the Torah in the same manner. The Sadducees formed a conservative religious party that believed that the Torah was a closed book. They also rejected all other books as divinely inspired Scripture, including the Prophets and the Psalms, and accepted only the Torah as the Hebrew Bible. In addition, the Sadducees dismissed relatively new ideas such as the resurrection of the dead. In this sense, the principal opponents of the Sadducees, the Pharisees, represented a more enlightened view, inspired by many new currents in Jewish thought during the so-called intertestamental period (roughly between the third century B.C.E. and the first century C.E.). The Pharisees actively debated and interpreted the application of the

These figures on the Maestà Altarpiece by Duccio di Buoninsegna (ca 1255/1260–ca 1318/1319) are believed to depict a group of Pharisees.

Torah to the changing needs of everyday life. In this, they drew inspiration not only from the Law itself but also from the writings of rabbis and sages in past generations. Over time, these discussions became a corpus of wisdom teachings known as the Oral Law; some traditions suggest that the institution of the Oral Law had actually begun with Moses on Mount Sinai and continued under Joshua and the Judges.

The Pharisees and Jesus had many ideas in common, including the messianic expectation of a new age, the resurrection of the dead, and the need to propagate and educate the (mostly illiterate) Jewish people about the proper understanding of biblical precepts. According to Josephus, the Pharisees represented the largest religious sect in Roman Palestine, which, unlike the Sadducees, enjoyed broad support among the Jewish population. ∎

WHEN WOULD THE KINGDOM COME?

How did Jesus plan to establish his Kingdom, his great new society under the rule of God? Did he expect it to occur in his lifetime? Traditional messianic expectations envisioned the restoration of Israel in eschatological terms, as the result of a military liberation campaign or by virtue of a major disaster such as a flood or an earthquake, but Jesus appears to have anticipated a very different process.

The first question, however, is whether the Kingdom concept was meant as a blueprint for a new society on Earth, or an illustration of the ideal conditions that would exist in heaven as a reward for faithful followers after death. The problem is that Jesus' many statements about the Kingdom, including his parables, are rather ambiguous, with subtle differences among the Gospels themselves. Many statements depict the Kingdom as a corporeal reality, a physical construct to be experienced by those who accepted the Kingdom's code of behavior. Some Gospel passages suggest that Jesus saw the Kingdom as an imminent reality in his lifetime (Mark 1:15; Luke 17:21), a belief that Paul would later share.

But other statements suggest something different. "The kingdom of God is not coming with things that can be observed," Jesus says in the Gospel of Luke; "Nor will they say, 'Look, here it is!' or 'There it is!' For in fact, the kingdom of God is *among you*" (Luke 17:20-21). The Gospel of Thomas has a similar passage, and adds, "The Father's kingdom is spread out upon the earth, and the people don't see it" (Thomas 113). This may imply that for Jesus, the Kingdom was a social and spiritual revolution of the heart, a deeply personal commitment that had social and political implications but not in the traditional sense of territorial conquest. Perhaps we may conclude, then, that the Kingdom of God was a new social covenant by which Jews pledged to return to the quintessential virtues of the Law: the pursuit of social justice, compassion toward one another, and love and faith in a merciful God. ■

A prutah coin struck during the reign of Herod Archelaus (r. 4 B.C.E.–6 C.E.), ethnarch of Judea and Samaria, depicts a grapevine.

A high-rimmed wooden plate with walnuts, dated to the first century B.C.E., was found intact near the Nahal David in En Gedi, close to the Dead Sea.

For I tell you, unless your righteousness exceeds that of the scribes and Pharisees, you will never enter the kingdom of heaven.

MATTHEW 5:20

FOLLOWING PAGES: *Jesus' Sermon on the Mount is the subject of this large fresco by Danish artist Henrik Olrik (1830–1890) in St. Matthew's Church in Copenhagen.*

CHAPTER ELEVEN

THE POOR AND THE HUNGRY

*Blessed are you who are poor,
for yours is the kingdom of God.
Blessed are you who are hungry now,
for you will be filled.*

LUKE 6:20-21

S PAUPTAS

Jesus Confronts the Social Injustice of His Time

The Gospels feature an unusual amount of narrative material about the social ills affecting Lower Galilee, particularly poverty, hunger, and disease. Across all four Gospels there are 26 references to "the poor," 16 references to "the blind," 10 instances of "lepers," and 7 cases of people who are "lame." The unsuspecting reader might not find this remarkable. After all, Antiquity was a time of great social inequality; the city of Rome itself contained a seething mass of disenfranchised people. Hygiene was almost unheard of, the medical profession was in its infancy, and disease—particularly in the hot climate of the Middle East—was ubiquitous.

Especially for us, who have become inured to searing television images of disease and poverty in Third World countries, the Gospel passages simply illustrate what we image life in Lower Galilee to have been.

But such would be misleading. Roman Palestine was indeed a land where poor harvests, primitive living conditions, and high child mortality were facts of life. This is particularly true for the highlands of Judea, where wells and springs were few and far between, and the topsoil discouraged agriculture of anything but the hardiest crops. But that was certainly not true for Lower Galilee. In fact, throughout Israel's long history, Galilee had always served as the breadbasket of the region and surrounding territories.

Partly as a result, Galilee had a distinct political and geographical identity. As the northernmost region of the Israelite realm, it was surrounded by foreign lands. To the northwest was the Phoenician region of Sidon and Tyre, which in the centuries before

Jesus had served as the main conduit of Hellenistic influence (the culture of ancient Greece) percolating into Judea. To the northeast was Roman Syria, known as Aram-Damascus in biblical times, and to the east lay the territory of the predominantly Gentile Decapolis (today's Transjordan). As a result, Galilee had always been an enclave of sorts, insular and landlocked, though with access to the Sea of Galilee. Geographically it formed an almost perfect circle of land surrounded by foreigners—which is probably the root of the word "Galilee" *(ha-galil),* a presumed shortening of the Hebrew *galil ha-goyim,* meaning "circle of the peoples."

As Josephus tells us, Galilee was traditionally divided into two regions, Upper (or northern) Galilee and Lower (or southern) Galilee, following the natural contours of the area's geography. Upper Galilee ran roughly from the Litani River in Lebanon to the natural boundary of the Beit HaKerem Valley. A land of tall peaks and deep valleys, Upper Galilee was markedly more rugged than Lower Galilee, with limestone cliffs that rose as high as 3,000 feet. These mountains also served as the region's principal source of water, enjoying rainfall of up to 44 inches per year to this day, far more than in any other part of Israel. Below stretched Lower Galilee, the place that Jesus considered his native region. According to Josephus, this area ran from the plain of Ptolemais

ABOVE: *Even today, Galilee's legendary fecundity can be seen in countless fields filled with wildflowers, sustained by rainfall in winter and underground aquifers in summer.*

OPPOSITE: *This red burnished cup, used for water or wine, is typical of the type of earthenware implements used by the peasants of Galilee in the first century C.E.*

PRECEDING PAGES: *"Allegory of Poverty" is the work of a 14th-century artist known as the Master of the Vaulting Cells in the San Francesco church in Assisi, Italy.*

(or Akko) in the west to Mount Tabor and Beth She'an in the south, and the Sea of Galilee to the east. Remarkably, these boundaries underwent very little change through the thousand years of Israelite history, except for the loss of some northwest territory to the Phoenicians.

A LAND OF BOUNTY

The eastern part of Lower Galilee, past the boundary of the Jordan River, consisted of highlands with deep basalt deposits, a material that is not very conducive to natural growth other than low-level brush and grass. But the western region presented an entirely different picture. Here were prominent ridges and endless valleys covered with lush shrub and olive trees, which thrived on the chalk soil. This highly fecund region, known as the Naphtali after the Hebrew tribe placed here by Joshua, was by the standards of the Near East truly a Garden of Eden. Josephus's claim that almost everyone living in Lower Galilee was engaged in agriculture is therefore quite plausible. "Its soil is so universally rich and fruitful, and so full of the plantations of trees of all sorts," writes Josephus, "that it invites even the most indolent to engage in agriculture, because of its fruitfulness."

The secret of Galilee's great fertility was its almost year-round access to water. A 1992 survey conducted by Israeli geologists discovered no fewer than 25 major springs between the Nazareth Ridge and the plain of Gennesaret, some of which are presumed to go back as far as the Early Bronze Age. Combined with the abundant rainfall in winter and the proximity of the Jordan, this ensured that Galilean land could be cultivated year-round.

Farmers would start preparing their soil with plowing and seeding in the month of Tishri (September–October) or Marchesvan (October–November), when the first rains of the season softened the sunbaked topsoil. As we saw, the barley harvest took place in Nisan/Iyyar (April), followed by wheat in May. Barley was used as animal fodder, while wheat was made into bread. To mark the end of the grain harvest, farmers would celebrate the Festival of Weeks (*Hag*

> *What then will the owner of the vineyard do?*
> *He will come and destroy the tenants*
> *and give the vineyard to others.*

MARK 12:9

ha-Shavuot, also known as the Feast of Reaping, the Festival of First Fruits, or Pentecost).

Shortly after, the next growing season began. Leviticus refers to this as "the season of vintage," the time when "the trees of the field shall yield their fruit" (Leviticus 26:5), when Galilean farmers tended to their orchards. By early summer, during the month of Tammuz (June–July), their grapes and olives were ready to be harvested. This task required every member of the family as well as hired seasonal workers. Once the grape crop was harvested, a large part of it was pulped into juice for wine fermentation, and another portion was set aside for the production of raisins. Olives were pressed for varying qualities of olive oil. Most of these products were destined for sale on the local market rather than for consumption by the farmer's family.

Jesus often referred to the orchard harvest in his teachings, when swarms of workers descended on the vineyard to collect the ripened fruit before it spoiled. Luke, Mark, and Matthew all describe parables of the vineyard.

These threshing boards, studded with jagged stones or iron bits on the bottom, were driven over harvested sheaves so as to remove kernels of grain from the stalks.

OPPOSITE: *A statuette of a young girl holding a dove, found near Jericho, probably dates to the late Hellenistic or early Roman period in Israel.*

TITHES AND TRIBUTES

Of course, this cultivation did not occur on the near-industrial scale that we are used to today. A farmer would typically tend to a collection of small plots that his family had accrued over the centuries as the result of marriage and inheritance. These ancestral holdings were not seeded for single-purpose yields, for these were subsistence farmers. Their first priority was to meet the nutritional needs of their families with a varied diet of bread, as well as (vitamin-rich) vegetables such as onions, cabbage, squash, and beets, and occasionally grapes, olives, or figs, in the limited quantities that their lands would allow. Assuming that the average holding was between four and six acres and taking into account such factors as fallow periods, seed reserves, and bad harvests, that meant that the average farmer was barely able to meet the needs of a typical family of five or six: two parents and their (surviving) children.

Even then, Galilean farmers could not use of all their yields for their own consumption. Any surplus, no matter how small, was sold on market day in the nearest township so as to raise funds for the purchase of farm animals, tools, pottery, and yarn. These same meager funds were also needed to meet religious duties, such as the annual Temple tax and the so-called priestly tithes. According to the Book of Numbers, a full tenth of the harvest was to be handed over to the community of Levites, who, as we saw, were responsible for a variety of activities at the Temple (Numbers 18:21-26). Only once every seven years, during the sabbatical year, were farmers exempt from paying these tithes to allow the land to lie fallow and rest (Leviticus 25:2-7; Exodus 23:10-11). In addition, each farmer was expected to pay an annual Temple tax of half a shekel in the month of Adar (February–March). This was the equivalent of two Roman dinarii, or a worker's wages for two days, not an insignificant sum.

Last but certainly not least, farmers were also expected to pay a tribute to the authority governing the land.

A rural family from northern Syria plows its fields with a horse-drawn plow as farmers in the Near East have done since biblical times.

HOW MUCH LAND DID A FARMER OWN?

Archaeological surveys suggest that prior to the Herodian era, the typical landholdings of a peasant family probably ranged between four and six acres. Julius Caesar granted his legionnaires ten *jugura* of land, equal to some six acres, which was considered the absolute minimum to sustain a family. A farmer in Antiquity probably realized a return of 1:5, that is, five times the original seed planted. Archaeologist Ze'ev Safrai has calculated that the annual yield of a single acre was around 1,320 pounds. Allowing for crop rotation, this means that the average farmer would have needed at least 0.625 acre per person to feed his household. Professor Douglas Oakman agrees that Galilean families of five needed at least 5.5 to 6.5 acres of land to feed their families, and this was *before* taxes. Recent UN studies of Third World feudal societies that resemble ancient Galilee, such as Burma (now Myanmar), have reached the same conclusion. This underscores the fact that most rural families in Galilee labored at or below subsistence levels. ■

After the Assyrian conquest, Galilee was taxed as part of the newly created Assyrian province of Megiddo. The Persians ruled Galilee as a subprovince of a Persian satrapy known as *Abar nahara* ("Beyond the [Euphrates] River"), while the Ptolemies taxed Galilee as a hyparchy named Galila. The purpose of these geographical subdivisions was to facilitate the exploitation of local agricultural resources—if not in coin, then certainly in the form of agricultural yields. Scholars such as E. P. Sanders have estimated that such tribute could range as much as 15 to 20 percent of harvests. Taken together, this meant that even in the best of times, farmers were forced to surrender as much as 25 to 30 percent of their yields.

In sum, Galilean farmers effectively lived at the margins of human existence. After they paid their taxes as well as the cost of immediate maintenance and household needs, they were left with nothing. There was, quite simply, no room for error; it took only a minor upset to destroy this delicate ecosystem. And when Herod came to power, that is exactly what happened.

A sixth-century mosaic from the St. Apollinare Nuovo in Ravenna, Italy, depicts the offering of the poor widow as described in the Gospel of Luke.

THE HERODIAN EXPLOITATION

Herod's father, an Idumean nobleman named Antipater, was serving as a key official in the Hasmonean administration of Queen Alexandra when the Roman General Pompey invaded the region and turned Judea into a Roman province. Antipater immediately saw an opportunity to advance his family's fortunes, and rushed to pledge his fealty to the Roman conqueror. Pompey rewarded him by appointing him as *epitropos,* a title comparable to that of prime minister, under the new vassal ruler, Hyrcanus II. Antipater then solidified his position by appointing his sons, Phasael and Herod, as provincial governors. Fatefully, Herod was placed in charge of Galilee.

It so happened that some time thereafter, Julius Caesar was assassinated and civil war broke out in Rome. One of Caesar's assassins, Cassius, appealed to vassal governors, including Antipater, to help him raise funds for new legions. Herod, eager to ingratiate himself with his Roman masters, took to this task with a vengeance. He understood that Galilee's agricultural bounty was the only important resource in the region and decided to impose ruinous

Barley was traditionally used as animal fodder, but as shown in the miracle of the multiplication of loaves and fishes, it was also used by the poor for baking bread.

taxes so as to raise the cash for Cassius. Those communities that were unable to pay, such as the villages of Gophna, Thamna, and Emmaus (which would later feature in the story of Jesus' resurrection), were sold into slavery.

This was the first of many calamities that Herod would inflict on the farmers of Galilee, and in response they took the only recourse available to them: They rose in revolt. Led by a man called Hezekiah, the revolt spread rapidly throughout the area and was finally suppressed with the bloodiest reprisals imaginable.

This sealed Galilee's fate. When years later, Herod returned to the region as the newly minted king of Roman Judaea, he imposed a brutal tax regime that quite literally was designed to squeeze the farmers dry. On top of the 25 to 35 percent they were obligated to pay to the Temple, the Levites, and

During late March and early April, the Jewish month of Nisan, the hills around the Sea of Galilee explode in a profusion of spring colors.

the Romans (as tribute), they were now burdened with a fourth layer of taxation to pay for Herod's lavish courts and his vainglorious building projects. Estimates vary, but Richard Horsley believes that the tax burden was now increased to between 45 and 50 percent. As we saw before, this was utterly unsustainable for Galilee's subsistence farmers, who were already teetering on the edge of existence.

The result was a spiral of debt. Farmers borrowed heavily to pay the tax collectors with their harvest as collateral, using the only capital source available: the tax collectors themselves. When inevitably they defaulted on the loan, their land was confiscated. If they were lucky, they were allowed to continue to work on their land as mere serfs, as tenant farmers, in return for

And he said to them, "Take care!
Be on your guard against all kinds of greed;
for one's life does not consist in
the abundance of possessions."

LUKE 12:15

a small share of the harvest. In Jesus' parable of the vineyard, the anger of the tenants toward their master prompts them to beat his slaves and even plot to kill the master's son (Luke 20:9-15). In this context, the frequent references in the Gospels to the "creditor" *(danistés)* and "landowner" *(kurios),* to "debtors" *(opheiletés)* and "tenant farmers" *(georgoi),* gain a whole new meaning.

Over more than three decades of Herodian rule, large numbers of farmers were displaced from their lands in this manner. Deprived of their harvests, they tried to subsist on the cheapest foodstuffs available: barley bread (made from animal fodder) and the occasional dried fish. It is not by accident that these poor foodstuffs would feature prominently in one of Jesus' most significant miracles: the multiplication of loaves and fishes.

The sharp reduction in the quality of the farmers' diet soon led to malnutrition, particularly among children. Modern science tell us that a child needs to take in between 1,500 and 2,000 calories per day, with a minimum of protein, carbohydrates, calcium, and vitamins, in order to develop into a healthy individual. Deprived of broad-spectrum crops, these children now grew to be stunted, with a high immunodeficiency against infection and disease. In the years to come, they would become the blind, the sick, and the lame who flocked to Jesus' words and touch. By that time, Galilee, the erstwhile Garden of Eden, had become a land of hundreds, perhaps thousands, of poor, hungry, and displaced farmers, as the Gospels so vividly attest. No wonder, then, that Jesus chose these words from Isaiah to launch his ministry: "The Spirit of the Lord is upon me, for he has anointed me to preach the Gospel to the poor; he has sent me to heal the brokenhearted, to preach deliverance to the captives" (Luke 4:18). ■

The Gospels describe how after the multiplication miracle, the remaining pieces of fish and bread filled "twelve full baskets," such as this one from the Cave of Letters.

FOLLOWING PAGES: In this dramatic depiction by Michelangelo Caravaggio (1571–1610), completed around 1600, Jesus calls on Matthew to follow him as a disciple.

CHAPTER TWELVE

JOURNEYS AROUND THE SEA OF GALILEE

*He told his disciples to have a boat
ready for him because of the crowd,
so that they would not crush him.*

MARK 3:9

Jesus Extends His Ministry Throughout Lower Galilee

As we saw in the Introduction, the people in Antiquity did not care as much about time, or the specific chronology of events, as we do today. It is therefore up to us to see whether we can identify a particular progression in Jesus' movements throughout Lower Galilee. Fortunately, there are important clues that can help us. First, the Gospels by and large agree that Jesus launched his ministry in Capernaum, a town strategically located at the intersection of both land and seaborne traffic. Capernaum was situated in an area known as the valley of Gennesaret, which featured a number of small townships and villages that could easily be reached from Capernaum by foot. Since the Sermon on the Mount and the multiplication of loaves and fishes, one of the few miracles attested in all four Gospels, both occurred in this area, it is not implausible to suggest that all of these took place in the first phase.

As the fame of Jesus as both a teacher and miracle worker spread, he was emboldened to move out of the valley of Gennesaret and bring his teachings to places throughout the region of the Sea of Galilee and its hinterland. This involved distances that could not be covered by foot in a single day, but as we saw, some of the Apostles were professional fishermen, with access to a boat. The sheer cost of such a vessel—one large enough to hold most or all of Jesus' immediate disciples—was probably beyond the means of any individual. That is the reason ancient fishermen owned or leased a boat in partnership, thus pooling its rent and maintenance as well as the cost of nets and other gear. Luke confirms exactly such a

cooperative relationship when he writes, "James and John, sons of Zebedee . . . were partners *(koinōnoi)* with Simon" (Luke 5:10).

Furthermore, the Gospels suggest that in this early phase, discipleship for Jesus was not yet a full-time, dawn-to-dusk occupation. Luke writes how one day, when "Jesus was standing beside the lake of Gennesaret, and the crowd was pressing in on him to hear the word of God, he saw two boats there at the shore of the lake." Apparently the fishermen had left their boats and were busy washing their nets. Jesus then "got into one of the boats, the one belonging to Simon, and asked him to put out a little way from the shore." And then, using the water as a sound platform to amplify his voice and carry it to all the people standing on the shoreline, he "sat down and taught the crowds from the boat" (Luke 5:1-3).

This charming passage shows us that Jesus was not only capable of improvisation on the spot, but also that he needed to adapt as his renown grew and the appeal of his teachings began to extend well beyond the Gennesaret area.

ABOVE: *This modern photo of a fisherman's vessel on the Sea of Galilee at sunrise is a close approximation of similar scenes during the time of Jesus.*

OPPOSITE: *During the Imperial era, Roman oil lamps could be cast in elaborate shapes, such as this one, discovered near Jerusalem, in the form of a boy riding a fish.*

PRECEDING PAGES: *Italian Renaissance artist Domenico Ghirlandaio (1449–1494) painted this fresco of "The Calling of St. Peter and St. Andrew" in 1481.*

THE EASTERN SHORE

Jesus' first foray may have taken him to Bethsaida, the city where he found refuge in the dark days after the arrest of John the Baptist. Jesus' reputation as a man of miracles had preceded him, for right away, says Mark, "some people brought a blind man to him and begged him to touch him." Jesus then took the blind man by the hand and led him out of the village, away from the prying eyes of the crowd, and healed him.

The richly cultivated eastern shore of the Sea of Galilee is referred to as the "country of the Gerasenes" in the Gospels.

From Bethsaida, Jesus sailed "across to the other side [of the sea]," which Mark identifies as the "country of the Gerasenes." This was Gentile territory, the region around the city of Gerasa, one of the cities of the Decapolis. The Decapolis was not sovereign territory, but rather an affiliation of ten major urban centers with close commercial ties. Most of these cities, including Gerasa, were located to the east of the Jordan River and the Sea of Galilee, near the eastern frontier between the Roman Empire and the Arabian peninsula, in the territory now occupied by southern Syria and the Kingdom of Jordan. Some ancient versions of Mark's Gospel, however, refer to the "country of Gadarenes" rather than "Gerasenes," which also appears in Matthew's version of the event (Matthew 8:28). This would point to the city of Gadara, today's Umm Qays, also located in Jordan.

Either way, the trip represented an unusual foray into Gentile territory, perhaps in response to the fact that many people from this area had come to see Jesus in Galilee. But the visit did not turn out as Jesus may have hoped. As soon as he set foot on land, he was approached by a possessed man "with an

> *Such a very large crowd gathered around him that he got into a boat on the sea and sat there, while the whole crowd was beside the sea on the land.*

MARK 4:1

This chair, belonging to the sixth-century Bishop Maximian of Ravenna, includes a panel of wood and ivory showing Christ healing the blind.

unclean spirit" who lived in a graveyard. Mark adds that "he had often been restrained with shackles and chains," possibly because of his mental illness, "but the chains he wrenched apart, and the shackles he broke in pieces; and no one had the strength to subdue him."

A 15th-century illustration from an Italian illuminated manuscript shows Jesus after the miracle of the evil spirits turned into swine.

Jesus was unafraid, even when this powerful brute started to shout at him, "What have you to do with me, Jesus, Son of the Most High God? I adjure you by God, do not torment me." Here again it is the *demons* possessing the man, like Satan in the desert, who recognize Jesus as the "Son of God" even as those around him, including his own disciples, have yet to acknowledge him as such. Jesus asked the man, "What is your name?" "Legion," was the enigmatic response, "for we are many"—no doubt referring to the many demons tormenting him. A *legio*, or "legion," was a regiment of Roman

GERASA, MODERN JERASH

Miraculously, the ancient city of Gerasa, now named Jerash, remained largely undisturbed until it was discovered by the explorer J. L. Burckhardt in 1819. Amazed, Burckhardt described the largely intact remains of a Roman-style city, complete with temples, theaters, residences, a forum, and an impressive main avenue, the *cardo,* flanked by colonnades. Gerasa's remarkable condition was partly due to its remoteness. In 1925, archaeologist George Horsfield wrote that the "ruins were unapproachable except on foot" and noted that "gardens encroached on monuments and cultivation extended into the theaters," like a long-lost temple in the jungle. The restoration of this astonishing jewel did not begin until 1928 and continues today. The massive Triumphal Arch, some 65 feet high and 75 feet wide, was rebuilt only in the early 2000s. Most visitors to the Holy Land have never heard of Jerash, although as a Roman city from the time of Jesus, it has no parallel. ■

The theater of Gerasa, modern Jerash, still features its scaenae frons, *or marble stage, and ranks as one of the best preserved Roman theaters from the second century* C.E.

infantry, numbering around 5,000 men. Significantly, the Roman Tenth Legion was stationed not far from the Gadarene area, in Antioch, Syria.

Jesus then spotted "a great herd of swine" on a nearby hillside. The "unclean spirits" saw it too and begged Jesus to "send us into the swine; let us enter them." In Judaism, swine were among the most unclean animals on Earth; the consumption of pork was strictly forbidden. Jesus agreed, and "the unclean spirits came out and entered the swine," but it did them little good. The herd, now possessed by the demons, went mad and "rushed down the steep bank into the sea, and were drowned in the sea" (Mark 5:1-13).

The swineherds promptly ran into the nearest town and told everyone what had happened. Soon a number of people came over to see the demoniac with their own eyes. But their reaction was not one of joy or wonder. When they saw the demoniac sitting there, "clothed and in his right mind," they became very afraid and begged Jesus to "leave their neighborhood" right away. Only the demoniac himself praised Jesus, and "began to proclaim in the Decapolis how much Jesus had done for him" (Mark 5:20). The story is a powerful example of the transformative power of Jesus to restore a severely disabled man to his place in society.

THE WESTERN SHORE

The western shore of the Sea of Galilee was more densely populated with towns and ports, serving the Galilean hinterland. One summer, during exceptionally low water levels, John Dominic Crossan documented the remains of no fewer than 15 fishing harbors that presumably dated from the first century, including Sennabris, Beit Yerah, Tel Samra, Duerban, Sussita, Ein Gofra, and Hammath. The ancient city of Hammath ("hot spring") was located close to the outlet of the Jordan River, which Josephus calls Ammathus ("warm baths"). It also appears in the Book of Joshua as one of the fortified towns on the periphery of Naphtali (Joshua 19:35). Today known as Hammath Tiberias, its impressive remains include no fewer than five successive layers of a basilica-type synagogue, the earliest of which may have been built in the time of Jesus. The synagogue was decorated with an amazing series of colorful frescoes, some of them in a remarkable state of preservation.

Just north of Hammath was the brand-new city of Tiberias, which Herod Antipas founded at some time after the death of Augustus in 14 C.E. Unlike the rebuilding of Sepphoris, in which Antipas showed some consideration toward the large and mostly devout Jewish population (as evidenced by the recent discovery of numerous stone vessels), Tiberias was designed as an unabashedly Greco-Roman city. Dedicated to Antipas's new patron, Emperor Tiberius (perhaps at the occasion of the emperor's 60th birthday in 18 C.E.), the city of Tiberias was equipped with baths, temples, a gymnasium, and other Roman institutions that observant Jews detested, for they were frequented by people in the nude. But Antipas was confident that no observant Jew would ever set foot in the city, for it had been

Sardines were one of the three main fish species caught in the Sea of Galilee and constituted the main source of protein for the Galilean poor.

This fresco in the Basilica di Santa Maria in Pomposa, Italy, by an anonymous 14th-century artist, depicts the raising of Jairus's daughter.

> *After Jesus had sent the crowd away,*
> *he got into the boat and went to the vicinity*
> *of Magadan.*
>
> MATTHEW 15:39

OPPOSITE: *A mosaic floor from the fourth-century synagogue of Khirbet es-Samarah depicts a temple facade with an Aron Kodesh, or Torah ark, the place where the Torah scrolls are kept.*

built (perhaps purposefully) on the site of an old Jewish cemetery, which made it ritually unclean. It thus became a thoroughly Gentile town, which may explain why Jesus never visited it. Nevertheless, word about Jesus' remarkable deeds had certainly reached the city, for John writes that at one point, "some boats from Tiberias" sailed to the place where Jesus had last been seen, carrying people who were hoping to catch a glimpse of him (John 6:23).

HEALINGS ON THE WESTERN SHORE

The western shore of the sea was more predominantly Jewish than the eastern side, so it is likely that Jesus would have spent more time on these shores. Mark writes that when Jesus left the land of the Gerasenes and "crossed again in the boat to the other side," he was met by a large crowd standing along the waterfront. Before Jesus had a chance to address the people, one of the "leaders of the synagogue," probably one of the elders in the local town, stepped forward. His name was Jairus. "My little daughter is at the point of death," he pleaded, "come and lay your hands on her, so that she may be made well, and live" (Mark 5:21-24). Jesus immediately made to follow him, but he made slow progress as the crowd "pressed in on him." No doubt they were filled with excitement over the chance to witness this miracle worker, this Jesus they had heard so much about, produce another "sign" with their own eyes.

The so-called Galilee boat, which was discovered along the shore of the Sea of Galilee in 1986, has been dated to the early first century C.E.

Among the crowd was a woman who had suffered from continuous hemorrhage for 12 years. Under the Jewish Law, a woman who had her period was considered ritually unclean. A woman with a *continuous* blood flow suffered from ritual impurity in perpetuity, without the chance to purify herself or to be integrated into her community. Her affliction therefore involved not only physical discomfort but great psychological stress as well. The woman came up behind Jesus and touched his cloak, thinking, "If I but touch his clothes, I will be made well." And she was right: Her hemorrhage stopped at that moment. Jesus acutely felt that "power had gone forth from him." He confronted the woman, who fell on her knees and trembled with fear. Jesus looked kindly on her, and said, "Daughter, your faith has made you well; go in peace, and be healed of your disease" (Mark 5:27-34).

Unfortunately, this incident had delayed Jesus just when Jairus's daughter was on the verge of death. As the crowd moved ponderously toward Jairus's house, a few people appeared with the dreadful news that the child had passed away. "Your daughter is dead," they told Jairus, "why trouble the Teacher further?" But Jesus turned to them and said, "Do not fear, only believe." He told the crowd to stay and rapidly walked to the house with only Peter, James,

The ruins of ancient Tiberias, founded by Herod Antipas between 14 and 20 C.E., are visible today on the southwestern shore of the Sea of Galilee.

and his brother John—the inner Apostolic circle, as it were—by his side. When he entered, the house was filled with weeping and wailing; presumably, the professional mourners who were often hired to attend to such tragic events had already arrived. Jesus asked them, "Why do you make a commotion and weep? The child is not dead, but sleeping." At those words, the wailers begin to laugh at him—an indication that these mourners were not close members of the family, who certainly would have rallied at Jesus' words. At that, Jesus shooed them out of the house, took the child's father and mother, and went to the little girl's room. He stood by her lifeless body, took her hand, and "said to her, *'Talitha cum,'* which means, 'Little girl, get up!' And immediately the girl got up and began to walk about." It is interesting that Mark, who wrote in Greek, cites Jesus in the original Aramaic, which suggests that he based this story on an original oral or written tradition (Mark 5:35-42).

THE TOWN OF MAGDALA

One port city that Jesus must have visited is Magdala, which Matthew refers to as "Magadan" and is located some three miles north of Tiberias. Here, he may have met the disciple who would become one of his most devoted followers, Mary of Magdala, or Mary Magdalene. Luke writes that she was one of several women who had been cured of evil spirits and infirmities, suggesting a chronic disease of some sort (Luke 8:2). The Gospels give us very little information about her background, but it is clear that she occupied a prominent social position in the city. Unlike most other Galilean women, she freely accompanied Jesus on his subsequent journeys, even though she was apparently unwed. In Galilee, unwed women did not leave their home without a relative as an escort. Luke adds that Mary Magdalene belonged to a group of women who "provided for [the Apostles] out of their own resources" (Luke 8:2-3). This would suggest that Mary was affluent and therefore enjoyed a greater independence than most other women. She remained with Jesus to the end, standing at the cross with two other fearless women, and according to the Gospel of John, she was the first to see Jesus after the resurrection (John 20:14-17). ■

THE TOWN OF MARY MAGDALENE

In Aramaic the town of Mary Magdalene was called Magdala Nunayya ("tower of fishes," a name that also appears in the Talmud), while Josephus and others referred to it by its Greek name, Tarichaea ("fish salters"). What these names suggest is that Magdala was a major center of the fish-processing industry on the Sea of Galilee, particularly fish sauce, a condiment prized throughout the Mediterranean.

The excavations of the residential section of ancient Magdala by the Universidad Anáhuac México Sur are ongoing.

Josephus writes that during the First Jewish War, when he served as rebel commander in Galilee, he fortified the city because of its strategic location on the lake. Today the ruins of ancient Magdala lie close to the Sea of Galilee resort of Migdal Beach. In the 1970s, archaeologist Virgilio Corbo was the first to excavate a synagogue using a basilica plan, with five rows of benches on the north side, similar to the synagogue built by Jewish rebels on the Herodian fortress of Masada. In 2009, Israeli archaeologist Dina Avshalom-Gorni discovered additional remains, which she dated to the early Roman period, which would have placed it in the time of Jesus.

Nearby is Nof Ginnosar, where in 1986 a prolonged drought exposed the hull of an ancient boat, 26 feet in length and 7.5 feet in beam. Now on display in the Yigal Allon Museum at Kibbutz Ginnosar, the boat has been carbon-dated to between 120 B.C.E. and 40 C.E., perfectly straddling the time of Jesus. Equipped with a mast and oars, the boat was capable of reaching all points along the lake, by day or by night. ■

CHAPTER THIRTEEN

THE HEALING STORIES

*That evening, at sundown,
they brought to him all who were
sick or possessed with demons.*

MARK 1:32

Jesus Gains Renown as a Man Capable of Healings

In the world of Jesus, medicine stood at its infancy, and only then in developed circles far removed from Galilee. Much of what the Romans believed or practiced about medicine was rooted in the experimental work of Greek physicians such as Hippocrates and Dioscorides, and further developed by Roman practitioners such as the famous Galen. The Greeks believed that the human body operates on four essential ingredients or humors: blood, phlegm, black bile, and yellow bile.

If a person fell ill, it was assumed that one or several of the four humors were out of balance. This idea dominated medical thought until well into the Middle Ages, and even into Shakespearean times.

Correcting the balance of humors was a difficult task. Nonetheless, given their superior grasp of mechanics and engineering, Roman doctors soon developed a number of procedures and instruments that are still in use today, such as the obstetric forceps, scalpel, catheter, and spatula. In addition, physicians such as Galen developed a broad spectrum of herbal medicine, including the use of fennel, aloe, rhubarb, and gentiana for many common ailments. And as we saw, Soranus published a series of books on gynecology in the second century, with some precepts that are still applicable today. But many of these potions and regimens were of practical use only for common and survivable afflictions, such as superficial inflammations, skin burns, breach birth, excessive menstrual flow, or bowel ailments. Against the chronic diseases described in the Gospels, Roman medicine was largely powerless—even if it had been available in rural Galilee, which was most certainly not the case.

As a result, medical doctors had a rather poor reputation in the ancient world, which in some ways would continue until the Renaissance and the birth of modern science. Their spotty record of success is vividly illustrated by the case of the woman who suffered from blood flow for 12 years, as we saw previously. "She had endured much under many physicians, and had spent all that she had," Mark notes sorrowfully, "and she was no better, but rather grew worse" (Mark 5:26). Jesus was aware of the general antipathy against doctors and their bizarre treatments. "Doctor, cure yourself!" he says mockingly in the Gospel of Luke, quoting from a popular proverb (Luke 4:23).

This may help us to understand why people flocked in such numbers to witness the healings and exorcisms that Jesus was reputably capable of. Parents of sick children, such as Jairus, were desperate to find a remedy, *any* remedy, to alleviate the suffering or even death of their loved ones. According to Josephus, this produced a large number of magicians, sorcerers, and charlatans who went from town to town, claiming to be able to heal the sick and exorcise demons. Knowing that desperation nurtures hope, these characters would typically engage in elaborate rituals, such as casting spells, dancing, or chanting to convince their audience of their magical powers. The Roman procurator Felix

ABOVE: *The gently undulating hills near the Sea of Galilee, also known as Lake Tiberias, lead to the city of Tiberias, founded by Herod Antipas between 14 and 20 C.E.*

OPPOSITE: *This depiction of Jesus healing the woman with continuous blood flow appears on a rare sarcophagus from the late fourth century, discovered in Turkey.*

PRECEDING PAGES: *"Jesus Opens the Eyes of the Man Born Blind" is a painting by Sienese artist Duccio di Buoninsegna (ca 1255/1260–ca 1318/1319); it was completed around 1311.*

A second-century Roman panel depicts a Greek physician named Jason with a boy. Most physicians working in Rome were either Greek or trained by Greek doctors.

(who some years later would sit in judgment on Paul) once engaged the services of a magician called Atomus to cast a spell on a woman named Drusilla, the sister of King Agrippa II. Felix hoped that the spell would persuade Drusilla to marry him rather than her fiancé.

The New Testament book the Acts of the Apostles reports the case of another sorcerer, "a certain man named Simon [who] had previously practiced magic in the city and amazed the people of Samaria, saying that he was someone great" (Acts 8:9). Justin Martyr adds that Simon, after being evicted by the Apostles, went to Rome, where he performed so many acts of magic that he was revered as a god and even had a statue dedicated to him. We also find many allusions to the power of magic in Hebrew Scripture. In the Book of Exodus, for example, Moses engages in a competition with Pharaoh's magicians to see who can pull off the most impressive feats. Similarly, the Babylonian Talmud mentions several rabbis who could produce rain or drought.

The belief in the healing power of magic was grounded in the belief that most birth defects and chronic diseases had a supernatural origin. If a child was born blind or deaf, for example, it was commonly believed to be the will of God as punishment for the sins of his or her parents. Man was formed in the image of God, says Genesis; it therefore followed that if a baby was malformed at birth, the baby must have been conceived in sin or doomed to suffer the punishment for the transgressions of his parents. When in the Gospel of John, the Apostles encounter a man who has been blind from birth, their first question to Jesus is, "Rabbi, who sinned, this man or his parents, that he was born blind?" (John 9:1-2)

He said to her, "Daughter, your faith has made you well; go in peace, and be healed of your disease."

MARK 5:34

Consequently, there was no clear distinction between healings and exorcisms, because chronic illness was often considered the work of evil spirits. Luke refers to "some women who had been cured of evil spirits and infirmities"; Mary Magdalene herself had been cured of no fewer than seven demons (Luke 8:2). But her condition may not have involved a mental illness, as in the case of the Gerasene demoniac. In Luke's story of the healing of Peter's mother-in-law, Jesus "stood over her and rebuked the fever, and it left her," which shows that demons could inflict physical suffering as well (Luke 4:39).

THE EXORCISMS

Compared to the exorcists of his era, Jesus operated very differently. Rather than engaging in all sorts of spells, Jesus simply *evicted* evil spirits by ordering them to leave, *now*. And without fail, these spirits and demons did. Of course,

OPPOSITE: *A ribbed bowl is typical of the type of glass ornaments with which affluent families in the first century began to advertise their cultural sophistication.*

"Christ Casting Out Devils" is a painting by Flemish artist Paul Bril (1554–1626), who worked for most of his career in Italy, under the influence of Italian art.

these reports carry a specific meaning. Satan and his acolytes, the demons, immediately recognize Jesus for what he is: the Son of God. They know they are powerless against the God-given powers that Jesus possesses. Therefore, when he confronts them, they are anxious to escape unscathed and fight him another day. This is the reason that the evil spirits in the Gerasene demoniac suggest that Jesus send them into the herd of swine in a nearby field. "Out of sight, out of mind," their reasoning appears to be. But as soon as they enter the swine, the crazed beasts start to run around like mad and ultimately hurl themselves into the Sea of Galilee.

This happy conclusion serves a further purpose: It shows that under Jesus' leadership, evil spirits will not be tolerated in the Kingdom of God. They will no longer torment human beings, just as all the evil that has vexed Israel for so long will come to an end. That is the deeper symbolic meaning of the exorcisms, but that doesn't rule out the possibility that the reports of Jesus' exorcisms are grounded in fact.

THE POWER OF ENERGY

Energy healing has long been dismissed in Western civilization, but recent interest among medical professionals in alternative therapies has led to a reassessment. Energy healing is rooted in ancient Eastern medicine. Both the Ayurvedic philosophy of the chakra and the Chinese concept of qi hold that the human body operates around certain energy concentrations that must be kept in balance in order to safeguard a person's well-being. Chinese practitioners maintain, for example, that qi uses dedicated channels, or *meridians,* to reach the 12 primary organs of the body. If the qi flow is blocked or unbalanced, a person develops a disease. To counter such imbalances, acupuncture or shiatsu massage is practiced; in Western medicine, this may take the form of electromagnetic radiation. Biofield energy healing takes this one step further by actively channeling energy into the patient's meridians. Some authors believe this could resemble the "healing by touch" therapies as described in the Gospels. ∎

"Christ Healing the Blind," also known as "The Blind of Jericho," was painted by renowned French Baroque artist Nicolas Poussin (1594-1665) in 1650.

*A leper came to him begging him,
and kneeling he said to him,
"If you choose, you can make me clean."
Moved with pity, Jesus stretched out
his hand and touched him.*

MARK 1:40-41

This extremely rare sheet of gold, probably produced in Syria around 200 C.E., contains a number of Jewish prayers for healing.

One thing is undeniably true: The stories of Jesus' healings belong to the oldest oral strata underlying the Gospels. That means that from the very beginning, people spoke about Jesus as capable of producing miraculous cures. Even Josephus, who had no particular sympathy for early Christians, writes, "Jesus, a wise man . . . was a doer of wonderful works, a teacher of such men as receive the truth with pleasure." John P. Meier, the author of a recent multivolume study

Italian Renaissance artist Sandro Botticelli (ca 1445–1510) painted this fresco, "The Purification of the Leper" (top), in the Sistine Chapel around 1481.

Aloe vera which grew naturally in the Near East because of its succulence, was prized as a medicinal plant by ancient authors, particularly for skin treatments.

of the historical Jesus, suggests that to dismiss the miracle tradition from Jesus' public ministry is to dismiss the Gospel tradition itself.

THE HEALINGS

There are striking differences between reports of healings and exorcisms in the Gospels. When it comes to healing people with chronic illnesses rather than demons, the intervention follows a predictable formula. "Do you have faith?" Jesus often asks. Only if the answer is affirmative can the miracle take place; Jesus even credits the patient by saying, "Your faith has healed you." In other words, the sufferer must believe in Jesus' power as an essential precondition for the miraculous cure; without it, the exercise comes to naught. This has led some historians to dismiss the healing stories as myths or parables whose sole purpose is to advance a theological message: the cardinal importance of faith. Others see them as allegorical stories that serve to illustrate the salvation offered by Christ as an earthly reflection of the great redemption in heaven.

But the second factor in Jesus' healing therapy is quite unprecedented. Jesus looks the patient in the eye and says (as in the case of Mark's paralytic from Capernaum), "Son, your sins are forgiven" (Mark 2:5). This statement goes to the heart of what we observed earlier: that chronic illnesses or defects were invariably judged as God's punishment for sinful living. A modern psychologist would recognize the purpose of Jesus' words: to eliminate the patient's sense of guilt, rooted in the belief that he suffered *because he deserved to,* because he (or his parents) had brought it upon him. Naturally these words were as much directed to the patient as to the villagers standing around him. After all, they are the ones who had condemned the sufferer to the margins of village society, to living in squalor, ill clothed and ill fed, alone with his pain or incapacity, bereft of the solace and comfort of the community. Imagine, for a moment, the joy of being told that the heavy yoke of that guilt, the intense trauma of that self-loathing, was now lifted.

"Christ at the Pool of Bethesda" is a painting by Spanish Baroque artist Bartolomé Esteban Murillo (1617–1682) between 1667 and 1670.

Note that Jesus does not say, "You never sinned, and so you were never responsible, so get on with it." Instead he says, "Your sins have now been forgiven," thus ordering the patient to put this period of suffering firmly behind him, both mentally and physically. That doesn't mean that Jesus himself believed that physical defects were the result of God's punishment. One day when the disciples met a blind man and asked Jesus, "Who sinned, this man or his parents?" Jesus rebuked them sternly. "Neither this man nor his parents sinned," was the emphatic response; "he was born blind so that God's works might be revealed in him" (John 9:1-3). In Luke, Jesus also referred to the collapse of the tower of Siloam, which killed 12 victims. "Do you think that

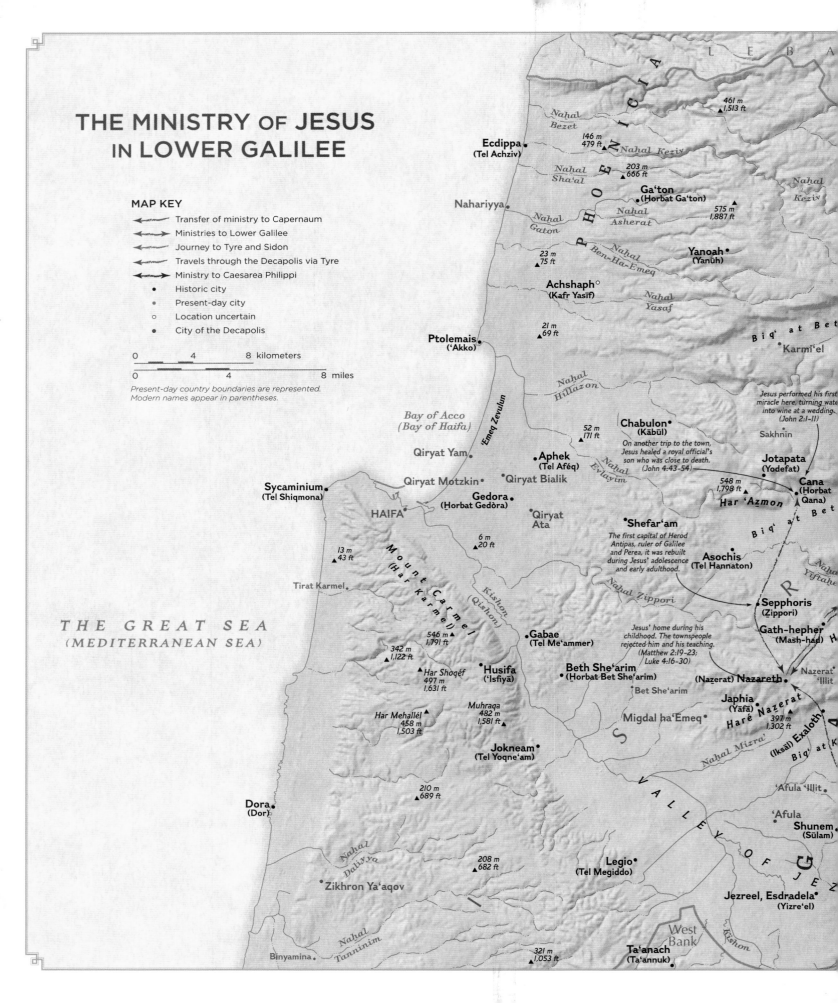

THE MINISTRY OF JESUS IN LOWER GALILEE

MAP KEY

⟵ Transfer of ministry to Capernaum
⟶ Ministries to Lower Galilee
⟵ Journey to Tyre and Sidon
⟵ Travels through the Decapolis via Tyre
⟶ Ministry to Caesarea Philippi

- • Historic city
- • Present-day city
- ○ Location uncertain
- • City of the Decapolis

0   4   8 kilometers
0   4   8 miles

Present-day country boundaries are represented.
Modern names appear in parentheses.

PHOENICIA

LEBA

461 m
▲ 1,513 ft

Ecdippa•
(Tel Achziv)

146 m
479 ft ▲

Nahal Bezet

Nahal Keziv

203 m
▲ 666 ft

Nahal Sha'al

Ga'ton
(Horbat Ga'ton)   ▲

Nahal Keziv

Nahariyya•

Nahal Gaton

Nahal Asherat

575 m
1,887 ft

Yanoah•
(Yanūh)

23 m
▲ 75 ft

Nahal Ben-Ha-Emeq

Achshaph○
(Kafr Yasīf)

Nahal Yasaf

Biq' at Bet

• **Karmi'el**

21 m
▲ 69 ft

Ptolemais•
('Akko)

Nahal Hillazon

52 m
▲ 171 ft

Chabulon•
(Kābūl)

Jesus performed his first miracle here, turning water into wine at a wedding. (John 2:1–11)

• Sakhnin

Bay of Acco (Bay of Haifa)

'Emeq Zevulun

Qiryat Yam•

On another trip to the town, Jesus healed a royal official's son who was close to death. (John 4:43–54)

• **Aphek**
(Tel Aféq)

Nahal Evlayim

Jotapata•
(Yodefat)

548 m
1,798 ft ▲

Cana•
(Horbat Qana)

Qiryat Motzkin•

• Qiryat Bialik

Har 'Azmon

Biq' at Bet

Sycaminium•
(Tel Shiqmona)

Gedora•
(Horbat Gedòra)

•Qiryat
Ata

•**Shefar'am**

Nahal Yiftahe

HAIFA•

The first capital of Herod Antipas, ruler of Galilee and Perea, it was rebuilt during Jesus' adolescence and early adulthood.

Asochis•
(Tel Hannaton)

R

13 m
▲ 43 ft

Mount Carmel (Har Karmel)

Kishon (Qishon)

6 m
▲ 20 ft

Nahal Zippori

Sepphoris•
(Zippori)

Tirat Karmel•

THE GREAT SEA
(MEDITERRANEAN SEA)

546 m ▲
1,791 ft

• **Gabae**
(Tel Me'ammer)

Gath-hepher•
(Mash-had)

H

342 m
▲ 1,122 ft

Jesus' home during his childhood. The townspeople rejected him and his teaching. (Matthew 2:19–23; Luke 4:16–30)

Nazareth
(Nazerat)

Nazerat
'Illit

Har Shoqéf
497 m
1,631 ft

• **Husifa**
('Isfiyā)

Beth She'arim•
(Horbat Bet She'arim)

Japhia
(Yāfā)

397 m
1,302 ft

Har Mehallél
458 m
1,503 ft ▲

Muhraqa
482 m
1,581 ft ▲

• Bet She'arim

Migdal ha'Emeq

Haré Nazerat

(Iksāl) **Exaloth**

Nahal Mizra'

Biq' at K

Jokneam•
(Tel Yoqne'am)

S

'Afula 'Illit

210 m
▲ 689 ft

Dora•
(Dor)

Nahal Daliyya

V A L L E Y

'Afula

Shunem•
(Sūlam)

208 m
▲ 682 ft

• Zikhron Ya'aqov

Legio•
(Tel Megiddo)

O F

J E Z

321 m
▲ 1,053 ft

Jezreel, Esdradela•
(Yizre'el)

West Bank

Kishon

Binyamina•

Nahal Tanninim

Ta'anach•
(Ta'annuk)

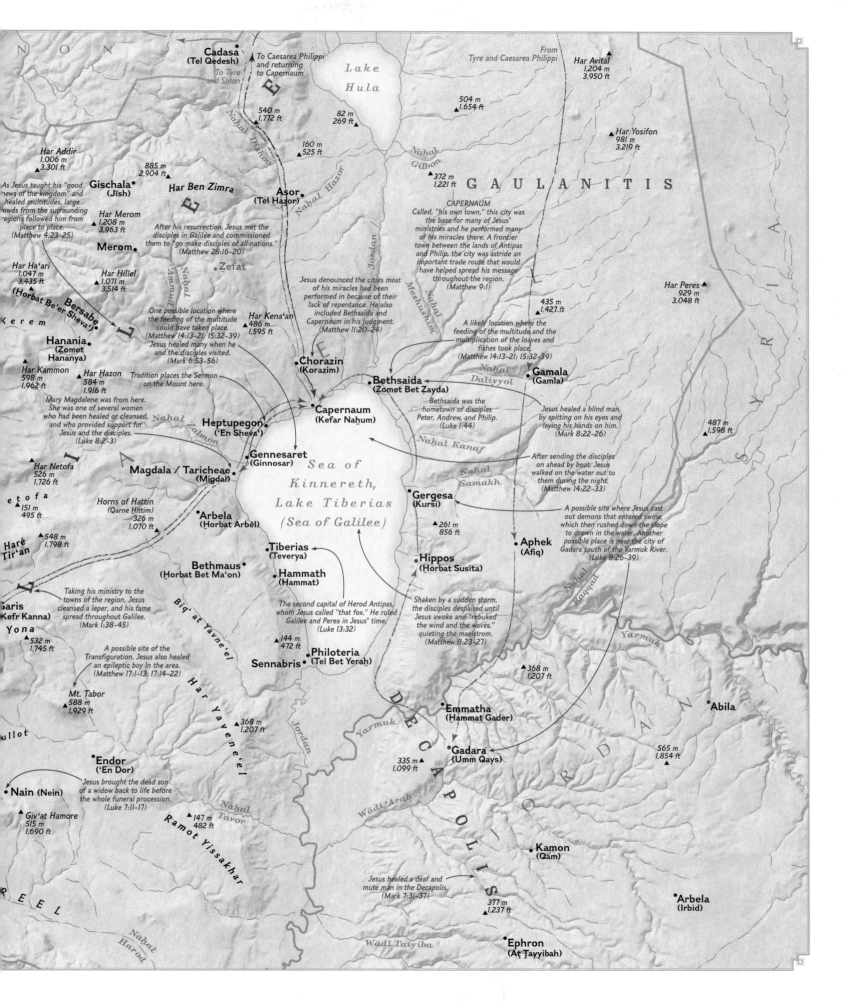

Traditional subsistence agriculture in Galilee yielded onions, squash, radishes, beets, and leeks, as well as citrus fruits, olives, figs, grapes, and dates.

The blue snake motif on this delicate Roman glass flask, found in Israel and dating from the first century c.e., may indicate that it was used for medicinal ointments.

they were worse offenders than all the others living in Jerusalem?" he asked (Luke 13:4).

But Jesus also recognized that such a response would not be particularly helpful in healing patients. For much of their lives, they had lived in the absolute conviction that their defects were the result of some transgression. Jesus adroitly turned that belief to his advantage by implicitly acknowledging it and telling the patient, "Now your sins are forgiven." With these words, the self-affirming motive for the disease was removed, and the patient realized that his life could begin anew as a fully recognized member of the community.

This is not to say that Jesus' healings are purely the result of psychotherapy, of treating or alleviating a psychosomatic condition, even though the psychological impact of his words should not be underestimated. For the third and perhaps most important factor in Jesus' healings is *touch*. Jesus often touches the patient, with no regard for ritual impurity or even contamination, as in the case of "lepers" (a term that probably referred to anyone with a skin disease). In this, as in so many other instances, Jesus rigorously places concern for human life above the precepts of the Law. For someone bereft of human intimacy for years, or possibly most of his life, the physical touch of Jesus must have been an electrifying experience. All of these elements would have produced a powerful stimulus to the natural healing process.

The purpose of Jesus' touch may also involve some exchange of power or energy. As we saw earlier, Jesus acutely felt that "power had gone forth from him" when the hemorrhaging woman touched his cloak. There is no precedent for this form of healing in Hebrew Scripture. Healing episodes are invariably the result of a prophet who consciously prays or invokes the power of God to help bring a miraculous event about. The idea that healing could take place through physical contact between two human beings and the resulting—unwitting—transfer of energy is rather rare in biblical literature, though it does appear in other ancient sources. This may further explain why people were ready to ascribe special, even magical, powers to Jesus.

It is not the purpose of this chapter to expose the "secret" of Jesus' healing techniques or to dismiss the essential message of these reports in the Gospels: that the healings are the product of divine intervention through the agency of Jesus' ministry. If Jesus is indeed the Son of God, as Christians believe, then his ability to summon supernatural healing powers is an obvious attestation of his divinity. Jesus seemed to indicate such when he said to the scribes, who accuse him of blasphemy, "so that you may know that the Son of Man has authority on earth to forgive sins." And then he turned to the paralytic and said, "I say to you, stand up, take your mat and go to your home" (Mark 2:10-11). A more dramatic proof of Jesus' remarkable healing powers can scarcely be imagined.

At the same time, we should not discount the powerful symbolic message of the healings. Curing the sick was perhaps the most vivid illustration of the great mercy that awaited the faithful in the reign of God. Seen from this perspective, the healing miracles are Jesus' Beatitudes made into flesh, the living proof that the Kingdom of God is at hand. ■

FOLLOWING PAGES: "Jesus Raising Jairus' Daughter" was painted by Prague-born Austrian artist Gabriel Max (1840–1915) in 1878; the fly on the girl's arm shows that she is truly dead.

HEALTH IN GALILEE

The presence of large numbers of disabled or diseased people in the Gospel stories may be related to a rapid deterioration of the peasant diet in the decades preceding the time of Jesus. Using a detailed analysis of ancient fecal matter, preserved in the remains of household "toilets" in areas of human habitation, paleoanthropologist Jane Cahill found evidence of a healthy diet of fruits, vegetables, and herbs from specimens dating *before* the Roman occupation of Palestine. Later archaeological periods, however, reveal not only a less balanced diet but also a dramatic increase in parasites and infectious agents, including traces of the parasite *Echinococcus granulosus,* or tapeworm. In their description of the miraculous multiplication of loaves and fishes, the Gospels explicitly refer to bread made of barley. "There is a boy here

Excavation campaigns at the Herodian stronghold of Masada, on the Dead Sea, continue to yield fascinating artifacts related to daily life in the first century C.E.

who has five barley loaves and two fish," Peter said to Jesus. "But what are they among so many people?" (John 6:9). Barley, however, was traditionally used for animal fodder, not human consumption. The confiscation of large tracts of arable land by Herodian elites may have forced many Galilean peasants to turn to this cheaper cereal instead. Compared to wheat, barley is notably deficient in vitamins A, C, and D, as well as minerals such as zinc. Modern studies of developing countries show that such vitamin deficiencies can produce blindness and even deafness in young children. Two skeletons excavated near the Villa Gordiani in Rome also revealed a strong link between low mineral counts and bone disease. Such deficiency among the Galilean children would have sharply lowered their resistance against infectious diseases. ■

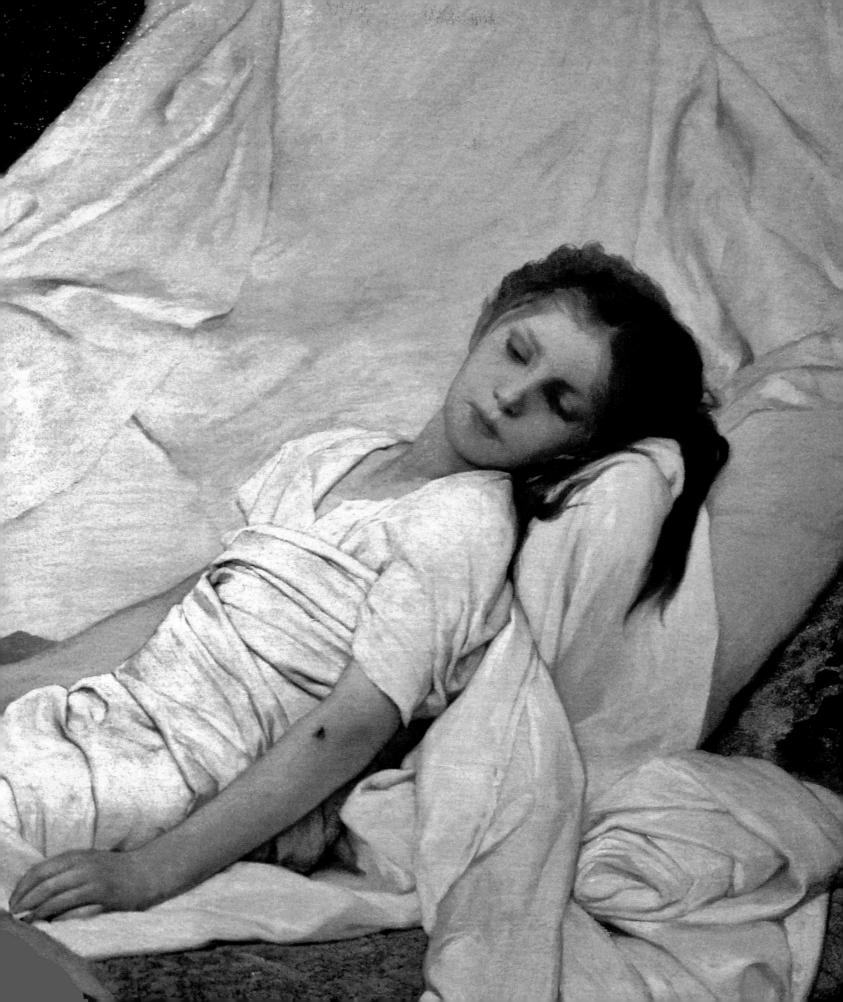

CHAPTER FOURTEEN

THE NATURE MIRACLES

*[They] said to one another,
"Who then is this, that even
the wind and the sea obey him?"*

MARK 4:41

Jesus Commands Miraculous Events in Nature

When the evening had come," Mark writes, "[Jesus] said to them, 'Let us go across to the other side.' And leaving the crowd behind, they took him with them in the boat, just as he was." But then, unexpectedly, "a great windstorm arose, and the waves beat into the boat, so that the boat was already being swamped." The Apostles began to panic, but Jesus gave no sign that anything was amiss. He was fast asleep in the stern of the boat, no doubt exhausted from speaking to the crowds all day. The disciples woke him up and said to him,

"'Teacher, do you not care that we are perishing?' Jesus stood up and said to the sea, 'Peace! Be still!' And the wind ceased, and suddenly there was a dead calm. Jesus then turned to the Apostles and said, `Why are you afraid? Have you still no faith?' And," Mark adds, "they were filled with great awe" (Mark 4:35-41).

This is the first so-called nature miracle in the Gospel of Mark after numerous reports of healings and exorcisms. The other Gospels feature nature miracles as well, such as the feeding of the five thousand (Matthew 14:13-21; Mark 6:32-44; Luke 9:10-17; John 6:1-15), the miraculous catch of fish (Luke 5:1-11; John 21:1-14), and the story of Jesus walking on water (Matthew 14:22-33; Mark 6:45-52; John 6:16-21). Another nature miracle is the conversion of water into wine, described in the Gospel of John (John 2:1-11).

It is doubtful that in ancient times, anyone would have made a distinction between these miraculous events and Jesus' exorcisms and healings. Once an individual was believed to be endowed with wondrous powers, he or she was assumed to be capable of virtually anything. But modern scholarship sees it differently and makes a clear distinction between the healings and meta-physical miracles. One reason is that healing stories abound in all four Gospels, whereas nature miracles appear only incidentally. Only one miracle, the feeding of the five thousand, is reported in all four Gospels. What's more, whereas the healing stories usually follow a distinct literary pattern, the nature miracles have no recognizable formula.

This by itself does not mean that these nature miracles have fewer historical roots. Nevertheless, there is obviously a vast difference between the ability to heal and the possession of supernatural powers to control stormy seas or walk on water. Were the evangelists aware of this difference? Or are these miracles the product of oral transmission and redaction, emphasizing the significance of Jesus' ministry for the early Church?

Some scholars believe the answer can be found in Hebrew Scripture. They suggest that the accounts of nature miracles seem to be consciously modeled on parallel episodes in Scripture, including passages featuring Elijah and Elisha, who often serve as prophetic models for the evangelists.

A case in point is Mark's story of Jesus calming the stormy sea. It is possible that this miracle was inspired by the story of the prophet Jonah. While sailing

ABOVE: *Reeds and shrubs cover the western shore of the Sea of Galilee near the ancient town of Magdala, which Jesus very likely visited during his journeys in the region.*

OPPOSITE: *An earthenware jug with handle and spout was found in the vicinity of Jerusalem and is dated to the late first or early second century C.E.*

PRECEDING PAGES: *The "Transfiguration" by Italian Renaissance artist Raphael (1483–1520) was completed by his pupil Giulio Romano after the artist's death in 1520.*

from Joppa to Tarshish, Jonah was found sleeping in the hold of a ship in the midst of a storm. The captain woke Jonah up and said, "What are you doing sound asleep? Get up, call on your god! Perhaps the god will spare us a thought so that we do not perish." Jonah calmly suggested another remedy. He told the sailors to "pick me up and throw me into the sea; then the sea will quiet down for you; for I know it is because of me that this great storm has come upon you." The sailors did as Jonah suggested "and threw him into the sea; and the sea ceased from its raging" (Jonah 1:3-15).

Another passage in Hebrew Scripture in which a prophet, using his God-given powers, takes control of the waters is the story of Moses, who with the Israelite slaves found himself marooned between the Red Sea and Pharaoh's advancing chariots. "Lift up your staff," the Lord told Moses, "and stretch out your hand over the sea and divide it, that the Israelites may go into the sea on dry ground." Moses did as the Lord told him, and "the Lord drove the sea back by a strong east wind all night, and turned the sea into dry land; and the waters were divided" (Exodus 14:16-21). In the Book of Job, moreover, the prophet refers to God as he who "trampled the waves of the Sea" (Job 9:8).

For people living in the ancient Near East, water was a vital element. It could give life, nurture, and quench, but it could also rise in anger to destroy and kill. By demonstrating his command over water, the Gospels present Jesus not only as the heir to the prophets of Hebrew Scripture but also as the true Son of God, master over the Earth's elements.

THE MULTIPLICATION OF LOAVES AND FISHES

Another important symbolic message can be found in the story of the miraculous multiplication of loaves and fishes. It is first reported in the Gospel of Mark and faithfully recounted by Matthew, Luke, and John with very few discrepancies.

The setting is a large field near the shore of the Sea of Galilee. It is dusk; the sun has begun to set on a long day in which Jesus has taught and healed large numbers of people. Now everyone is tired and hungry, and looking for something to eat. The disciples come to Jesus and say, "This is a deserted place and the hour is now late; send the crowds away so that they may go into the villages and buy food for themselves" (Matthew 14:15). Jesus refuses to do so. He knows these people; they are famished and

Bread and fish—in this case, bread made from barley and either tilapia fish or sardines—formed the basic ingredients of the diet of Galilean poor.

A 15th-century illustration from an Italian illuminated manuscript (top) shows Christ calming the storm on the Sea of Galilee. A first-century basket (inset), made from woven willow twigs, was found in the Judean Desert.

malnourished for the simple reason that they have no money to buy food. During the Sermon on the Mount, he taught, "Blessed are you who are hungry now, for you will be filled." Now, surrounded by thousands of hungry people, the time has come to demonstrate the fulfillment of that most tangible, most fundamental human need. The Apostles disagree; they protest that "we have nothing here but five loaves and two fish." The four evangelists describe what happens next:

Mark: "Then he ordered them to get all the people to sit down in groups on the green grass . . . Taking the five loaves and the two fish, he looked up to heaven, and blessed and broke the loaves, and gave them to his disciples to set before the people; and he divided the two fish among them all. And all ate and were filled; and they took up twelve baskets full of broken pieces and of the fish." (Mark 6:39-43)

Matthew: "Then he ordered the crowds to sit down on the grass. Taking the five loaves and the two fish, he looked up to heaven, and blessed and broke the loaves, and gave them to the disciples, and the disciples gave them to the crowds. And all ate and were filled; and they took up what was left over of the broken pieces, twelve baskets full" (Matthew 14:19-20).

Luke: "And he said to his disciples, 'Make them sit down in groups of about fifty each.' They did so and made them all sit down. And taking the five loaves and the two fish, he looked up to heaven, and blessed and broke them, and gave them to the disciples to set before the crowd. And all ate and were filled. What was left over was gathered up, twelve baskets of broken pieces" (Luke 9:14-17).

John: "Jesus said, 'Make the people sit down.' Now there was a great deal of grass in the place; so they sat down, about five thousand in all. Then Jesus took the loaves, and when he had given thanks, he distributed them to those who were seated; so also the fish, as much as they wanted. When they were satisfied, he told his disciples, 'Gather up the fragments left over, so that nothing may be lost.' So they gathered them up, and from the fragments of the five barley loaves, left by those who had eaten, they filled twelve baskets" (John 6:10-13).

FISHING IN THE SEA OF GALILEE

The account of the miraculous catch of fish appears in the Gospel of Luke, but another version is found in the Gospel of John, right after the story of the Resurrection. After Jesus taught the crowds from a boat, he told Simon Peter to "put out into the deep water and let down your nets for a catch." Simon answered, "Master, we have worked all night long but have caught nothing. Yet if you say so, I will let down the nets." When they had done this, they caught so many fish that their nets were beginning to break" (Luke 5:4-6). Some historians believe that the failure of the Apostles to catch fish reflects the overharvesting of the Sea of Galilee in Jesus' time, possibly by amateur fishermen who had been displaced from their fields. Israeli scientists have identified 27 species of fish in the sea, many of which are also described in ancient sources. Of these, only a few types are truly edible, including sardines (possibly the "few small fish" in Mark's feeding of the four thousand), a carplike barbel fish, and the Galilean tilapia fish, which today is popular among visitors to Galilee as "St. Peter's fish." ∎

This modern fisherman's vessel is an approximation of the type of boat that would have plied the Sea of Galilee in Jesus' time.

A Roman lidded basket from woven leather and fiber probably contained cosmetics or other personal items.

It is quite possible, as some historians have suggested, that the miracle was inspired by Elijah's multiplication of the meal and oil at the house of the widow at Zarephath (I Kings 17:14) or Elisha's miraculous feeding of a hundred men (II Kings 4:42), just as Elisha's conversion of Jericho's toxic wells into fresh water may have been a model for John's story of the miraculous conversion of water into wine at Cana (II Kings 2:21; John 2:9). The reference to a "deserted place" may be another scriptural allusion, evoking the miraculous appearance of manna on the desert floor of Sinai during the Exodus.

But what is truly remarkable about these four passages is their exceptional similarity. It suggests that this story must have carried a message of vital importance, not only for the evangelists but also for their principal audience, the early Christian communities. All four versions faithfully report that (1) the people were asked to *sit down,* (2) that Jesus then *blessed the bread* and *broke it,* (3) that all ate *and were filled,* and (4) that the leftovers filled *12 baskets.*

It is likely that these features were inspired by the practice of the Eucharist, which was then taking shape among many early Christians. The faithful

The "Feeding of the Five Thousand" was painted by Flemish Renaissance artist Joachim Patinir (or Patenier; 1487–1524).

would meet in each other's homes to sit down (or recline) and share bread and wine in commemoration of Jesus' Last Supper ("Eucharist" is derived from the Greek word *eucharistia,* or thanksgiving). In this context, the story of the multiplication of loaves and fishes symbolizes the miraculous multi- plication of the budding Church, the early Christian *ekklesia,* in which Jesus, the "bread of life," offers spiritual fulfillment to all who believe in him. The 12 baskets, moreover, symbolize the 12 Israelite tribes, to emphasize that Jesus offers redemption to all of Israel, regardless of where the faithful may be in the far-flung Diaspora. ■

This fresco from a fourth-century Roman catacomb showing a banquet scene may be one of the first depictions of the Christian Eucharist.

When he had finished speaking, he said to Simon, "Put out into the deep water and let down your nets for a catch."

LUKE 5:4-6

FOLLOWING PAGES:
Renaissance artist Raphael (1483–1520) painted "The Miraculous Draught of Fishes" around 1515 as one of seven designs of tapestries for the Sistine Chapel.

CHAPTER FIFTEEN

THE PARABLES

With many such parables
he spoke the word to them,
as they were able to hear it;
he did not speak to them
except in parables.

MARK 4:33-34

Proverbial Stories That Illustrate the Kingdom of God

Listen," Jesus once said, "a sower went out to sow. And as he sowed, some seed fell on the path, and the birds came and ate it up." Other seeds fared no better: Some fell on rocky ground, and other seeds fell among thorns. Only a small portion of the seeds "fell into good soil and brought forth grain, growing up and increasing and yielding thirty and sixty and a hundredfold" (Mark 4:3-8).

Short proverbial stories like these abound in the Gospels. Confronted with a mostly uneducated and largely illiterate audience, Jesus must have felt the need to illustrate the abstract ideas he talked about with simple metaphorical stories. At first glance, they are easy to understand. Most parables are inspired by very common genre scenes taken from everyday life in rural Galilee. Many have to do with Galilee's agriculture, probably because, as Josephus tells us, almost everyone was engaged in cultivation in some form or another. Other parables take their cue from the debts that many farmers struggled with, or the egregious gap between rich and poor, such as the story of the talents and pounds (Matthew 25:14-30), the creditor (Luke 7:41-43), the rich fool (Luke 12:16-21), and the Pharisee and the tax collector (Luke 18:9-14). Other parables explore the importance of family and clan in Galilee, such as the story of two sons (Matthew 21:28-31), the prodigal son (Luke 15:11-32), and the wedding banquet (Matthew 22:1-14).

In most cases, however, the deeper symbolic meaning is not always obvious, and many stories leave the Apostles befuddled. In the case of the parable of the sower, for example, the Apostles must have been particularly clueless, because Jesus said to them, somewhat exasperated, "Do you not understand this parable? Then how will you understand all the parables?"

Jesus explained what he was trying to say. "The sower sows the *word,*" he said. "These are the ones on the path where the word is sown: when they hear, Satan immediately comes and takes away the word that is sown in them." Similarly, the word may fall on rocky soil, that is, among people who only have a superficial interest. In that case, "when trouble or persecution arises on account of the word, immediately they fall away." And when the word is sown among "the thorns," then "the cares of the world, and the lure of wealth, and the desire for other things, come in and choke the word." Thus, the seed of the word falls on good ground only if the listeners "accept it and bear fruit, thirty and sixty and a hundredfold" (Mark 4:15-20).

This passage in Mark is one of the few instances where Jesus offers an explanation of what he has in mind. It is possible that he offered many more such explanations for his parables, but they did not make it into the Gospels (or perhaps this midrashic material was lost in the oral tradition). Nevertheless, these parables are not only typical of Jesus' didactic method, but also offer tantalizing glimpses of life in Galilee.

ABOVE: *Wheat fields and olive groves such as these orchards outside Nazareth evoke the timeless beauty of ancient Galilee.*

OPPOSITE: *These five Roman rings, made of Egyptian ivory, may have been used as bracelets to ward off spells and evil spirits.*

PRECEDING PAGES: *"The Return of the Prodigal Son" is a work from the late period of Dutch 17th-century artist Rembrandt Harmenszoon van Rijn (1606–1669), completed in the year of his death.*

PARABLES IN HEBREW SCRIPTURE

The parables take up such a large part of the Gospels that the genre has spawned a separate movement of biblical scholarship that continues to debate their meaning. One reason is their sheer diversity. Amazingly, five parables are listed in all three synoptic Gospels. Matthew has 9 parables that don't appear anywhere else, and Luke includes no fewer than 12 parables that are unique to his Gospel. So the underlying oral traditions about Jesus' parables must have been vast.

The word "parable" comes from the Greek *parabolé*, which can mean comparison, proverb, analogy, illustration, or even riddle. As such it was a figure of speech that Greek philosophers sometimes used when making a particular point. Early Christian authors who may not have been aware of this precedent believed that the parable was Jesus' unique invention, so as to better illustrate the eschatological concepts he talked about. But scholars such as John P. Meier have shown that parables, or *mashalim* in Hebrew, also have a long tradition in Hebrew Scripture. A typical example is the parable told by the prophet Nathan to King David. "There were two men in a certain town, one rich and the other poor," Nathan said. "The rich man had a very large number of sheep and cattle, but the poor man had nothing except one little ewe lamb he had bought." The poor man then raised the lamb as if it was his daughter. One day, the rich man received a visit from a traveler. He wanted to prepare a meal from him, but he was loath to take his own sheep. So he took the lamb that belonged to the poor man and "prepared it for the one who had come to him" (II Samuel 12:1-4).

The image of the good shepherd, inspired by the Gospel of John (John 10:11), is one of the oldest Christian motifs, as shown in this statue from the late fourth century C.E.

And he said to them, "Do you not understand this parable? Then how will you understand all the parables?"

MARK 4:13

Upon hearing the story, David rose in anger. Who is this rich man? he wanted to know. "As surely as the Lord lives, the man who did this must die!" Then Nathan said to the king, "You are the man!" And he explained how God had given him all this wealth—the kingdom of Israel, a palace, and many wives—and that in spite of this, David had seen fit to have Uriah the Hittite killed, so that he could take his wife, Bathsheba. The king was deeply humbled by this analogy. "I have sinned against the Lord," he said. In response, God caused the child that Bathsheba bore to David to become ill and die—although a second son, Solomon, would succeed David as king (II Samuel 12:7-15). This story is a great example of the persuasive power of the parable: to frame a moral question in a way that listeners can understand.

PARABLES IN THE RABBINIC TRADITION

Modern research has argued that Jesus may have been introduced to parabolic poetry by the community that the Gospels often cast as his adversary: the Pharisees. As we saw in the Introduction, the Pharisees were engaged in an ongoing effort to debate and interpret the Jewish Law according to the changing needs of contemporary life. In these discussions, they often harked to examples or

TOP: *Olive trees such as these in northern Galilee yielded one of the most valuable products in Antiquity: olive oil.*

BOTTOM: *Sickles, made of wood and iron, were the principal tools for reaping the harvest, an activity often cited in Jesus' parables.*

Then Jesus told them a parable about their need to pray always and not to lose heart.

LUKE 1:18

situations that they had observed. One such parable is told by renowned rabbinical leader Yohanan ben Zakkai. He said, "A king once summoned his servants to a banquet without appointing a time. The wise ones adorned themselves and sat at the door of the palace . . . The fools went about their work." At that moment, the summons arrived. Inevitably, the wise ones entered properly dressed, "while the fools entered soiled." Thus, the wise were feted, while the foolish ones, in their dirty everyday garb, were forced to "stand and watch."

This rabbinic parable is reminiscent of the story of the wedding banquet in the Gospel of Matthew. "The kingdom of heaven may be compared to a king who gave a wedding banquet for his son," Jesus said. "He sent his slaves to call those who had been invited to the wedding banquet, but they would not come." Some of the guests went back to their farms, another to his business, "while the rest seized his slaves, mistreated them, and killed them." Enraged, the king burned down the city and ordered his slaves to go and invite everyone they could find on the streets. Thus, the banquet hall was filled. But one man was not wearing the festive garb that one would expect for a wedding. The king told his attendants, "'Bind him hand and foot, and throw him into the outer darkness, where there will be weeping

GOD'S PARABLE

In the Book of Ezekiel, it is God himself who uses a parable to warn the Israelites: "A great eagle with powerful wings, long feathers and full plumage of varied colors came to Lebanon. Taking hold of the top of a cedar, he broke off its topmost shoot and carried it away to a land of merchants, where he planted it in a city of traders." The seedlings brought forth a vine with many branches. But then "there was another great eagle with powerful wings and full plumage. The vine now sent out its roots toward him from the plot where it was planted and stretched out its branches to him for water." The meaning is as follows: The first eagle is King Nebuchadnezzar, who took the royal house of Judah into exile. The seed he planted is the Jewish vassal king, Zedekiah. The second eagle is Pharaoh Psammetichus II, to whom Zedekiah foolishly switched his allegiance. For this, Zedekiah would be destined to die in captivity. ∎

Jesus often used the orchard as a metaphor for the Kingdom of God, perhaps because of its bountiful supply of nourishing fruits.

The fields of western Galilee, known as the Naphtali after the Hebrew tribe placed here by Joshua, are covered with lush shrubs and olive trees, which thrive on the chalk soil.

and gnashing of teeth.' For many are called, but few are chosen" (Matthew 22:2-14). The parallels between this story and the one told by Rabbi Yohanan are evident. Both urge the listener to be ready for God, no matter the time and place.

THE PARABLE OF THE PRODIGAL SON

The rabbinic use of parables does not in any way diminish the fact that Jesus uses the parable tradition in new and unique ways. In his stories, Jesus appears to be focused on a single objective, namely, to explain his vision for the Kingdom of God: how to bring it about, how to enter it, how to thrive in it. To illustrate this rather abstract model, Jesus uses pithy stories that feature the types of characters everyone was familiar with: a widow, a son, a servant, a tenant farmer, a king. This is the cast of characters that also populate our own beloved fables, from the Brothers Grimm to Disney, for they are essential characters, salt-of-the-earth people we can identify with.

When the chief priests and the Pharisees heard his parables, they realized that he was speaking about them.

MATTHEW 21:45

But in using these stock characters, Jesus is retelling familiar themes in new ways—even in ways that some scholars have called "subversive." At first glance, the plot may be familiar, but the outcome, the final spin of the story, is not. In expressing Israel's longing for messianic delivery, Jesus must convince his audience that that time has come, that it is within their grasp, and that he is the one who has been charged by God to lead them into that kingdom.

Let us, for example, take one of the most famous parables from the Gospel literature, the story of the prodigal son. "There was a man who had two sons," Jesus said. "The younger of them said to his father, 'Father, give me the share of the property that will belong to me.' So he divided his property between them." What does the younger son do? He does what most teenagers today would do: travels to a faraway city (the ancient equivalent of Las Vegas, perhaps) and splurges on everything he can get his hands on. Inevitably there comes a time when his money runs out. He needs a job, but he can find only the most menial of occupations: feeding the pigs (which, as we saw earlier, are considered unclean and ritually impure in Judaism). While the pigs gorge themselves on the pods the son is feeding them, he himself has

This depiction of "The Return of the Prodigal Son" was painted by Italian late Baroque artist Pompeo Girolamo Batoni (1708–1787) in 1773.

This bronze sesterce was struck during the reign of Emperor Tiberius (r. 14–37 C.E.). Four sesterces made one denarius, about the equivalent of $18, usually a day's wages.

nothing. In a bout of self-pity, he thinks of home and tells himself, "How many of my father's hired hands have bread enough to spare, but here I am, dying of hunger!"

And so he resolves to go back. Perhaps he wonders whether his father will agree to take him on as one of his hired hands. But as he approaches his father's house, no doubt filled with dread and shame, his father comes running toward him. He throws his arms around the prodigal son and hugs him tight. He summons his servants to bring wonderful clothes, covers the son with fine jewelry, and tells his slaves to lay on a big feast. Naturally the other son, who has been diligently working in the fields while his sibling was living the high life, is very upset. "For all these years I have been working like a slave for you," he cries at his father, "yet you have never given me even a young goat so that I might celebrate with my friends!" And then, Jesus said, the father turned to him and replied, "Son, you are always with me, and all that is mine is yours. But we

THE GOOD SAMARITAN

Among all of Jesus' parables about his vision of the Kingdom of God, the story of the Good Samaritan in the Gospel of Luke is perhaps one of the most popular. A Jewish man who "was going down from Jerusalem to Jericho . . . fell into the hands of robbers, who stripped him, beat him, and went away, leaving him half dead" (Luke 10:30). Two people passed the unfortunate victim: a priest and a Levite. They both looked the other way and refused to come to the man's aid. Then a Samaritan passed by. Most Jews in Jesus' time avoided contact with Samaritans, the inhabitants of Samaria, for their bloodlines were believed to have been contaminated by intermarriage with Babylonian settlers. And yet it was the Samaritan who took pity on the man. He "bandaged

"The Good Samaritan Heals the Traveler" was painted by Dutch artist Nicolaes Roosendael (1634–1686) around 1665.

his wounds, having poured oil and wine on them," and then took him to an inn, where he gave the innkeeper two denarii (about $40) for the victim's care (Luke 10:30-37).

The parable is meant to illustrate a specific tenet of the Kingdom: the absolute concern for one's neighbor, one's fellow human being, regardless of racial prejudice. Jesus is prompted to tell the story by "a lawyer," who asks him what he must do to inherit eternal life. Jesus answers by referring the lawyer to the Torah, which commends one to love the Lord your God, and to love your neighbor as yourself (Deuteronomy 6:5; Leviticus 19:18). For Jesus, "there is no other commandment greater than these," emphasizing selfless love as the cardinal pillar of the Kingdom (Mark 12:28-31). ∎

had to celebrate and rejoice, because this brother of yours was dead and has come to life; he was lost and has been found" (Luke 15:11-32).

On the surface, this is a wonderful story about the power of forgiveness and the fathomless depths of a father's love—something that every parent with wayward children can empathize with. But the real meaning of the parable goes well beyond that. One interpretation is that the younger son is Israel itself, which chose to turn away from God so that it could pursue sinful living with foreigners and found mercy when it chose to repent. But other authors have suggested that the parable refers to tensions within the early Christian Church: The older, faithful brother refers to Jewish Christians, while the younger son may symbolize newly converted Gentiles.

THE PARABLES OF THE KINGDOM

Most of Jesus' other parables continue this theme of translating the prerequisites of the Kingdom of God into rather challenging stories, using metaphors that his audience of Galilean peasants and workers could identify with. "The Kingdom of God," Jesus explained, "is like a mustard seed, the smallest of all the seeds on earth, that, when sown, becomes the greatest of all shrubs" (Matthew 13:31). Or "The Kingdom of God is like a seed that sprouts while the farmer is asleep; it grows into a stalk, the head, and finally the grain, which the farmer cuts with his sickle" (Mark 4:26-29).

Taken together, these Kingdom parables also set up an essential conflict: that between Jesus and the Jewish authorities, particularly the priestly group of the Sadducees, who had a very different idea about what redemption in Judaism meant. For the Sadducees, the Temple was the ultimate place of redemption, and the combination of tithes and sacrificial rites was the only way to secure it. That is why some scholars believe that the parables are essentially subversive. It may also be the reason that Jesus couches his sermons about the Kingdom of God in the veiled language of simple, folksy stories: He was well aware of the risks he was taking. In the Gospel of Mark, Jesus even states quite plainly that he is comfortable talking about the Kingdom of God with his Apostles, but not with "those outside" his immediate circle of followers. For those outsiders, he says that "everything comes in parables in order that they may indeed look, but not perceive, and may indeed listen, but not understand" (Mark 4:11-12). ∎

The scene on this round panel depicts "The Parable of the Sower," painted by Flemish late Renaissance artist Abel Grimmer (ca 1570–ca 1620).

FOLLOWING PAGES: *Renaissance artist Paolo Veronese (1528–1588) completed this vast canvas, "The Wedding Feast of Cana," in 1563 for the Benedictine monastery of San Giorgio Maggiore in Venice, Italy.*

CHAPTER SIXTEEN

JESUS AND THE PHARISEES

*The scribes and the Pharisees
began to be very hostile toward him
and to cross-examine him about
many things, lying in wait for him,
to catch him in something
he might say.*

LUKE 11:53-54

Are the Pharisees Adversaries . . . or Allies?

The Pharisees make their first appearance when they challenge Jesus about a topic often debated in Pharisaic circles: the proper observance of the Sabbath. "One Sabbath," says Mark, "[Jesus] was going through the grain fields; and as they made their way his disciples began to pluck heads of grain." This was either observed by or, more likely, reported to the Pharisees, who took umbrage at such behavior. The Sabbath was devoted to rest; no form of work, not even an effort as minor as plucking heads of grain or removing the husks so as to eat the kernels, was permitted.

So the Pharisees challenged Jesus on this issue. "They said to him, 'Look, why are they doing what is not lawful on the Sabbath?' And he said to them, 'Have you never read what David did when he and his companions were hungry and in need of food? He entered the house of God, when Abiathar was high priest, and ate the bread of the Presence, which it is not lawful for any but the priests to eat, and he gave some to his companions'" (Mark 2:23-26).

In other words, Jesus was making the argument that a person has to eat, and if circumstances prevented the Apostles from having ready-to-eat bread on the Sabbath, then they were surely entitled to pluck the grain. As the Mishnah (which may include material from Pharisaic debates) and the later Talmudic literature indicate, such topics were often the subject of discussion. In the Babylonian Talmud, for example, second-century Rabbi Judah ben El'ai is cited as saying that "[on the Sabbath] one may pluck [grain] by hand and eat, but only if one plucks without a utensil; and one may rub [a husk] and eat, but only if one does not rub a lot with a utensil."

Mark, who probably wrote his Gospel in Rome in the late 60s, may not have been familiar with the Pharisaic movement of Jesus' time or with the Book of Samuel. His comparison with the story of David, for example, is not entirely correct. David's transgression was not that he harvested grain or performed any type of work on the Sabbath, but that he used "the bread of the Presence," that is, the ceremonial bread placed in YHWH's shrine, to feed himself and his "young men," his soldiers (Samuel 21:1-6). Regardless of these discrepancies, the point that Jesus was trying to make is obvious: "The Sabbath was made for humankind," he said, "and not humankind for the Sabbath."

> *Some of the Pharisees said, "This man is not from God, for he does not observe the Sabbath." But others said, "How can a man who is a sinner perform such signs?"*

JOHN 9:16

"The Man with the Withered Hand" was painted by French artist James Jacques Joseph Tissot (1836–1902) for a series of illustrations known as "The Life of Christ," circa 1894.

The purpose of the Sabbath as a day of rest had been ordained by God in the Book of Genesis and later incorporated into the legal corpus of the Torah as one of the Ten Commandments. "You shall keep my Sabbaths, for this is a sign between me and you throughout your generations, given in order that you may know that I, the Lord, sanctify you," God told Moses (Exodus 31:13). But what such Sabbath observance entailed in practice was (and still is) a matter of debate among various Jewish traditions. The tractate *Shabbat* in the Talmud specifies 39 categories of prohibition; one of these is the "gathering" of edible foodstuffs from their place of origin, in a field or an orchard.

What Jesus is saying, however, is that there are reasonable exceptions, based on basic human needs. Plucking and eating grain, when there is no other food available, is such a need, and it should be allowed. As the Talmud suggests, there were at least some rabbis who would have agreed with him, provided one avoided tools that would qualify the activity as *melakha*, as a physical effort, as *work*.

MATTERS OF LIFE AND DEATH

Mark then writes that the Pharisees tried to catch Jesus in another Sabbath violation. They followed him into the synagogue, presumably in Capernaum, to see if Jesus would be tempted to heal a man among the congregation who suffered from a withered hand. If he did, they would promptly denounce him. But Jesus was on to them. He told the man, "Come forward," and then immediately turned to the Pharisees, challenging *them* instead. "Is it lawful to do good or to do harm on the Sabbath," he asked them, "to save life or to

> *So the Pharisees and the scribes asked him,*
> *"Why do your disciples not live according*
> *to the tradition of the elders,*
> *but eat with defiled hands?"*

MARK 7:5

kill?" Jesus knew he had them there. The rabbinic tradition clearly accepted that any danger to human life could override the prohibitions of the Sabbath. For example, if someone's house caught on fire on the Sabbath, no one was allowed to intervene and extinguish the flames. But if someone was trapped in the house, then it would become an obligation for everyone to rush in and try to put out the fire.

What makes Mark's story so interesting is the ambiguity of the case. Did the man's affliction, of having a withered hand, constitute a life-threatening condition? Many Jews would have argued that it did not, that this was apparently a chronic condition, and that Jesus, if he wanted to help the man, could simply wait until sundown, when the Sabbath would come to an end and he could do whatever he liked. Others would have argued that the man's grievous disability had an urgency of its own.

It's precisely this ambiguity that led the Pharisees not to challenge Jesus. "They were silent," Mark says. This aggrieved Jesus deeply. For him, the physical suffering of a human being was as much cause for immediate intervention as a life-threatening danger, trumping any restrictions that the Sabbath might impose. Ignoring their "hardness of heart," Jesus turned to the man and said, "Stretch out your hand." He stretched it out, and his hand was restored (Mark 3:2-5).

A stained-glass window of 1248 from Sainte-Chapelle in Paris depicts the resurrection of the dead on Judgment Day, an idea that was debated in Pharisaic circles.

Significantly, the healing did not involve any *melakhot;* Jesus neither touched the man nor performed any other physical act. He simply spoke, and the hand was healed. The Pharisees, however, were undeterred. They continued to harass Jesus on other presumed transgressions of the Torah.

PHARISEES, SCRIBES, AND TAX COLLECTORS

The other Gospels continue the theme of the Pharisaic opposition. In the Gospel of Matthew, the Pharisees go so far as to compare Jesus to Satan, saying, "It is only by Beelzebul, the ruler of the demons, that this fellow casts out the demons" (Matthew 9:34; 12:24). Jesus fires back by calling them "a brood of vipers" and accusing them of speaking "good things, even when you are evil" (Matthew 12:34); elsewhere, he explicitly warns his audience not to pay heed to "the yeast of the Pharisees," their teachings (Matthew 16:6). Finally, after Jesus heals the man with the withered hand on the Sabbath, the situation escalates: The Pharisees "went out and conspired against him, how to destroy him" (Matthew 12:14).

In Luke's stories, the Pharisees are often lumped together with the other "usual suspects": the scribes and tax collectors. All three were groups that played an important role in the world of Jesus: the Pharisees, because of their leading role in teaching the people about proper religious observance; the scribes, because of their service as public notaries; and the tax collectors, or "publicans," because of their pivotal role in the lending, brokering, and collection of funds. Of the three, only the tax collectors were truly despised because they were widely believed to be corrupt.

But the Gospels present a very different attitude. They see the publicans as wayward people who can be saved. A case in point is Zaccheus, a wealthy toll collector in Jericho. Jesus persuaded him to give back all the monies he had defrauded and to donate half of his possessions to the poor (Luke 19:8). Christian tradition even holds that Matthew

THE PHARISEES AND FASTING

In the Gospel of Mark, another confrontation between Jesus and the Pharisees takes place over the issue of fasting. "Why do John's disciples and the disciples of the Pharisees fast," the people asked, "but your disciples do not fast?'" An interesting question. The Apostles, after all, were hardworking fishermen who needed their nutrition, in contrast to more ascetic Jews who could afford the luxury of solitude. What's more, fasting was not prescribed in the Law, though Jews did fast on occasion, such as Yom Kippur—the Day of Atonement (Leviticus 16:29). Jesus replied, "The wedding guests cannot fast while the bridegroom is with them, can they?"—a metaphorical reference to his teachings as the essential "bread of life." Jesus then added, "The days will come when the bridegroom is taken away from them, and then they will fast on that day" (Mark 2:18-20). This is probably an allusion to early Christian communities, where—as the evangelists may have known—fasting was regularly practiced. ∎

This reconstruction of a Greco-Roman–style villa in Sepphoris suggests the opulence and wealth enjoyed by the upper classes in the time of Jesus.

was originally a tax collector himself, a man named Levi.

The Gospels also have some good things to say about scribes, a group of professionals not otherwise known for their charity. "Every scribe who has been trained for the kingdom of heaven," says Jesus in Matthew, "is like the master of a household who brings out of his treasure what is new and what is old" (Matthew 13:52).

But when it comes to the Pharisees, the judgment in the Gospels is resolutely harsh. "Woe to you Pharisees!" Jesus cries in Luke's Gospel no fewer than three times. He calls them people who "rejected God's purpose for themselves," who are obsessed with the minutiae of the Law, while "neglect[ing] justice and the love of God" (Luke 7:30; 11:42). They are "like unmarked graves" (an egregious example of defilement), men who care for nothing but "to have the seat of honor in the synagogues and

A sixth-century C.E. mosaic depicts the "Parable of the Pharisee and the Publican" in the church of St. Apollinare Nuovo in Ravenna, Italy.

> At that very hour some Pharisees came and said to him, "Get away from here, for Herod wants to kill you."
>
> **LUKE 13:31**

This barrel-shaped jar with a ribbed body and two loop handles is dated between 50 B.C.E. and 50 C.E. Such jars were often used to store provisions.

to be greeted with respect in the marketplaces." They may clean the outside of the cup and of the dish, "but inside," Jesus says, they "are full of greed and wickedness" (Luke 12:39-44).

These are serious accusations. Why do the Gospels levy them? What is the reason for this deep animus between Jesus and the Pharisees?

COULD THE PHARISEES HAVE BEEN ALLIES?

When seen from a historical perspective, the conflict between the Pharisees and Jesus' movement doesn't make much sense, because both groups had much in common. As we saw, the Pharisees were prepared to debate the Law and make allowances for particular human needs, just as Jesus sought to do. The Pharisees were also the first to talk about a rather revolutionary idea: the immortality

"The Conversion of Zaccheus" is a painting by Italian Baroque artist Bernardo Strozzi (1581–1644), who mostly lived in Venice and Genoa.

of the soul and the belief in the resurrection after Judgment Day. These two concepts, vigorously opposed by the Sadducees, are also present in the teachings of Jesus. It also explains the great popularity enjoyed by the Pharisees in Roman Judea, particularly in urban areas. In contrast to the inflexible and arrogant attitude of the Sadducees, the Pharisees brought a progressive attitude to the question of how first-century Jews should observe the Law.

All this suggests that Jesus and the Pharisees *should* have been natural allies, aligned in their progressive ideas while unified in their opposition to the corrupt Sadducee class. And some scholars believe that this was exactly the case. The numerous stories of the Pharisees challenging Jesus on Torah observance, they argue, actually prove that they genuinely welcomed his opinion. Spirited debate on matters of Law was the bread and butter of Pharisaic life; lively, even heated discourse is what they practiced among themselves. To approach Jesus on these matters, then, would suggest that they respected his knowledge and believed his ideas had merit. Luke, for example, acknowledges that on several occasions, Pharisees invited Jesus to dine with them (Luke 7:36; 11:37).

Luke also writes that when Herod Antipas became alarmed over Jesus' activity in Galilee, it was a group of Pharisees who came to warn Jesus about the threat. "Get away from here," these Pharisees urged, "for Herod wants to kill you" (Luke 13:31). This appears to contradict Matthew's assertion that the Pharisees "conspired against him, how to destroy him" (Matthew 12:14). Finally, it was a Pharisee and "a member of the Council," Joseph of Arimathea, who would intercede with Pilate to release Jesus' body and allow a proper burial in his tomb. This clearly shows that at least one group of Pharisees had considerable sympathy for what Jesus was trying to accomplish.

Why, then, would the Gospels depict the Pharisees as his principal adversaries? We have to remember that the evangelists probably wrote in the wake of the Jewish War, when much of the world that Jesus knew had been destroyed. The Temple was burned down. The Sadducees were gone. Only the Pharisees remained. In the decades to come, their focus on the Oral Law, the ongoing interpretation of the Torah, would lay the basis for a new form of Judaism known as

Rabbinic Judaism. By the end of the first century, the Jewish rabbinate, heirs to the Pharisees, had become the dominant religious authority in Roman Palestine.

But this same period was also a time of escalating tensions between observant Jews and Christian Jews—Jews, in other words, who continued to honor the Torah while also celebrating Jesus as the Messiah. According to the Book of Acts of the Apostles, this conflict began soon after the Resurrection, when the Apostles decided to continue Jesus' mission. At that time, the Sadducees were the principal antagonists. But after the Jewish War, the rabbinical hierarchy seemed to have perpetuated this prejudice against Jewish Christians. This may explain the negative attitude of the evangelists toward the Pharisees. Particularly for oppressed Christian communities, it reinforced the idea that Jesus as well had felt the pains of persecution—even though historically, that may not always have been the case. ◼

FOLLOWING PAGES:
"The Parable of the Blind Leading the Blind" was painted by Flemish artist Pieter Brueghel the Younger (1564/5–1636) in 1616, after an original painted by his father.

THE CONFLICT BETWEEN THE PHARISEES AND SADDUCEES

The movement of the Pharisees (derived from the Greek *pharisaois,* based on the Hebrew *perushim,* or separated ones) came about during the Hasmonean era, after the Maccabean Revolt succeeded in restoring a Jewish kingdom in Israel. At one point, the Pharisees, which consisted of both laymen and priests, were the leading political and religious party in Judea. But when the Hasmonean king, Alexander Jannaeus (r. 103–76 B.C.E) decided to place the more conservative Sadducees in sole control over the Temple, the Pharisees lost their power and were left with a minority position on the Great Jewish Council, the Sanhedrin. This only boosted their popularity among the educated class in the country. After King Herod assumed power, he kept the Sadducees in charge of the Temple in

A detail from "The Finding of the Savior in the Temple" by Pre-Raphaelite artist William Holman Hunt (1827–1910) shows a group of Pharisees and other scholars seated in the Temple.

order to curtail the Pharisees' influence. But the king also undermined the Sadducees by importing priestly families from Babylonia and appointing them to top positions at the Temple. One such family was the house of Ananas—a man whose son-in-law, the high priest Caiaphas, would soon sit in judgment of Jesus. The Sadducees continued to insist that the sacrificial cult at the Temple was the only conduit to salvation and that the Torah was a closed book. The Pharisees disagreed. They tried to make the Torah more meaningful in the life of ordinary people. One way to do that was to apply Temple ritual to everything a person did, including washing, tithing, and Sabbath observance. Josephus estimated that by the middle of the first century, there were some 6,000 Pharisees in Roman Judea. ◼

CHAPTER SEVENTEEN

GOD AS ABBA

He said, "Abba, Father, for you all things are possible; remove this cup from me; yet, not what I want, but what you want."

MARK 14:36

A New Way of Seeing God

In many ways, Jesus was a man of his time. Like the leaders of other reformist movements, including the Essenes, the Pharisees, and John the Baptist, Jesus' teaching offered the promise of redemption to his followers, provided they abandoned their selfish ways and returned to the covenantal principles of the Torah. But in two very significant aspects, Jesus broke with the prevailing traditions of Judaism of his time to create an entirely new foundation for men and women to live in obedience to the will of God.

The first, as we saw, was Jesus' concept of the much sought restoration of the Kingdom of God. Many historians agree that Jesus envisioned the Kingdom not as a political entity but, rather, a social and spiritual one. In most of his teachings, Jesus talks about the Kingdom of God in strictly social, ethical, and religious terms. Whereas John the Baptist saw the Kingdom as the product of an apocalyptic clash between good and evil, a period of moral cleansing, Jesus did not emphasize eschatological upheaval, political violence, or ethnic strife. In other words, Jesus did not see the Kingdom as the restoration of an independent political entity, but as the realization of traditional Jewish solidarity within Galilean society.

That is not to say that the Gospel descriptions of the Kingdom philosophy are entirely devoid of eschatological ideas, as some scholars have argued. Rather, such eschatology may have been inspired by apocalyptic sentiments in early Christian communities rather than the actual words of Jesus.

THE NAME OF GOD

The second innovation of Jesus' teachings is his radical reinterpretation of how we should see God and communicate with him. This topic is particularly relevant when we remember that Judaism, unlike all other Near Eastern religions, never developed a cultic image of its God. There are no paintings or statues of God in traditional Jewish culture, as there would be in later Christian traditions. The Law forbade the worship of images of any living thing, and certainly a depiction of God himself.

By contrast, Western civilization was rooted in the anthropomorphic conceptions of Greek and Roman mythology, which had no problem visualizing divine beings. In fact, the Greeks and Romans delighted in expressing the divine nature of their gods by the sheer perfection of their physical beauty. Using Greek and Roman art as a model, Christianity eventually developed its own artistic tradition to satisfy the European desire for an *Andachtsbild,* a visual image of the saintly or divine being to whom one is praying. The result is the rich tradition of Christian painting and sculpture that we have today.

But the ancient Jewish world never developed such a tradition, being content to contemplate God in transcendent and intangible terms, beyond the realm

ABOVE: *Spring showers over the southern end of the Sea of Galilee nourish the astonishing fecundity of this region.*

OPPOSITE: *This Roman earthenware oil lamp, with a circular body, four small filling holes, and a Medusa head in the center, is typical for lamps of this period.*

PRECEDING PAGES: *Breaking with Baroque paradigms, Dutch artist Rembrandt Harmenszoon van Rijn (1606–1669) painted this intimate and human portrait of Jesus between 1648 and 1650.*

RIGHT: *"He Who Is God Hears the Word of God" was painted by French artist James Jacques Joseph Tissot (1836–1902) for a series of illustrations known as "The Life of Christ," circa 1894.*

BELOW: *A figurine in bronze of an unidentified deity, excavated near Jerusalem, reveals the artistic virtuosity of Greek artists working in Roman Palestine.*

of human comprehension. This gave the specific form of address, the very *name* by which individuals could turn their mind toward God, a very special and symbolic meaning that is sometimes difficult for us to grasp.

In Hebrew Scripture, God appears under several names. In the oldest strain of Genesis and other books of the Torah, he is referred to by the four-letter construct known as YHWH (since biblical Hebrew was written only in consonants), usually pronounced YAH-weh. Some historians believe the name refers to God's quality as "Creator," whereas others believe that God himself explained the meaning when he confronted Moses in the form of a burning bush. God said to Moses, "Say this to the people of Israel, 'I AM has sent me

[Jesus] said, "I thank you, Father, Lord of heaven and earth, because you have hidden these things from the wise and the intelligent and have revealed them to infants."

LUKE 10:21

to you'" (Exodus 3:14). In either case, the name is deeply implicated in the verb "to be" and refers to God as the cause or the very essence of being.

A second strain in the Hebrew Bible refers to God as *Elohim,* the majestic plural of the noun *El,* even though the name is grammatically used as a singular. The meaning of this name may be "powerful," possibly because El was worshipped as the supreme, all-powerful god in Ugaritic and Canaanite culture.

At the early stages of the Second Temple period, perhaps during the third century B.C.E., the use of YHWH was discontinued out of reverence for the holiness of God. If God's name was not to be taken in vain (Exodus 20:7), then it would make sense not to use it at all in everyday speech. Only the High Priest was allowed to pronounce YHWH in the inner sanctum of the Temple, the Holy of Holies, and then only once a year: the Day of Atonement during Yom Kippur. Instead, the epithet Adonai became the accepted form for addressing God, which in English is usually translated as "the Lord," a custom that was continued in the Gospels.

The Mishnah, the written collection of the Oral Law tradition first compiled around 200 C.E., uses a third variant, Ha-Shem, which literally means "the Name," so as to create a further reverential distance between humans and the unfathomable mystery of God. To this day, most Jews substitute Adonai for YHWH in prayer and liturgical reading of Hebrew Scripture, while using Ha-Shem in everyday speech.

THE LORD'S PRAYER

In the Gospels of Matthew and Luke, Jesus teaches his followers how to pray. "Lord," said one of his disciples, "teach us to pray, as John taught his disciples." The Gospels give us two versions of this prayer that are remarkably similar:

MATTHEW	LUKE
Our Father in heaven,	Father,
hallowed be your name.	hallowed be your name.
Your kingdom come.	Your kingdom come.
Your will be done,	
on earth as it is in heaven.	
Give us this day our daily bread.	Give us each day our daily bread.
And forgive us our debts, as we also have forgiven our debtors.	And forgive us our sins, for we ourselves forgive everyone indebted to us.
And do not bring us to the time of trial, but rescue us from the evil one.	And do not bring us to the time of trial.
(Matthew 6:9-13)	(Luke 11:2)

According to John Meier, the short and simple structure of the prayer makes it ideal for memorization. At the same time, it is also a powerful summary of Jesus' principal tenets: the hope for the coming of God's kingdom, the social justice of sharing food and resources, the importance of mutual forgiveness, protection from Satan, and the love of God as a merciful father. ■

The aureus, the most valuable currency unit in the Roman Empire, was worth 100 sesterces and carried the image of the emperor—in this case, Vespasian (r. 69–79 C.E.).

But which name was Jesus taught to use? After all, Joseph and Mary spoke neither Hebrew, the language of Hebrew Scripture, nor Greek, the language of the Gospels. Instead, they spoke Aramaic. Which name would they have used?

The answer hinges on the question of whether Galileans in Jesus' time used the Aramaic version of Elohim, which is Elah or Elahah, or that of YHWH, which is usually transposed as Maryah. Given the reluctance to use the tetragrammaton YHWH in the Second Temple period, it is likely that Jesus was taught to pray to God as either Elah or Elahah. Evidence may be found in Mark's passage in which Jesus, in his final moments on the cross, cries out the opening verse from Psalm 22 in Aramaic: *"Eloi, Eloi, lema sabachthani?*—My God, my God, why have you forsaken me?" (Mark 15:34; Psalms 22:1). Mark wrote in Greek, probably in Rome, so it is unlikely that he would have understood Aramaic. Therefore, Eloi is probably a rendering of Elahiy by Greek-speaking Christians.

A NEW VIEW OF GOD

Jesus developed a very different and deeply personal view of God. For Jesus, God was not an awesome, unapproachable deity far removed from the daily toil of mortals, but a kind and gentle presence, to whom Jesus could turn as if to a father. Jesus began to refer to God as Abba, an Aramaic term that in this context may mean something between the English word "Father" and the more familiar "Papa." This feeling of deep intimacy with the divine, this sense of God as a caring and loving father, may have been motivated by a number of factors.

In modern synagogues, as here in "Jews Praying in the Synagogue on Yom Kippur" by Polish artist Maurycy Gottlieb (1856–1879), the word Ha-Shem is used for Scripture references to God.

Christian theology, for example, holds that such an intimate relationship between Jesus and God is obvious, given that Jesus is God's only son. From a Jewish perspective, however, the idea of God as a father figure is not unprecedented. Hebrew Scripture often uses the metaphor of God as the father of the nation of Israel (for example, Deuteronomy 32:6). In the first century, rabbinic miracle workers such as Honi the Circle Drawer and Hanina ben Dosa were called sons of God because of their obvious closeness to God's power; Honi also referred to God as Abba. But perhaps the most important source for Jesus' vision of God were the eighth- and seventh-century prophets who served as a

model for his ministry, men like Hosea, Micah, and Jeremiah. These prophets rejected the idea that God could be mollified with sacrificial rites. "Will the Lord be pleased with thousands of rams?" Micah asked. On the contrary, the prophet said; "What does the Lord require of you but to do justice, and to love kindness, and to walk humbly with your God?" (Micah 6:7-8). Jeremiah echoed this sentiment. "I, the Lord, test the mind and search the heart," reads one of Jeremiah's verses, "to give to all according to their ways, according to the fruit of their doings" (Jeremiah 17:10).

This idea of God desiring a person's *heart* rather than the carcass of a sacrificial animal lies at the core of Jesus' vision. To him, Elah was not a distant being but a loving father, an Abba, to whom he could confide his innermost fears and dreams. Time and again, Jesus impressed on his audience that God is both approachable and forgiving, and that this divine compassion should serve as a model for the way human beings behave toward one another (Luke 6:35). In other words, Jesus deliberately extended his vision of God as a loving father to his disciples; the privilege of calling God "Abba" was not exclusively his but available to all who followed him. This idea was enshrined in the prayer that he taught his followers. Its opening words are, "Our Father." ■

The synagogue of Chorazin, a township in Lower Galilee identified in the Gospels, was built of the black basalt stone in the late third century and rebuilt in the sixth century.

FOLLOWING PAGES: *This panel of "Christ Preaching on the Sea of Galilee" was painted by Flemish Renaissance artist Jan Brueghel the Elder (1568–1625).*

CHAPTER EIGHTEEN

THE JOURNEY TO PHOENICIA

*Jesus left that place
and went away to the
district of Tyre and Sidon.*

MATTHEW 15:21

Jesus in the Land of the Gentiles

While some of us may find it difficult to believe, Jesus' ministry in Galilee may not have lasted more than some 18 or 20 months. This hypothesis is based on the fact that the synoptic Gospels have only one reference to Passover, the most important religious festival in the Jewish liturgical year. If our original assumption is correct—that Jesus joined the movement of John the Baptist around 28 c.e.—then it is reasonable to assume that his ministry began around 29 and culminated in Jerusalem during the Passover Festival of 30 c.e. Of course, none of these dates is written in stone, and scholars continue to debate them, but they offer an idea of the incredibly short time span in which Jesus sought to establish the Kingdom of God on Earth.

This begs the question: What prompted Jesus to leave his native region and turn to communities outside Galilee?

A CHRONOLOGY OF JESUS' MINISTRY

If we follow the narrative of the synoptic Gospels closely, it is possible to distinguish three separate phases. In the first phase, Jesus delivered his sermons in synagogues and meeting places in the immediate vicinity of Capernaum, including the townships of Bethsaida and Chorazin. Emboldened by the response to his teachings and healing, Jesus then entered a second phase, in which he used the boat of his fishermen Apostles to travel into areas bordering the eastern and western coasts of the Sea of Galilee. This brought him into contact with a far greater and more diverse audience—one that represented almost every layer of Galilean society, from day workers and tenant farmers to

tax collectors, scribes, and Pharisees. As a result, his fame spread rapidly—so rapidly, in fact, that even foreigners from lands outside Roman Palestine came to see him.

Jesus must have been intrigued by this, as any teacher or prophet would have been. From the very beginning, Jesus had always insisted that his message was destined only for Jews—for people who understood the Law and pledged their faith to one God, and God alone. "Go nowhere among the Gentiles," he had urged his Apostles (Matthew 10:5). As Mark Chancey has shown, there were plenty of Gentiles living in Galilee at the time, although the ethical, cultural, and spiritual gulf between them and observant Jews was often vast.

But if that was the case, why did crowds from "beyond the Jordan, and the region around Tyre and Sidon" travel long distances to hear him speak? (Mark 3:8). Tyre and Sidon were located near the coast of Phoenicia, a Gentile territory north of Galilee that had always been famous for its trading prowess. In many ways, its population enjoyed a higher living standard than that of

ABOVE: *The ancient city of Tyre, in today's Lebanon, was once a major port for Jewish Diaspora pilgrims traveling to Jerusalem from cities throughout the Mediterranean.*

OPPOSITE: *This slender ribbed jar with a short neck and a splayed rim was excavated in lower Judea and was probably made between 50 B.C.E. and 50 C.E.*

PRECEDING PAGES: *"Jesus and the Syrophoenician Woman" is taken from the illuminated manuscript* Très Riches Heures of Jean, Duke of Berry, *created by the Limbourg Brothers around 1416.*

Then he returned from the region of Tyre, and went by way of Sidon towards the Sea of Galilee, in the region of the Decapolis.

MARK 7:31

rural Galilee. Why would people from these sophisticated urban areas brave the rigors of travel through Galilee to hear the sermons of a Jewish rabbi?

Jesus decided to find out, and this signaled the third phase in his ministry—one in which he moved beyond the traditional borders of his native region to test his teachings in lands unknown. He first set out for the port city of Tyre (today's Tyre in Lebanon). Mark's Gospel doesn't explicitly state that Jesus visited the city of Tyre itself, but that he traveled in "the region of Tyre," including the coastal enclave. Jesus was on a reconnaissance mission of sorts. Accordingly, says Mark, "he did not want anyone to know he was there." That gambit failed, however, when "a woman whose little daughter had an

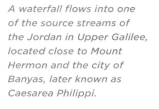

A waterfall flows into one of the source streams of the Jordan in Upper Galilee, located close to Mount Hermon and the city of Banyas, later known as Caesarea Philippi.

unclean spirit immediately heard about him, and she came and bowed down at his feet" (Mark 7:26). This posed a dilemma. Not only was Jesus hoping to remain incognito; he also despaired how a woman "of Syro-Phoenician origin," a *Gentile* woman, could possibly summon the necessary faith to make a healing possible. And so he told her, "It is not fair to take the children's food and throw it to the dogs." These were very harsh words, but the woman came back with a quick rebuttal. "Sir," she said, "even the dogs under the table eat the children's crumbs." What she meant was that even those who were *not* chosen by God might still yearn for his grace. Jesus was deeply impressed. "Woman," he said, "great is your faith! Let it be done for you as you wish." And her daughter was healed instantly (Matthew 15:26-28).

THE JOURNEY TO BANYAS

It is possible that this encounter marked a turning point of sorts. Although Jesus had always believed that his mission was intended only for "the lost sheep of the house of Israel" (Matthew 15:24), in practice it had not turned out that way. He had been genuinely surprised by the faith shown by a Roman centurion in Capernaum, for example (Matthew 8:5), and this impression may have been reinforced by his experience in Tyre.

Thus, Jesus decided to continue his journey into foreign territory. He moved to Sidon, another Phoenician city, before turning south for a visit to the Decapolis, the Gentile territory east of the Jordan. Along the way, he traveled along the base of Mount Hermon, one of the sources of the Jordan River, and in due course he arrived in Banyas.

Of all the places he had visited on this journey, this was by far the most

SON OF MAN: ANGEL OR MESSIAH?

Scholars are divided over whether the character of the Son of Man in the Book of Daniel refers to the Messiah or to an angel such as the archangel Michael. The Hebrew Bible recognized many beings who shared in the divine character of God: not only angels but also messengers and other celestial beings who bring tidings to favored individuals (Genesis 6:2). Some historians point out that in later Jewish writings—notably Enoch and IV Esdras, both written less than a century before Jesus— the term "Son of Man" is more explicitly associated with the Messiah. For Jesus, however, the distinction may not have mattered. Daniel's vision gave him not only a clear sense of destiny, but also a confirmation of the strong kinship he felt with God as Abba. What's more, given the high tensions produced by Pilate's ruthless rule in Judea, the title Son of Man may have been less incendiary politically than the far more dangerous epithet of Messiah. ∎

Flemish artist Josse Lieferinxe (active 1493–1508) painted this panel of "St. Michael Slaying the Dragon," based on a reference in the Book of Revelation (12:7–9).

pagan. Banyas was built around a mountain spring that served as a cult center for the Greek god Pan, a deity associated with everything that was wild, rural, and untamed, including a zest for young and attractive nymphs. Since 14 C.E., Tetrarch Philip had made a number of improvements to Banyas in an effort to turn it into a Roman resort under the name of Caesarea Philippi. It was as unlikely a place for a Gospel story as we can imagine, but it is here, in neutral Gentile territory, that Jesus paused to reflect on his experiences and to take stock of his ministry.

OPPOSITE: *A sixth-century icon of Christ* Pantokrator *("All-powerful") from the fourth-century Monastery of St. Catherine in Sinai, Egypt, is one of the oldest portraits of Jesus.*

What had Jesus accomplished over the preceding months? Had people harkened to his words to join the Kingdom of God? Or had they merely followed him as thrill seekers, hoping for a miracle? The memory of the Gentile woman in Tyre and her unshakable faith may have stood in stark contrast to the ambiguous response he had received among his fellow Jews in Galilee.

According to Mark, this is when Jesus turned to his Apostles and asked them a blunt question: "Who do people say that I am?" A difficult question, perhaps. The Apostles were reluctant to answer it, for fear of hurting Jesus' feelings, and so they equivocated. "John the Baptist," said one. "Elijah," another chimed in. Others hedged their bets, calling him a prophet. Not a very impressive performance. "But," said Jesus at length, "who do *you* say

Little remains of the Banyas temple dedicated to Pan, a Greek god in the shape of a satyr. The temple was once a major pilgrimage destination as well as a Roman resort.

The northern shore of the Sea of Galilee, close to the ancient city of Capernaum, has changed little from the days of Jesus' ministry.

that I am?" Silence ensued. Then Simon Peter stood up and said, "You are the Messiah."

Whether Jesus was pleased with this answer, Mark doesn't tell us. According to his Gospel, Jesus then "sternly ordered them not to tell anyone about him" (Mark 8:30). But Matthew reports the scene differently. In his version, Jesus was clearly gratified by Peter's response. "Blessed are you, Simon son of Jonah!" he exclaimed, and added a pun on Peter's nickname (*Petros* in Greek, or rock): "You are Peter, and on this rock I will build my Church" (Matthew 16:17-18).

THE SON OF MAN

What is missing from this riveting story is the ultimate question: How did Jesus see himself? Since Paul, it has been a foundation of Christian theology that Jesus is the Son of God. In principle, this concept was not incompatible with Jewish ideas. Hebrew Scripture often referred to the nation of Israel as God's progeny (Exodus 4:22). Any "anointed one" (the very meaning of the word *Mashiach* or Messiah), such as a Jewish king, was by definition a "son of God" (Psalm 2:7). As God said to the prophet Nathan, referring to David, "I will be a father to him, and he shall be a son to me" (II Samuel 7:14).

Jesus also experienced a deep sense of intimacy toward God, and there is no question that these feelings were akin to that of a son toward a loving father. And yet Jesus never brought himself to state unequivocally, "I am the Son of God." This was probably a source of some frustration to the evangelists as well as to early Christian communities, particularly in the Greco-Roman world, for whom Jesus' divinity was an article of faith. It may also have prompted the need for the evangelists to have *others* call Jesus the Son of God—particularly Satan and demons, who were supernatural beings themselves and therefore in a position to know.

Jesus, by contrast, referred to himself as the Son of Man. In all of the four canonical Gospels combined, the term "Son of Man" appears some 80 times.

THE CITY OF TYRE

Tyre, the city that Jesus may have visited during his sojourn abroad, was one of the oldest urban centers on the Phoenician littoral. Founded in the third millennium B.C.E., it became a flourishing center of international trade. Phoenicians from Tyre ranged across the known world, settling in places as far as Memphis, Egypt. Their mercantile prowess was boosted by their devel-

The Phoenician galley is based on the Greek word galloi, tubs, *to denote the tublike shape of these flat-bottomed ships, capable of sailing most Mediterranean routes.*

Before Herod's construction of Caesarea, Tyre had served as the principal harbor through which Jewish pilgrims from around the empire passed on their way to Jerusalem. Conquered by the Romans in 64 B.C.E., around the same time that the Roman general Pompey took control of the Jewish kingdom, Tyre had continued to flourish as an autonomous region under Roman tutelage.

opment of the galley, a sleek vessel powered by sails as well as manned oars. Apart from trade, Tyre also became known for its manufacture of purple dye, an expensive pigment used exclusively for togas and garments of the nobility. Its stupendous wealth drew the ire of the prophets, notably Ezekiel. "Your heart was proud because of your beauty," the prophet said; "You corrupted your wisdom for the sake of your splendor" (Ezekiel 28:17).

Tyre later proved receptive to Christian ideas. A Christian community was established in the mid-30s. It was visited by Paul upon his return from his third missionary journey (Acts 21:3-7). By the late second century, Tyre had acquired its own bishopric, but it suffered from persecutions under Emperor Diocletian. The community recovered and hosted one of Constantine's synods in 335. ■

This would indicate that Jesus chose the title deliberately. Moreover, it is a title that is used by Jesus himself—and almost never by those around him.

But what does it mean, Son of Man? The version that appears in the Gospels is a transposition of the Aramaic *bar-nasha,* itself based on the Hebrew *ben-adam.* The Hebrew term appears throughout Hebrew Scripture, particularly in passages of a poetic or prophetic character. In the Book of Ezekiel, for example, where *ben-adam* appears some 90 times, the title is used by God to emphasize Ezekiel's mortal nature and illustrate the vast distance between the prophet and the divine (Ezekiel 2:1).

But in the Book of Daniel, written around the second century B.C.E., "Son of Man" appears to have a very different meaning. In one of his visions, Daniel sees "one like the Son of Man coming with the clouds of heaven. And he came to the Ancient One and was presented before him" (Daniel 7:13). In Daniel's version, in other words, the character is not a mere mortal but a figure of considerable importance: one who is carried on clouds of heaven to the presence of God. Moreover, his appearance in the story is auspicious. It follows the destruction of several allegorical beasts, each symbolizing the terror of a foreign ruler in Israel's past. The last to be destroyed is the fourth kingdom, that of the Greek Seleucid dynasty, which ruled over Judea from 198 to 140 B.C.E. With Israel thus cleansed of foreign invaders, Daniel's vision welcomes the Son of Man as the figure to whom God will give "dominion and glory and kingship."

The close analogy between Daniel's vision of foreign terror and the harsh reality of Roman-occupied Judea in Jesus' time is obvious. It is therefore not a leap of faith to suggest that Jesus saw himself as the figure foretold in Daniel's prophecy: as the Son of Man whom God himself had designated to restore the Lord's dominion over Israel, in the form of the Kingdom of God. The Gospels seem to agree with this idea. In one passage known as the "synoptic apocalypse," Jesus told his disciples that "they will see 'the Son of Man coming in a cloud' with power and great glory" (Mark 13:26; Matthew 24:30; Luke 21:27). The phrase is an almost a word-for-word quotation of Daniel's great vision.

THE ROAD TO JERUSALEM

And so it happened that, after his journey abroad, Jesus came to the conclusion that his sermons and healings had not accomplished what he had hoped: attract broad support for refashioning Galilean society as a Kingdom of God. Luke and Matthew suggest that this tipping point was indeed the sojourn to

Delicate Roman glass flasks found throughout Roman Palestine and dating from the mid- to late first century C.E. were used for perfumed oils.

Phoenicia. For on his return to Galilee, Jesus lashed out at the cities where his campaign had begun. "Woe to you, Chorazin!" he cried. "Woe to you, Bethsaida! If the powerful deeds performed among you had been done in Tyre and Sidon, they would have changed their ways long ago, sitting in sackcloth and ashes!" (Matthew 11:21; Luke 10:13).

If that were the case, where should he go now? What to do next? Jesus may have remembered that Jeremiah, with whose teachings he had much in common, had experienced a similar crisis of self-doubt (Jeremiah 20:7; 14-15). But God had told the prophet, "Jeremiah, stand at the gate of the Lord's house. Teach this message at the gate: 'Hear the message from the Lord, all you people of the nation of Judah!' "

Jesus resolved to do the same. He would go to the Lord's house, the Temple in Jerusalem, and make the same dramatic appeal that Jeremiah had delivered: "If you change your lives and do good things, I will let you live in this place" (Jeremiah 7:5).

And so Jesus and his Apostles set out on their fateful journey south, to Judea. "They were on the road, going up to Jerusalem," Mark says, "and those who followed were afraid" (Mark 10:32). ∎

BELOW: *Jerusalem's Temple Mount, where the Second Temple once stood, is today marked by the seventh-century Dome of the Rock, one of the oldest examples of Islamic architecture.*

FOLLOWING PAGES: *French classicist painter Jean-Germain Drouais (1763–1788), a pupil of Jacques-Louis David, completed "Christ and the Canaanite Woman" in 1784.*

CHAPTER NINETEEN

THE ROAD TO BETHANY

When Jesus had finished saying these things, he left Galilee and went to the region of Judea beyond the Jordan.

MATTHEW 19:1

Jesus and the Apostles Travel to Judea

There were two major routes by which Galileans could reach Judea. The first one, the central road, skirted the hills along the western shore of the Sea of Galilee and turned south just past the newly built city of Tiberias. From there the road led past Mount Tabor and into the Jezreel Valley, also known as the Valley of Esdraelon, and continued within sight of the ancient fortress site of Megiddo before turning southeast. It was a pleasant route that avoided the hardships and extreme temperatures of the Jordan Valley, as well as the attention of the forces of Herod Antipas. But it had one disadvantage: Before reaching the hills of Jerusalem, the road led through Samaria, populated by Samaritans. In Jesus' day, Jews generally

avoided Samaritans because they were believed to be of mixed blood. Early on, Jesus too had instructed his disciples, "Enter no town of the Samaritans" (Matthew 10:5).

And yet Luke's Gospel suggests that Jesus chose this route. But Jesus was aware of the hostility that he and his disciples might encounter once they entered Samaritan territory, so he sent an advance party to test the mood among the local residents. The disciples duly "entered a village of the Samaritans to make ready for him," says Luke. But the village refused to extend any hospitality, even though the Galileans were clearly tired, hungry, and thirsty. Two disciples, James and John, got angry. "Lord," they said to Jesus, "do you want us to command fire to come down from heaven and consume them?" Jesus sternly rebuked them for even suggesting such nonsense (Luke 9:52-55).

In the next episode, Jesus showed that prejudice had no place in the Kingdom of God. "On the way to Jerusalem," Luke continues, "as he entered a village, ten lepers approached." As we saw, lepers and other sufferers of chronic disease typically lived on the periphery of their village, forbidden to join the community because of their impure status. This is why they kept their distance from Jesus but pleaded with him, saying, "Jesus, Master, have mercy on us." Jesus took pity on them. He said simply, "Go and show yourself to the priests." As described in Leviticus, only a priest could determine whether a person had been healed from his skin affliction and be certified as ritually clean (Leviticus 13:1-23). "And as they went," says Luke, "they were made clean."

Overjoyed, the men ran off. Only one stopped, dropping to his knees and thanking Jesus. As it turned out, he was the only Samaritan in the group. "Were not ten made clean?" Jesus asked him. "Was none of them found to return and give praise to God, except this foreigner?" (Luke 17:11-18). This last comment was not directed at the Samaritan but at the Apostles, including James and John. Once again, it had not been a Jew but a "foreigner," one ostracized from the Jewish community, who had shown the deepest faith in Jesus.

ABOVE: *A rocky outcropping near the old city of Samaria, renamed Sebaste by King Herod, offers a stunning view of the valley through which ran the ancient road to Jerusalem.*

OPPOSITE: *A delicate blue-tinted glass flask is a fine example of Roman glassblowing techniques developed in the mid-first century C.E.*

PREVIOUS PAGES: *"The Raising of Lazarus" was painted by Italian Mannerist artist Mirabello Cavalori (1520–1572), an associate of Giorgio Vasari.*

THE ROAD TO JERICHO

Mark and Matthew suggest a different scenario for the journey to Jerusalem. In their version, Jesus takes the shorter but much more strenuous 80-mile route along the Jordan Rift. The Rift Valley is a fault in the terrestrial surface that runs from the Orontes River Valley in Syria through the Bekaa Valley in Lebanon before reaching its deepest depression along the Jordan River, on its way to the Dead Sea. At first, the road moved past Beth Shemesh to enter the territory of the Decapolis, the League of Ten Cities. The principal city in this area, and indeed the only Greek city on the west side of the Jordan, was Scythopolis, the biblical Beth She'an. Thereafter, the route dropped deep into the Jordan Valley. Rolling hills and soothing pastures abruptly changed to the dry, craggy cliffs of the Judean Desert.

Eventually they reached Jericho. A large crowd of Jewish pilgrims had already gathered here, mentally girding themselves for the steep road up to Jerusalem. Although the distance was only some 18 miles, the road forced travelers to

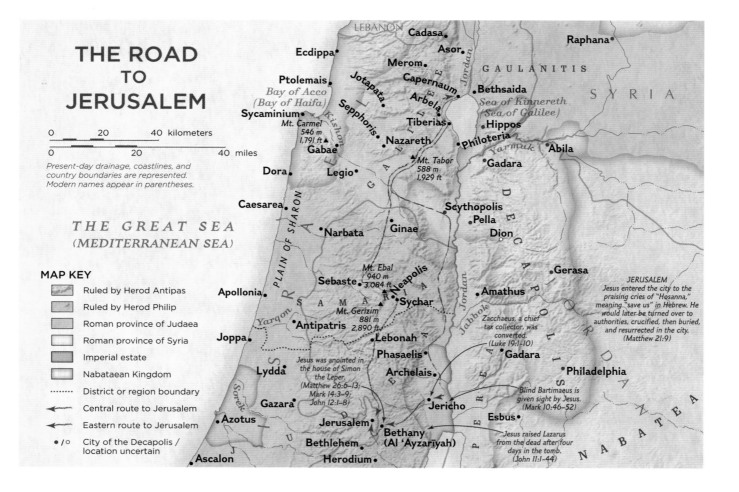

THE ROAD
TO
JERUSALEM

0   20   40 kilometers

0   20   40 miles

Present-day drainage, coastlines, and country boundaries are represented. Modern names appear in parentheses.

THE GREAT SEA
(MEDITERRANEAN SEA)

MAP KEY

- Ruled by Herod Antipas
- Ruled by Herod Philip
- Roman province of Judaea
- Roman province of Syria
- Imperial estate
- Nabataean Kingdom
- ·········· District or region boundary
- ← Central route to Jerusalem
- ← Eastern route to Jerusalem
- • / ○ City of the Decapolis / location uncertain

JERUSALEM
Jesus entered the city to the praising cries of "Hosanna," meaning "save us" in Hebrew. He would later be turned over to authorities, crucified, then buried, and resurrected in the city. (Matthew 21:9)

Zacchaeus, a chief tax collector, was converted. (Luke 19:1–10)

Jesus was anointed in the house of Simon the Leper. (Matthew 26:6–13; Mark 14:3–9; John 12:1–8)

Blind Bartimaeus is given sight by Jesus. (Mark 10:46–52)

Jesus raised Lazarus from the dead after four days in the tomb. (John 11:1–44)

*Our friend Lazarus has fallen asleep,
but I am going there to awaken him.*

JOHN 11:11

negotiate an elevation increase of some 3,400 feet, all through the harsh terrain of the Judean Desert. As Jesus and his disciples prepared to join the other pilgrims, a voice rang out: "Jesus, Son of David, have mercy on me." It was the voice of Bartimaeus, a blind beggar. The people around him told him to be quiet, but Jesus had heard him. "What do you want me to do for you," Jesus asked. "My teacher," the blind man said, "let me see again." "Go," said Jesus, "your faith has made you well." And immediately he regained his sight (Mark 10:46-52).

A sixth-century mosaic from the Byzantine church of St. Apollinare Nuovo in Ravenna, Italy, depicts Jesus healing the blind of Jericho.

THE RESPITE IN BETHANY

Exhausted, Jesus and his disciples eventually reached Bethany at the summit of the Mount of Olives, less than two miles from Jerusalem. Here lived two sisters, Mary and Martha, with their brother, Lazarus.

Jesus was very close to this family. Luke tells us that during one of his visits to the Bethany house, Jesus began to teach, while Mary "sat at the Lord's feet and listened to what he was saying." In agrarian societies such as Galilee, educational opportunities for women were few, yet Jesus treated Mary, as well as Mary Magdalene and the other women in his entourage, as disciples, on an equal footing with the men. There was one problem, however: While Mary sat and listened, her sister, Martha, had to work twice as hard to get the house ready for Jesus' visit. She finally turned to Jesus and said, "Lord, do you not care that my sister has left me to do all the work by myself? Tell her then to help me."

Jesus replied, "Martha, Martha, you are worried and distracted by many things; there is need of only one thing. Mary has chosen the better part"

OPPOSITE: *The 18-mile road from Jericho to Jerusalem runs through the forbidding terrain of the Judean Desert with an elevation increase of some 3,400 feet.*

(Luke 10:39-42). Discipleship, Jesus appears to say, is a gift that should be treasured and placed above all other worldly concerns—a message that would have resonated with Luke's early Christian readers.

The Gospel of John uses the setting of the Bethany house for a very different story. While Jesus was still "across the Jordan," writes John, Lazarus fell ill, and his sisters feared for his life. They promptly sent a message to Jesus, saying, "Lord, he whom you love is ill" (John 11:3). We would expect Jesus to drop everything and make haste, but he chose not to do so. He stayed on the East Bank of the Jordan for "two days longer," before finally deciding to proceed to Judea.

This rather callous response does not sound like the Jesus we know. What does it mean? Some authors suggest that Jesus realized that Lazarus was already dead by the time the message reached him and that he needed time to mourn. Others interpret Jesus' words that he deliberately waited for Lazarus to die so that his intervention would be even more astonishing and attest to the greater glory of God. Indeed, when the group finally broke up to walk to Judea, Jesus said, "Lazarus is dead. For your sake I am glad I was not there, so that you may believe" (John 11:14-15).

But Jesus was unprepared for what awaited him in Bethany. Martha met him halfway and couldn't help but reproach him for his tardiness. "Lord, if you had been here, my brother would not have died," she said. Jesus was greatly distraught by her grief and began to weep himself. At last he went to the tomb, which was placed in a cave with a stone blocking the entrance. He asked that the stone be removed, then looked upward and prayed to the Father, "so

THE ANOINTING

In addition to the story of Lazarus, Bethany is also the place of another prelude to Jesus' Passion. Shortly before Passover, Jesus was invited to visit the house of "Simon the leper." And "while he sat at the table, a woman came with an alabaster jar of very costly ointment of nard, and she broke open the jar and poured the ointment on his head" (Mark 14:3). Affluent homes sometimes offered their guests luxurious perfumes such as nard or "spikenard," an aromatic oil, as a refreshment to cover the inevitable smells of a hard day of travel in the sun. But in Mark's story, the anointing has a very different meaning: It prepares Jesus' body for his death on the cross. When other guests grumbled that this precious liquid could have been put to better use by giving it to the poor, Jesus explained that "she has performed a good service for me." He added, "She has anointed my body beforehand for its burial" (Mark 14:8). ■

A banded alabaster flask with a rounded base and outsplayed rim, recovered near Jerusalem, was probably used for precious perfumed oils.

that they may believe that you sent me." And then he cried in a loud voice, "Lazarus, come out!" And "the dead man came out, his hands and feet bound with strips of cloth, and his face wrapped in a cloth" (John 11:42-44).

For John, the story of Lazarus is the seventh in the series of seven miracles or "signs" that form the backbone of his narrative. Quite possibly, these signs were inspired by the seven-day Creation cycle in Genesis. The seventh sign is particularly important, because the resurrection of Lazarus is a foretelling of the greatest sign to come, the resurrection of Jesus himself. ▪

FOLLOWING PAGES: *"Martha and Mary Magdalene," also known as "Martha Reproving Mary," was painted by Italian Baroque artist Michelangelo Caravaggio (1571–1610) in 1598.*

CHAPTER TWENTY

THE TEMPLE DISRUPTION

*Tell the daughter of Zion,
Look, your king is coming to you,
humble, and mounted on a donkey,
and on a colt, the foal of a donkey.*

MATTHEW 21:5

Jesus Lashes Out Against the Money Changers

As soon as dawn broke over the house in Bethany, Jesus and the Apostles prepared to walk down the Mount of Olives and enter the Temple. Many in the group were filled with excitement. From the summit of the Mount, they could see the Temple complex shimmering in the early sunlight, rising like a mirage of marble and gold over the ocher-brown mass of ancient Jerusalem. When Jesus had visited the Temple at age 12, much of the large open esplanade, the Court of the Gentiles, had still been under construction. Now, 49 years after King Herod had begun the project, the massive sanctuary was finally completed (John 2:20).

Already, throngs of pilgrims were passing by the Bethany house on their way to the Temple. Some of the men and women were singing hymns and waving palm fronds, taken from the large palm tree plantations in Jericho. Jesus and his Apostles decided to follow them. It was only a one-hour walk down the Mount and into the Kidron Valley, from where the road slowly wound up to the city gate. But then Jesus turned to two of his disciples and said, "Go into the village ahead of you, and immediately as you enter it, you will find tied there a colt that has never been ridden; untie it and bring it" (Mark 11:1). As soon as they had done so, Jesus seated himself on the colt and joined the stream of humanity pouring down to Jerusalem.

Did the pilgrims and bystanders recognize the rabbi from Galilee? Had his fame preceded him? Mark tells us that they did. "Many people spread their cloaks on the road," the evangelist writes, "and others spread leafy branches

that they had cut in the fields." In the excitement, some began to sing "Hosanna! Blessed is the one who comes in the name of the Lord! Blessed is the coming kingdom of our ancestor David!" (Mark 11:7-10).

This must have been a very special moment for Jesus. Coming so soon after his moment of despair in Galilee, the ecstatic welcome at the gates of Jerusalem bolstered his spirits, precisely because here, in Judea, the people *did* recognize him as the Son of Man, as the herald of "the coming kingdom." Some of the Pharisees in the crowd became nervous and urged Jesus to maintain a low profile. They knew full well that the Roman forces in the city would take a keen interest in a man being hailed as "a king." "Teacher," they said, "order your disciples to stop." Jesus would have none of it. He was overcome by this surge of popular enthusiasm that had intoxicated his followers. How could he possibly silence them? "I tell you," Jesus replied, "if these were silent, the stones would shout out!" (Luke 19:39-40).

Some historians have cautioned that this wonderful Palm Sunday episode appears to be inspired by a prophecy in the Book of Zechariah, where the king of a restored Israel is hailed as "triumphant and victorious . . . humble and riding

ABOVE: *Jesus would have passed through this valley, known as the Kidron Valley, on his way from Bethany on the Mount of Olives to Temple Mount in Jerusalem.*

OPPOSITE: *A Tyrian silver shekel, dated around 68 C.E. and inscribed with "Jerusalem the Holy," was the only type of currency permitted within the Temple.*

PRECEDING PAGES: *"Christ Driving the Moneychangers from the Temple" was painted in 1626 by Dutch Golden Age artist Rembrandt Harmenszoon van Rijn (1606–1669).*

This coin, struck during the Second Jewish War against the Romans between 132 and 135 c.e., shows the facade of the Second Temple in Jerusalem.

A model of Herod's Second Temple sanctuary shows all of the key areas featured in the Gospel stories.

on a donkey, on a colt" (Zechariah 9:9). But the story of Jesus' triumphal entry is repeated in all four Gospels, which strongly argues for its authenticity, at least in the original oral tradition.

THE VISIT TO THE TREASURY

Once inside Jerusalem, Jesus took the Apostles to the monumental staircase leading up to the Double Gate at the south side of Temple Mount. While the height of each step was roughly the same, the depth alternated between 12 inches and 35 inches. This was deliberate, for it forced pilgrims to ascend carefully, mindful of the sanctity of the ground they were about to enter. Another gate, to the right, known as the Triple Gate, was reserved for priests and their assistants and used to reach the storage and administrative rooms of the Royal Stoa, towering high above the wall.

Passing through the Double Gate, Jesus and the Apostles entered a dark tunnel, lit by torches; their voices echoed against the smooth limestone ashlars. And then, at last, they emerged into the large outer courtyard. They were standing in the Temple. As far as the eye could see, pure white marble stretched in all directions, surrounded by a vast colonnade of twin rows of Corinthian columns. For disciples who had never before visited the Temple, indeed had never seen a monumental building of this size, it must have been an overwhelming experience.

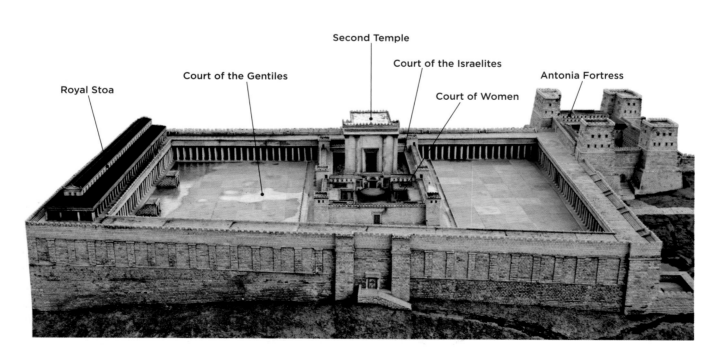

Second Temple

Court of the Israelites

Court of the Gentiles

Court of Women

Antonia Fortress

Royal Stoa

They wanted to arrest him, but they feared the crowds, because they regarded him as a prophet.

MATTHEW 21:46

Jesus led them past the forecourt and the *soreg,* the boundary beyond which no Gentile could pass, and entered the first of two inner courts: the Court of Women. Here was the *korban,* the treasury, where the Temple authorities collected the tithes—the half-shekel Temple tax, as well as a variety of other donations. To receive these funds, the court was ringed by 13 horn-shaped depositories, or *shoparoth,* each earmarked for a particular offering. As the crowd fanned out, Jesus "sat down opposite the treasury, and watched the crowd putting money into the treasury" (Mark 12:41). He silently observed how many rich pilgrims deposited vast sums while, by contrast, a poor widow put in two small copper coins or *mites.* "Truly I tell you," he said, "this poor widow has put in more than all of them; for the others contributed out of abundance, but she in her poverty has put in all she had to live on" (Luke 21:1-4).

Jesus and his entourage spent the rest of the day in the Temple, and Mark uses the opportunity to stage a final appearance of all of Jesus' principal opponents: the Sadducees, including the chief priests, the scribes, the Pharisees, and even some Herodian officials. One by one, they step forward to interrogate Jesus in an effort to "entrap him" (Mark 12:13), but Jesus deftly parries their questions. For Mark, this is both the final act of Jesus' ministry and the overture to the next act, the dramatic conclusion of the story in the form of Jesus' Passion. Whether it actually took place as Mark describes is irrelevant. The point that the evangelist wants to make is that at

An early Christian sarcophagus from the Villa Felice in Rome and dated around 312 C.E. shows the entry of Jesus in Jerusalem.

long last, the religious elites of the nation were drawing together to condemn the rabbi from Galilee.

As the disciples left the Temple through the Double Gate, some were still giddy with excitement. "Teacher, what large stones and what large buildings!" one gushed. "Do you see these great buildings?" Jesus replied. "Not one stone will be left here upon another; all will be thrown down" (Mark 13:1-2). That may have put a damper on the disciple's spirit, but Jesus was right: Forty years later, in 70 C.E., this magnificent complex was burned down by a vengeful Roman legion.

THE ANTONIA FORTRESS

If Jesus and his followers had looked toward the north while they were standing on the Temple forecourt, they would have seen a large citadel rising above the Temple, known as the Antonia Fortress. King Herod had built this complex adjacent to the Temple to station troops for the purpose of maintaining law and order throughout the sanctuary. He had anticipated that the vast esplanade of the forecourt could also serve as a convenient rallying point for demonstrations or even riots. In this, Herod was proven right. In 4 B.C.E., upon the king's death, protesters had staged a demonstration against Herod's heir, Ethnarch Archilaus, in this very forecourt, pelting a Roman cohort with stones. The riot led to reprisals that left 3,000 worshippers dead. Significantly, this incident had taken place during the feast of Passover. Ever since, Passover was a time when the Roman forces stationed at the Antonia barracks went on high alert. ■

A model of the Antonia Fortress, which stood on the northern side of Temple Mount, shows the interior court between two towers.

THE EVE OF PASSOVER

And then it was the 14th day of the month of Nisan, the eve of Passover, the festival that celebrates Israel's release from bondage in Egypt, after the Israelites had been told to sacrifice a lamb and paint the door lintel with its blood. All of these homes were "passed over" by the angel sent by God to slay all of Egypt's firstborn sons (Exodus 12:6-7). The Israelites were also told to roast a lamb and eat it with unleavened bread while waiting for the signal to leave Egypt. Moses later decreed that Jews should "observe this rite as a perpetual ordinance" (Exodus 12:24).

As Mark writes, it was also the beginning of the Week of Unleavened Bread (Mark 14:1). During this holy week, all bread made with leavened dough is to be avoided. Instead, Jews eat matzo, the flat bread made from unleavened dough (Deuteronomy 16:3).

On this day, the afternoon of Nisan, the festival had once again brought thousands of Jewish pilgrims to the Temple to offer a lamb as a Passover sacrifice. Scholar E. P. Sanders has estimated that it may have attracted as many as 300,000 worshippers. As part of the rite, each head of a household would bring a lamb into the inner court of the Temple, the Court of the Israelites, and tie the animal to one of 30 upright stakes. At the signal of the Levite choir, the pilgrim would kill the animal with a sharp cut to the throat, and a Levitical assistant caught the warm blood in a special silver vessel. The lamb carcass was then butchered. Organs destined for sacrifice—such as the neck, the liver, and the stomach—were carried to the huge altar and thrown onto the flames by priests. A portion of the meat would be presented to the priests and the rest given to the pilgrim, who would take it home, roast it, and eat it during the Seder, the Passover meal.

Jesus and his disciples also left the house in Bethany and followed the large crowds into Jerusalem for this all-important festival. At the same time, the Roman forces in Jerusalem, stationed at the Antonia Fortress, went on high alert. There had been several bloody riots since the death of King Herod, and almost all of them had occurred in the large Temple forecourt during festivals, an ideal place for staging popular protests. What's more, Passover was particularly volatile, since it celebrated Israel's liberation from a despotic tyrant—the Egyptian Pharaoh. It didn't take much to see the Roman emperor in exactly the same role.

A view of the southeastern supporting walls of Temple Mount in Jerusalem, excavated in the late 1960s, shows the remnant of an archway known as Robinson's Arch.

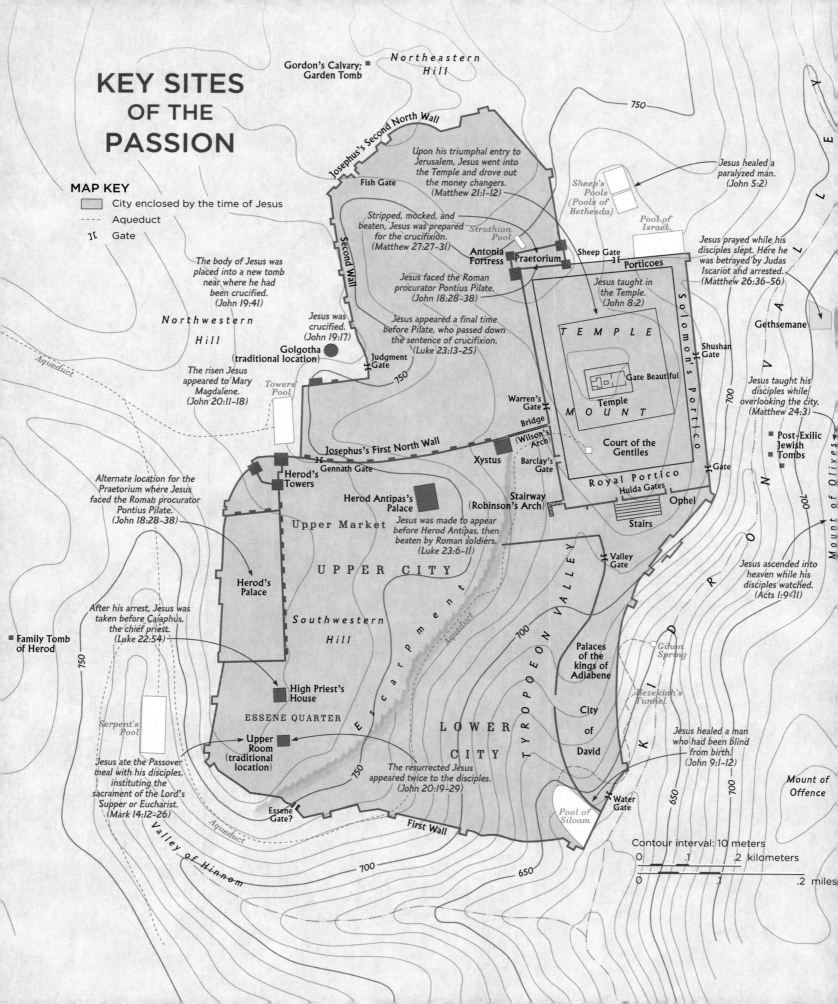

KEY SITES OF THE PASSION

MAP KEY

City enclosed by the time of Jesus

- - - - Aqueduct

✗ Gate

Gordon's Calvary; Garden Tomb

Northeastern Hill

Josephus's Second North Wall

Fish Gate

Upon his triumphal entry to Jerusalem, Jesus went into the Temple and drove out the money changers. (Matthew 21:1-12)

Jesus healed a paralyzed man. (John 5:2)

Sheep's Pools (Pools of Bethesda)

Pool of Israel

Second Wall

Stripped, mocked, and beaten, Jesus was prepared for the crucifixion. (Matthew 27:27-31)

Struthion Pool

Antonia Fortress

Praetorium

Sheep Gate

Porticoes

Jesus prayed while his disciples slept. Here he was betrayed by Judas Iscariot and arrested. (Matthew 26:36-56)

The body of Jesus was placed into a new tomb near where he had been crucified. (John 19:41)

Jesus faced the Roman procurator Pontius Pilate. (John 18:28-38)

Northwestern Hill

Jesus was crucified. (John 19:17)

Golgotha (traditional location)

Jesus appeared a final time before Pilate, who passed down the sentence of crucifixion. (Luke 23:13-25)

Jesus taught in the Temple. (John 8:2)

T E M P L E

M O U N T

Gethsemane

Shushan Gate

The risen Jesus appeared to Mary Magdalene. (John 20:11-18)

Judgment Gate

Towers Pool

Gate Beautiful

Temple

Jesus taught his disciples while overlooking the city. (Matthew 24:3)

Aqueduct

Warren's Gate

Bridge (Wilson's Arch)

Barclay's Gate

Josephus's First North Wall

Gennath Gate

Xystus

Court of the Gentiles

Solomon's Portico

Gate

■ Post-Exilic Jewish Tombs

Alternate location for the Praetorium where Jesus faced the Roman procurator Pontius Pilate. (John 18:28-38)

Herod's Towers

Herod Antipas's Palace

Stairway (Robinson's Arch)

Royal Portico

Hulda Gates

Ophel

Stairs

Upper Market

Jesus was made to appear before Herod Antipas, then beaten by Roman soldiers. (Luke 23:6-11)

U P P E R   C I T Y

■ Family Tomb of Herod

Herod's Palace

Southwestern Hill

Valley Gate

Jesus ascended into heaven while his disciples watched. (Acts 1:9-11)

After his arrest, Jesus was taken before Caiaphas, the chief priest. (Luke 22:54)

E s c a r p m e n t

Aqueduct

TYROPOEON VALLEY

Palaces of the kings of Adiabene

Gihon Spring

Hezekiah's Tunnel

High Priest's House

City of David

Jesus healed a man who had been blind from birth. (John 9:1-12)

Serpent's Pool

ESSENE QUARTER

Upper Room (traditional location)

L O W E R   C I T Y

The resurrected Jesus appeared twice to the disciples. (John 20:19-29)

Mount of Offence

Jesus ate the Passover meal with his disciples, instituting the sacrament of the Lord's Supper or Eucharist. (Mark 14:12-26)

Essene Gate?

Aqueduct

First Wall

Water Gate

Pool of Siloam

Contour interval: 10 meters

0   .1   .2 kilometers

0   1   .2 miles

Valley of Hinnom

KIDRON VALLEY

Mount of Olives

THE SALE OF PASCHAL LAMBS

The rules for the lambs were strict. They had to be male, between eight days and one year old, and free of any physical blemish (Exodus 12:5). Priests were posted at the Temple gates to inspect the lambs and to reject any specimens that were found to have an injury or a blemish, no matter how small. For pilgrims who had traveled long distances or tried to negotiate the dangers of Jerusalem's overcrowded streets, that was a major problem.

> *Making a whip of cords, he drove all of them out of the Temple, both the sheep and the cattle.*
>
> **JOHN 2:15**

The Temple authorities recognized this. Therefore, they themselves offered such lambs for sale, guaranteed to pass priestly muster. In his 2000 book, scholar Bruce Chilton argued that the sale of sacrificial animals, including lambs and doves, had traditionally taken place at the Chanuth market on the Mount of Olives, to prevent nervous animals from soiling the Temple with their waste. But apparently the high priest Caiaphas had decided to bring this trade within the Temple precinct itself. That introduced another complicating factor: In order to buy animals within the Temple walls, pilgrims couldn't use Roman or local currency (which sometimes carried the image of the emperor). They had to change their money into the only coin permitted at the Temple, the Tyrian shekel. This meant that in addition to large pens holding lambs, there would also be innumerable stands of money changers pitching their services.

We may speculate on Caiaphas's motives for taking all this business inside the Temple. Perhaps he wanted to exert greater control over the quality of the lambs being sold, or perhaps he sought to minimize the chaotic conditions at the city gates, where previously pilgrims and their animals had struggled to get through. Bringing the sales inside would also have ensured that the Temple received a commission.

A Greek-style golden necklace features a rosette on the lock and a gemstone pendant on the bottom.

French history painter Louis Felix Leullier (1811–1882) painted "The Entry of Christ into Jerusalem" using 19th-century studies of Palestinian dress.

What we do know is that when Jesus emerged into the forecourt with his disciples, he was shocked to see this rampant commerce sprawled across the marble esplanade and hear the cacophony of bleating animals, the loud cries of money changers proclaiming their rates, and the haggling of pilgrims over the inflated prices of the lambs.

Jesus was incensed. He had planned to deliver a great speech, as Jeremiah before him had done—a Temple sermon for the ages, addressed to all of the thousands of pilgrims now converging on the Temple. But he had been upstaged by a ragged collection of money changers and animal peddlers. His anger welled up, and he "began to drive out those who were selling and those who were buying in the temple, and he overturned the tables of the moneychangers and the seats of those who sold doves" (Mark 11:15).

As the bewildered traders scattered in all directions, Jesus stood up and cried, quoting the Book of Isaiah, "Is it not written, my house shall be called a house of prayer for all the nations?" (Isaiah 56:7). "But you," he continued, looking at the priests in their white linen robes and tubular hats, "you have made it a den of robbers." That last sentence was also a citation, taken from Jeremiah's Temple speech (Jeremiah 7:11), but it sealed Jesus' fate. Jesus may not have known this, but just two years earlier, the Roman prefect Pontius Pilate (presumably in collusion with Caiaphas) had been accused of illegally appropriating funds from the Temple Treasury—ostensibly to build a Roman aqueduct. Jesus' accusation struck a nerve. As Mark writes, as soon as "the chief priests and the scribes heard it, they kept looking for a way to kill him" (Mark 11:18). Jesus was now a marked man.

While the evangelists portray the arrest of Jesus as the result of a carefully hatched conspiracy by Jewish elites, many historians concur that it was probably Jesus' attack in the Temple that prompted it. This is underscored by the fact that it was the Temple Guards, not Roman soldiers, who served the arrest warrant. Caiaphas could not ignore the possibility that this Galilean rabbi might stage another violent demonstration, particularly during the volatile Passover festival. He needed to be removed. ■

FOLLOWING PAGES: *"Christ Driving the Money-Lenders From the Temple" is an oil painting by French Baroque artist Valentin de Boulogne (1594–1632), completed around 1618.*

THE WEEK OF UNLEAVENED BREAD

Mark's Gospel tells us that Jesus was in Jerusalem "on the first day of Unleavened Bread, when the Passover lamb is sacrificed" (Mark 14:12). During this holy week, coinciding with Passover, all bread made with leavened dough was to be avoided. The "leaven" is yeast, which in Jesus' time was the remains of old dough that had become fermented; without it, bread would not rise in the oven. Jesus referred to this practice when he compared the Kingdom of Heaven to "yeast that a woman took and mixed in with three measures of flour, until all of it was leavened" (Matthew 13:33).

The Jewish calendar reckons a day from sunset to sunset. On the night of the 14th of Nisan, that is, *after*

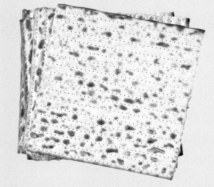

Matzo, or matzah *bread, is a crackerlike flat, unleavened bread that is not allowed to rise during baking.*

nightfall on the evening *before* Passover Eve, the head of every Jewish household would search his home and gather any remaining crumbs of *chametz*—leavened bread made from wheat, oats, or barley dough that had risen through contact with water. Not a single morsel of leaven should remain to despoil the house during the Passover festival. During the next seven days, Jews in Roman Palestine and throughout the Diaspora would consume the hard, crackerlike bread made from unleavened dough, called matzo (Deuteronomy 16:3). This would remind them of the day when their forefathers hastily prepared to flee from Egypt, with no time to wait for the dough to rise (Exodus 12:8). ■

CHAPTER TWENTY-ONE

THE LAST SUPPER

*So Jesus sent Peter and John,
saying, "Go and prepare
the Passover meal for us
that we may eat it."*

LUKE 22:8

Jesus and His Apostles Share a Final Meal

The sun's shadow was lengthening as Jesus and the Apostles made their way through the narrow alleys of Jerusalem's Lower City. All over town, families were busy preparing for the Seder, the Passover meal. No doubt Mary and Martha would also be fully absorbed in the preparation, but Jesus had decided to stay in Jerusalem for the time being rather than return to Bethany. The Gospels do not give us the reason; perhaps the Apostles feared that the gates and roads would be heavily patrolled by Roman soldiers and Temple Guards, and undoubtedly they were. In the meantime, however, they had no place where they could stay or share a meal themselves.

Jesus asked two disciples to go and find a room. They were to follow a man with a jar of water, and when they saw him entering a house, they were supposed to say, "The teacher asks, where is my guest room where I may eat the Passover with my disciples?" (Mark 14:14). The phrasing of this sentence suggests that the home owner may have known "*the* teacher" and that he was either a sympathizer or a disciple himself. As we will see later on in the story, the Gospels indicate that there were individuals in Jerusalem who knew Jesus and were sympathetic to his teachings even though his ministry had been mostly confined to Galilee. Some authors even suggest that the home owner was Joseph of Arimathea, who reappears in the Passion story. Others have identified this mysterious individual as the disciple John Mark, who according to the Book of Acts lived in a house in Jerusalem with his mother,

Mary. John Mark may be a plausible candidate, for his mother's house would later become an important gathering place for the disciples (Acts 12:12-13).

THE PASSOVER MEAL

The two Apostles followed Jesus' instructions to the letter and "found everything as he had told them." And, Mark adds, they then "prepared the Passover meal" (Mark 14:16). First, the lamb meat was roasted on skewers made of pomegranate wood, using an open oven that was usually set up for Passover in the courtyard of the house. The meat was spiced with garlic cloves and repeatedly basted with honeyed olive oil. Cakes of unleavened bread were baked in another oven, while inside the house, experienced hands created several dishes of bitter herbs, such as parsley, mallows, chicory, and radishes. The purpose of these bitter herbs was to remind the Jews of their bitter time in Egypt. During the meal, the herbs would be dipped in a sop called *charoseth,* which consisted of various fruits pounded into a paste and mixed with vinegar and salted water.

Given that a Seder was often shared by a large group and the lamb portions were usually small, there would also be plenty of starch, usually in the form of

ABOVE: *The Room of the Last Supper, located on Mount Zion, is traditionally believed to be the location where Jesus and his disciples shared their last meal together.*

OPPOSITE: *A Roman gold cup with tapered top, made between 50 B.C.E. and 25 C.E., once belonged to an affluent or aristocratic household in Judea.*

PRECEDING PAGES: *"Jesus Washing Peter's Feet" is the work of British Pre-Raphaelite artist Ford Madox Brown (1821–1893), painted between 1852 and 1856.*

"Christ Washing the Feet of the Disciples" is one of the frescoes painted by Giotto di Bondone (1266–1337) in the Scrovegni Chapel in Padua, Italy, around 1305.

a stew of lentils and barley, spiced with onions, celery, garlic, and carrots. If the home was of modest means, these dishes would be served on simple wooden or earthenware plates with high rims, so as to better contain the food; several such plates were found near the caves near Qumran. More affluent homes would use special Passover dishes of copper or silver, and the wine would be savored in cups of glass, silver, or gold. By contrast, Jesus and the Apostles probably tasted the wine in unadorned terra-cotta cups.

Wine was an important component of the Passover meal. The Mishnah decrees that everyone, including the poor, should have "no fewer than four cups of wine, even if [the funds] come from public charity," to allow everyone to share in the joy of Israel's release on Passover night.

Mark's account of the Passion, which Matthew and Luke adopted, clearly states that the Last Supper was a Passover meal, taken on the eve of Passover. John's Gospel, however, differs in two important respects. He places this event a day earlier, that is, on the 13th of Nisan (John 13:1; 19:14). Some historians have argued that this change served a theological purpose; by moving the sequence up by one day, Jesus died on the cross on the 14th, at the same time that the Paschal Lambs died in the Temple. In John's symbolic vision, Jesus thus became the über-Paschal Lamb, the ultimate sacrifice that erased man's sins and obviated the need for any subsequent sacrificial rites. Another interpretation suggests that John may have been urging early Christians to stop associating Last Supper celebrations with the Jewish Seder.

John also relates an episode that is not found in the other Gospels. "During the supper," says John, Jesus "got up from the table, took off his outer robe, and

[Judas] went away and conferred with the chief priests and officers of the temple police about how he might betray [Jesus] to them.

LUKE 22:4

TOP: *A simple earthenware pitcher with ribbed body, wide neck, and splayed rim suggests the type of vessel that would have been used to serve wine during the Last Supper.*

BOTTOM: *This "Last Supper" fresco from 1480 in the refectory of the Ognissanti in Florence is one of several versions by Renaissance artist Domenico Ghirlandaio (1449–1494).*

tied a towel around himself. Then he poured water into a basin and began to wash the disciples' feet and to wipe them with the towel that was tied around him." The Apostles, and particularly Simon Peter, were aghast. The washing of feet, a necessity in a land where the roads were dusty and unpaved, was usually a service performed by the lowest servant or slave in the household. "Lord," asked an incredulous Simon Peter, "are you going to wash my feet?" The unstated question was: Why? Why would the Teacher engage in such a menial task, when it should be the disciples who washed their Teacher's feet? "You do not know now what I am doing," Jesus replied to him, "but later you will understand" (John 13:4-7).

A collection of Jewish and Tyrian shekels, dating from the Second Jewish War (ca 132–135 C.E.), illustrates the 30 pieces of silver paid to Judas for his betrayal of Jesus.

This mysterious response suggests that Jesus was talking about his impending death: A corpse was usually washed before it was wrapped in a shroud and laid to rest. Some, however, interpret the scene as a reference to Jewish purification rites. Other authors believe that the feet washing serves as an allegorical version of baptism, a practice that would soon become a key part of the Apostolic mission to the nations (Acts 1:5). Yet another interpretation sees the event as a token of Jesus' deep humility.

JUDAS ISCARIOT

When Jesus was finished, he rose and said, "Not all of you are clean." Thus, John introduces the most shocking development in all of the Gospel stories: the discovery of a traitor in the midst of Jesus' following. John's depiction of this episode is by far the most harrowing. His first enigmatic words, *not all of you are clean,* primes his audience for the bombshell announcement to follow. "Very truly, I tell you," Jesus declared, "one of you will betray me."

The Apostles, who were reclining on benches around the table as was the custom at the time, were shocked. They were too stunned—or perhaps too afraid—to respond. One of the disciples, "the one whom Jesus loved," was reclining at the place of honor, next to Jesus, sharing his couch. Simon Peter, who knew the great affection that Jesus bore this young disciple, motioned to him that he should "ask Jesus of whom he was speaking." He did so, and Jesus replied, "It is the one to whom I give this piece of bread when I have dipped it in the dish" (John 13:21-26). The Apostles held their breath as Jesus took the piece of matzo bread, dipped it—and wordlessly handed it to Judas, son of Simon Iscariot.

WHO IS THE BELOVED DISCIPLE?

The Gospel of John makes four references to a mysterious figure named "the beloved disciple," to whom Jesus is very attached. This disciple plays a significant role. It is he who reclines next to Jesus at the Last Supper and stands at the cross when Jesus tells his mother, Mary: "Woman, here is your son" (John 13:23; 19:26). Who is this character, and why doesn't John identify him? Christian tradition holds that the disciple is John the Evangelist himself. But this is less likely when we remember that the Fourth Gospel was composed at least 60 years after the Passion events. The evangelist writes that "[the beloved disciple] is the disciple who is testifying to these things and has written them, and we know that his testimony is true" (John 21:24). That would suggest that this Apostle, presumably named John, was a follower who wrote a memoir or sayings document about Jesus, which then served as the principal source for the Fourth Gospel. ∎

A detail from the "Last Supper" by Sienese artist Duccio di Buoninsegna (ca 1255/1260–ca 1318/1319) shows Jesus and the Beloved Disciple.

Judas took the bread and immediately left. "It was night," says John, and Judas set about his grim task. He had promised to betray the location of Jesus to the chief priests in exchange for 30 pieces of silver (Matthew 26:14-16).

THE INSTITUTION OF THE EUCHARIST

After Judas had left and the group had recovered from the shock, the disciples waited for Jesus to bless the food, a common Jewish practice at meals. Jesus took the bread, blessed it, and gave it to the disciples, saying, "Take; this is my body." Then Jesus took a cup, and after giving thanks, he gave it to them, saying, "This is my blood of the covenant, which is poured out for many" (Mark 14:22-24).

With these words, Jesus instituted the quintessential Christian ritual of the Eucharist. It would be reenacted among scores of early Christian communities; some scholars believe that Mark's version, probably written after the destruction of the Temple in 70 C.E., actually reflects the type of Eucharist then being celebrated among Christian communities. For one, it closely matches the description Paul provided in his letter to the Corinthians (I Corinthians 11:23-26).

The Apostles then sang hymns, as was customary during the Passover meal, got up, and quietly left the house. It was well into the night. They slipped out of the city under the cloak of darkness and made their way to the Mount of Olives. ■

A detail of Judas, Peter, and the Beloved Disciple is taken from a copy of Leonardo da Vinci's "Last Supper" fresco, painted by Andrea Solario (1460–1524) around 1507.

FOLLOWING PAGES: *A 20-year restoration of the "Last Supper" fresco by Leonardo da Vinci (1452–1519), completed in 1999, has revealed many intriguing details.*

CHAPTER TWENTY-TWO

THE ARREST AND INDICTMENT

Then Jesus went with them to a place called Gethsemane; and he said to his disciples, "Sit here while I go over there and pray."

MATTHEW 26:36

Jesus Is Accused of Blasphemy and Rebellion

Our traditional image of Jesus during the final hours before his arrest shows him in solitude, abandoned by his Apostles, and surrounded by the pastoral stillness of the Mount of Olives. This traditional iconography, established in the early Renaissance, became so ingrained that it is still featured in modern film and television specials about the Passion. But the reality was very different.

As we saw previously, the vast majority of Passover pilgrims had neither the money for an inn nor relatives in the city to spend the night with. Instead, they would congregate on the Mount of Olives, there to find a grassy patch in the shade of an olive tree. On this night, the hill would have been teeming with campfires, the smells of hundreds of cooking pots, and the cries and laughter of countless children. It was through this mass of humanity that Jesus and the Apostles slowly made their way up the mountain, careful not to step on the bundles of sleeping men and women scattered along their path. It was dark, and it was cold: Night temperatures in the middle of Nisan could fall as low as 40 degrees Fahrenheit.

This is why Jesus, in search of a quiet place to reflect and pray, made his way to a place he must have visited before: a *gat-shemanim,* the root of the word Gethsemane. A *gat-shemanim* was an oil press, used to crush olives from the orchards that gave the mount its name. It was usually set up in a cave so as to keep the oil cool in summer months and protect the wooden press from the elements. It was here that Jesus spent his final moments of freedom—tormented by agony and self-doubt. "Abba, Father, for you all things are possible," he prayed; "remove this cup from me." But then he paused and added, "yet, not what I want, but what you want" (Mark 14:36).

Soon after Jesus went looking for his disciples in the hope that they could console and strengthen him in this supreme hour of need. Earlier, he had warned them that they would all become deserters. When Peter had hotly defended himself, saying, "I will not," Jesus told him, "This day, this very night, before the cock crows twice, you will deny me three times" (Mark 14:30). And now that desertion had begun. Just when he needed them most, they were all sound asleep, "for their eyes were very heavy, and they did not know what to say to him." Here, the theme of alienation and abandonment that runs the length of Mark's tragic story finds its sad conclusion.

At long last, Jesus accepted the inevitable. "Enough!" he said, as much to himself as to his followers; "the hour has come; the Son of Man is betrayed into the hands of sinners" (Mark 14:41).

THE ARREST

The instrument of that betrayal, Judas Iscariot, was at that moment picking his way through the thousands of eating and sleeping pilgrims on the mountain, closely followed by a detachment of Temple Guards. This was precisely the reason that the Guards needed Judas: to help identify their

ABOVE: *This garden on the Mount of Olives is located close to the traditional place of Gethsemane, the place where Jesus was arrested.*

OPPOSITE: *A Roman silver vessel with tapered top from the first century C.E. may have once served as a wine pitcher or cooler.*

PRECEDING PAGES: *Dutch Golden Age artist Gerrit van Honthorst (1592–1656) painted "Christ before Caiaphas" around 1617 under the influence of Italian painter Michelangelo Caravaggio.*

Then they seized him and led him away, bringing him into the high priest's house.

LUKE 22:54

"The Agony in the Garden" by Renaissance artist Andrea Mantegna (ca 1431–1506), painted around 1460, is closely related to Giovanni Bellini's treatment of the same subject, shown on pages 292–293.

quarry among the multitudes who crowded the hills of Jerusalem. As soon as Judas spotted Jesus near the Gethsemane cave, he rushed toward him and kissed him—the ultimate betrayal. Pupils habitually kissed their teacher as a sign of respect. Judas, however, turned this gesture of affection into a cynical token of treason.

Recognizing the signal, the guards moved in and arrested Jesus. And then, at long last, one of the disciples roused himself from his apathy. He "drew his sword and struck the slave of the high priest, cutting off his ear" (Mark 14:47). Jesus immediately intervened before the violence could spread. "No more of this," he said firmly, and restored the ear to the man's head (Luke 22:51).

Normal practice dictated that Jesus should be interned in one of the cells or near the Temple, there to await the time of his hearing in front of the full Sanhedrin, the Jewish Council. This is exactly what happened when, many months later, Peter and John were arrested for the crime of blasphemy. They were placed in custody at the Temple until such time that "Annas the [former] high priest, [and] Caiaphas" could preside over a full session of the Sanhedrin (Acts 4:15). The same process was repeated when Peter and some of the Apostles were found preaching in the Temple once again, near Solomon's Portico: They were arrested, placed in the Temple stockade, and eventually interrogated by the Sanhedrin.

THE SANHEDRIN PROTOCOL

In Jesus' case, something strange happened: He was not taken to a prison cell, but dispatched with unseemly haste to the private residence of the high priest Caiaphas himself. As soon as he arrived there, he was instantly subjected to an indictment hearing.

This was entirely without precedent, for a number of reasons. First, it was Passover eve; if indeed a verdict was reached, it would have to be confirmed in a statutory follow-up session the following day. But this was Passover, a feast day, when any session of the Sanhedrin was out of the question. Second, as Caiaphas well knew, anyone accused of a religious crime could be tried only by a panel of 71 judges—the full quorum of the Sanhedrin (Mishnah Sanhedrin 1:5). But to gather this quorum on such short notice, on the eve of the most important feast day in the year, would have been impossible. And finally, sessions of the Sanhedrin were invariably scheduled during the day, not at night, and these are believed to have taken place at the Lishkat La-Gazit, the Chamber of Hewn Stones in the Temple Stoa, never at someone's home.

And yet Caiaphas was determined that the rabbi from Galilee should be tried and condemned forthwith, *immediately,* without waiting for the Passover festival to end. This begs the question: Why? Why was Caiaphas in such a hurry to put Jesus away?

This stone marked the soreg, the boundary at the entrance to the Temple beyond which no Gentile could pass, and warned trespassers of the penalty of death.

This ossuary, a box for the second burial of skeletal remains after the body has decomposed, is believed to have contained the bones of the high priest Caiaphas.

A beautiful first-century glass flask with yellow bands and a tall, tapered top would have been used as a container for cosmetic oils.

The answer is simpler than we might think. Caiaphas and his Sadducee brethren did not control the full Sanhedrin. There was a sizable and rather vocal minority on the council that was composed of Pharisees, and Pharisees tended to go against the grain of Sadducean opinion whenever it suited them. What's more, Caiaphas may have known enough about Jesus to know that in many respects, his teachings were rather similar to those espoused by Pharisees. Josephus agrees; he too writes that the Pharisees on the Sanhedrin were less rigid and more merciful than the Sadducees. Therefore, the outcome of a vote by the full Sanhedrin would have been entirely unpredictable.

Later developments bear this out. Twice, Peter and the Apostles were tried by the full Sanhedrin, and twice they were allowed to go free. During the second hearing, it was a highly regarded Pharisee, Rabbi Gamaliel, who came to the Apostles' defense and argued for moderation (Acts 5:59).

But Caiaphas knew he had to act. Just as Herod Antipas had sensed that John the Baptist was a political threat, so too could Caiaphas ill afford the risk that Jesus might be the leader of a movement that, once unleashed, could cause the thousands of pilgrims in the Temple to stage a revolt. As the high priest said in the Gospel of John, "It is better for you to have one man die for the people than to have the whole nation destroyed" (John 11:50). That is why Caiaphas decided on a highly unusual course of action. He would indict Jesus in *secret,* at his own private residence, and in front of a few of his own handpicked Sadducee associates: "the chief priests, the elders, and the scribes" (Mark 14:53). This way, if the Pharisees ever got wind of it, it would be too late.

There was only one problem with this plan: No high priest had the power to condemn a man to death on his own authority without the backing of the Sanhedrin. But Caiaphas had thought of that as well. He wasn't planning on putting Jesus to death; he was going to let the Romans do it for him.

"The Kiss of Jesus" is a polychrome wood carving by a Netherlandish artist from Brabant, completed between 1475 and 1500.

THE CAIAPHAS INDICTMENT

Much to Caiaphas's surprise, the session at his house did not unfold as planned. At issue was the nature of the crime that Jesus was accused of: disturbing the peace in the Temple. That was a serious matter, but not one that would be of much interest to the Romans. According to the uneasy pact brokered between the Romans and the Jewish religious authorities, the Sanhedrin dealt with domestic or religious cases, while the Romans occupied themselves with crimes against the Roman state, such as nonpayment of tribute or political agitation. The challenge for Caiaphas, therefore, was to steer the indictment from the *religious* to the *political* sphere, to such a degree that Pontius Pilate, the Roman prefect, would be compelled to intervene.

To accomplish this, Caiaphas had recruited some trustworthy "eyewitnesses." But as Mark writes, the testimony of these false witnesses "did not agree." Some stood up and said, "We heard him say, 'I will destroy this temple that is made with hands, and in

When they had kindled a fire in the middle of the courtyard and sat down together, Peter sat among them.

LUKE 22:55

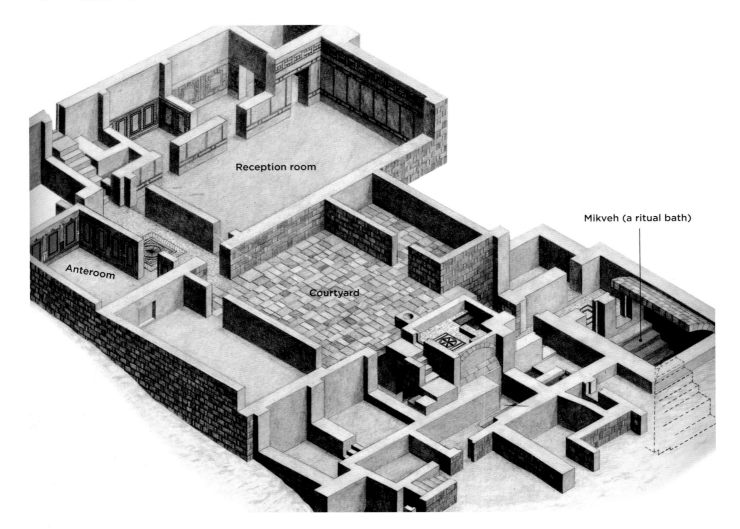

Reception room

Mikveh (a ritual bath)

Anteroom

Courtyard

The 700-square-yard Priestly House in the Upper City in Jerusalem, excavated by archaeologist Nahman Avigad in the late 1960s, included a courtyard and a large reception room.

OPPOSITE: *Gerrit van Honthorst (1592–1656), an artist from the Dutch Golden Age, painted "The Denial of St. Peter" around 1623.*

three days I will build another, not made with hands'" (Mark 14:58). In itself, that was hardly a crime. Many Jewish prophets, from Isaiah to Jeremiah, had made similar doomsday predictions about Jerusalem and the Temple. Nor was it a piece of evidence that would get the Romans excited. And even on this point, says Mark, the witnesses "did not agree."

In desperation, Caiaphas decided to interrogate Jesus himself, in the hope of eliciting something that would incriminate him. "Have you no answer?" he taunted Jesus. "What is it that they testify against you?" Jesus knew better than to respond.

But then Caiaphas played his last card. "Are you the Messiah," he asked slyly, "the Son of the Blessed One?" As a pious Sadducee, he did not pronounce the word God but rather a euphemism, *Blessed One.* This was a question Jesus could not ignore. He straightened and replied, *"I am."* And then he went on to quote the famous passage from Daniel that had inspired him throughout his ministry: " 'You will see the Son of Man seated at the right hand of the power,' and 'coming with the clouds of heaven' " (Mark 14:62, quoting from Psalms 110:1 and Daniel 7:13-14).

It was beautiful, rousing poetry, but Caiaphas didn't care about that. What mattered was that Jesus had just spoken the words the high priest wanted to hear—words that would enable him to transfer the case to Roman jurisdiction, as a capital crime.

PETER'S DENIAL

Meanwhile, Peter had followed the party that took Jesus to Caiaphas at a safe distance (Luke 22:54). Like many of the other chief priests, Caiaphas maintained a palatial residence in the Upper City of Jerusalem. One such priestly home was excavated by Israeli archaeologists in 1970. It featured not only a private suite of *mikva'ot,* or ritual baths, but also a large reception hall, lavishly decorated with colorful frescoes, and a central courtyard. It was in one such courtyard that Peter now found himself, surrounded by servants and guards, while inside the mansion the hearing against Jesus was in progress.

This richly detailed oil lamp from the third century c.e. features symbols from the temple and altar on Mount Gerizim in Samaria.

Peter was torn. On the one hand, he knew he should try to make his way inside and forcefully speak up in Jesus' defense. But on the other, he was afraid that by doing so, he would incriminate himself and most likely wind up being arrested as well. And so he tarried, warming his hands at the fire in the courtyard (Luke 22:55).

As his face was lit by the flames, one of Caiaphas's servant girls looked at him more closely. "You also were with Jesus, the man from Nazareth," she said accusingly. Peter looked up, shock in his eyes. "I do not know or understand what you are talking about," he stammered, his Galilean accent thick with fear, and he quickly turned away just as a cock began to crow.

The servant girl wouldn't let it go. She turned to the other people in the courtyard and said loudly, "This man is one of them!" Some of them, intrigued now, stepped closer and looked at Peter intently. "Certainly," one said, "you are one of them; for you are a Galilean." Peter hotly denied it and began to curse. "I do not know this man you are talking about!" he cried.

At that moment, the cock crowed for the second time, and Peter suddenly remembered what Jesus had said to him: "Before the cock crows twice, you will deny me three times." And, says Mark, "he broke down and wept" (Mark 15:66-72). He had failed his master in his greatest moment of need.

THE VERDICT

Inside the mansion, the indictment session was drawing to a close. Caiaphas was satisfied: The witnesses had very nearly botched the proceedings, but

THE JUDAS BETRAYAL

The story of betrayal at the very heart of Jesus' following is one of the most unusual and surprising developments in the Gospels. What motivated Judas to betray Jesus to the chief priests? The question has occupied scholarship for many decades, and a few plausible hypotheses have emerged. One argues that Judas's name, Iscariot, indicates that he was man *(Ish)* from Kerioth, a town in southern Judea. That made Judas the only non-Galilean in Jesus' inner circle. As a Judean, Judas may have thought himself to be uniquely qualified to broker a deal with the Temple authorities—one that would result in Jesus' arrest but allow all of Jesus' followers to go free. Another hypothesis points to the fact that Judas was the treasurer of the group, entrusted with the money box (John 12:6). Perhaps he was purely motivated by money—particularly since his price of 30 silver shekels was quite substantial. Yet another suggests that Judas simply fulfilled a key role in the story. Without Judas, the Temple Guards would have never found Jesus among the thousands of Passover pilgrims crowding the city. A second- or third-century Gnostic text, the "Gospel of Judas," argues that this is the reason that Jesus actually *asked* Judas to betray him so as to fulfill his destiny by dying on the cross. According to this document, Judas is not a traitor but a deeply loyal and obedient follower. The historicity of this version of events is, however, in question. ∎

A Tyrian silver shekel was minted in the second year of the Second Jewish War (132-135 c.e.)

"The Kiss of Judas" is a detail from a fresco painted by Giotto di Bondone (1266–1337) in the Scrovegni Chapel in Padua, Italy, around 1305.

Jesus himself had spoken the words that, Caiaphas knew, would incriminate him in the eyes of Rome. Anyone who declared himself to be "seated at the right hand of power" would immediately be suspected of political activity, possibly sedition. "Why do we still need witnesses?" Caiaphas grandly declared. "You have heard his blasphemy! What is your decision?" Of course, the verdict was a foregone conclusion. Caiaphas had picked his fellow judges well. "All of them," says Mark, "condemned him to death" (Mark 14:63-64).

As soon as it was morning, the chief priests held a meeting in which the verdict was ratified (Mark 15:1). This was the statutory "second meeting," required in capital cases, but it did not involve "the whole council"—for the simple reason that it was a feast day, when no plenary sessions of the Sanhedrin could be scheduled. Thus, no one intervened as Jesus was bound and led away, to be transferred into Roman custody. ∎

FOLLOWING PAGES:
"The Agony in the Garden" by Venetian Renaissance artist Giovanni Bellini (ca 1430–1516) was painted between 1459 and 1465.

CHAPTER TWENTY-THREE

THE PILATE HEARING

When morning came, all the chief priests and the elders of the people conferred together against Jesus in order to bring about his death.

MATTHEW 27:1

Jesus Is Condemned to the Cross

Of all the Gospel passages related to the Passion, the trial by Pilate is perhaps the most controversial. It is here that the evangelists try to grapple with the ultimate mystery of their story: *Who killed Jesus?* In the final analysis, who was responsible for his murder? The question is important not only for our understanding of Jesus and the history of Christianity; it was of critical importance for the evangelists who, after all, wrote when the Roman Empire, and the system of Imperial governance in the occupied territories, was still very much in force.

As a result, these authors faced a unique quandary. Their task was to show that Jesus was the Messiah foretold in Hebrew Scripture, the Son of God, who had sought to establish a Kingdom of God on Earth—a Kingdom that would ultimately embrace all the people within the Roman realm. But they also had to confront the fact that this same Jesus, this Messiah, had been tried and executed as a political revolutionary, an enemy of Rome. He had been crucified—a barbaric form of execution that Rome reserved for the worst political offenders—after due process, presided by Rome's highest representative in the territory, the prefect Pontius Pilate himself.

How to reconcile these narratives? How could the evangelists be true to the oral and written traditions about Jesus without potentially running afoul of the Roman authorities by implicitly challenging the legality of his execution? This was the essential dilemma that Mark faced, and it is his solution that would ultimately be adopted, and further elaborated on, by Matthew, Luke, and John.

THE PRAETORIUM PROCEEDINGS

Given the immense importance that Mark's account would have for the Gospel tradition and Christianity in general, his chapter on the Pilate hearing is almost unbelievably short. There are none of the intriguing details with which Mark so vividly sets the stage for the Caiaphas indictment. There is no indication of where the trial took place, for example, or at what time. Nor are we told who was present at the hearing other than Jesus' accusers, the chief priests. Most important, we don't know what set the trial in motion, what charges were brought, or why Pilate agreed to hear the matter to begin with. After all, this was the beginning of Passover, the most politically volatile day in the year, when keeping order in the city should have been foremost on the prefect's mind.

Instead, Mark begins his story by having Pilate ask a blunt question: "Are you the King of the Jews?" Jesus simply answered, "You say so" (Mark 15:2).

The other evangelists were keenly aware of this paucity of detail, and so they added their own refinements, possibly based on sources not available to Mark. Luke, for example, opens the trial with a proper reading of the charges: "We found this man perverting our nation, forbidding us to pay taxes to the emperor, and saying that he himself is the Messiah" (Luke 23:2).

ABOVE: *These caverns are believed to have formed part of the lower level of the Antonia Fortress, even though they were later incorporated in a Roman city gate built in the second century C.E.*

OPPOSITE: *An ancient door knocker in the shape of a lion's head was a popular motif for doors of official Roman buildings, including those belonging to the praetor, or Roman magistrate.*

PRECEDING PAGES: *French academic artist William-Adolphe Bouguereau (1825–1905) painted "The Flagellation of Our Lord Jesus Christ" in 1880, based on meticulous research.*

They bound Jesus, led him away, and handed him over to Pilate.

MARK 15:1

In addition, Matthew and John specify the location of the trial. John writes, "They took Jesus from Caiaphas to Pilate's headquarters" (John 18:28). John uses the word *praitorion* or praetorium, literally "the office of the praetor," who was the second ranking official in the territory, below that of governor or prefect. This has prompted a lively discussion in scholarly circles about where this praetorium could have been located. One school believes it was Herod's old palace in the southwestern part of the city, just south of today's Jaffa Gate. Because of its association with the king, it was the most prestigious and certainly the most comfortable residence in the city.

But another group believes it would have been more plausible for Pilate to stay in another of Herod's palaces, the one adjoining the Antonia Fortress as described by Josephus. One of the Antonia's towers, says the historian, was "seventy cubits" or around 100 feet high, and offered a "commanding view of the whole area of the Temple." From there, Pilate could keep a watchful eye on all the pilgrims below—the very reason he had come up from his home base in Caesarea. The choice for the Antonia is even more plausible when we consider that two Gospels place the scourging "in the courtyard . . . of the governor's headquarters," in the presence of "the whole cohort" (Mark 15:16; Matthew 27:27). As Josephus writes, that cohort, consisting of around 200 soldiers, was permanently stationed at the Antonia.

THE HISTORICAL PILATE

The Gospels describe Pontius Pilate as a compassionate man who is convinced of Jesus' innocence but is forced by the crowd to condemn him to death. This portrayal, however, does not agree with the historical data. Pontius Pilate was a Roman knight, not a senator, who sought to deliberately antagonize the Jewish population from the moment he took office in Judea in 26 C.E. and ruthlessly pursued anyone suspected of posing a political threat. Ten years after the trial of Jesus, Jewish historian Philo wrote that Pilate was a man of "supremely grievous cruelty" who "constantly ordered executions without trial." Even Josephus, who wrote at the behest of the Romans, admitted that Pilate committed outrageous acts. Significantly, Pilate was removed from his office in 36 C.E. for the excessive violence with which he tried to suppress a religious gathering of Samaritans, a rather unprecedented event in the history of Roman overseas governance. ■

A stone from the Roman theater in Caesarea bears the dedication "[To the Gods This] Tiberium [Has Been Dedicated by] Pontius Pilate, Prefect of Judea."

In Mark's version, Jesus refuses to answer the charges. "The chief priests accused him of many things," says the evangelist, so that even Pilate was compelled to ask, "Have you no answer? See how many charges they bring against you." But Jesus made no further reply (Mark 15:3-5).

John, however, gives a far more dramatic version of the proceedings. In his Gospel, Jesus and Pilate engage in a learned and almost friendly debate. "What have you done?" Pilate asked. "My kingdom is not from this world," Jesus answered; "if my kingdom were from this world, my followers would be fighting to keep me from being handed over to the Jews."

Pilate nodded. "So are you a king?" he wondered. "You say that I am a king," Jesus replied. "For this I was born, and for this I came into the world, to testify to the truth." Ah, said Pilate, "What is truth?" And with that, the prefect got up, turned to the accusers, and said, "I find no case against him" (John 18:35-38).

Matthew's and Luke's Gospel present the hearing in very similar terms. But whereas Mark notes that Jesus' accusers are the chief priests—the senior Sadducee leadership, in other words—Luke and Matthew expand this group to include "the leaders, and the people" (Luke 23:13). By the time John writes his version, near the end of the century, he no longer makes any distinction whatsoever. Jesus' accusers, he says, are simply "the Jews" (John 19:14-15).

Then Pilate said to the chief priests and the crowds, "I find no basis for an accusation against this man."

LUKE 23:4

A pair of toga-clad men from the middle of the first century C.E. probably depicts two senators or other high officials in the Roman government.

WHO IS TO BLAME?

Unbeknown to the evangelists, this argument that the Jewish community bore collective responsibility for the murder of Jesus would lay the seeds for centuries of Jewish persecution in Europe, from the massacres of the First Crusade to the anti-Semitism of the 19th century and, ultimately, the unfathomable crime of the Holocaust. Matthew pushes the concept of Jewish culpability even further when he has the crowd cry out, "His blood be on us, and on our children!" (Matthew 27:25). But is this what happened? Why would the evangelists attempt to shift the blame from Caiaphas and Pilate to the Jewish community of Jerusalem—the same community that had so warmly welcomed Jesus just a week before?

The answer may lie in the extraordinary conditions in which early Christian communities found themselves in the latter part of the first century, when the Gospels were written in their midst. From the 30s onward, the Sadducee leadership launched a concerted campaign to eradicate the early Christian movement in Judea. Stephen, one of the early disciples, was stoned to death around 34 C.E. James, the son of Zebedee, was executed by King Agrippa I

(r. 37–44 C.E.) in 44. Paul was nearly killed by a mob in 57. James, the brother of Jesus, was stoned to death on orders of the high priest Ananus in 62 C.E. By the time the Jewish War broke out in 66, the Christian movement in Judea had all but ceased to exist. As the evangelists saw it, the Jews of *their* time, in the latter part of the first century, had rejected the Messiah—the very man who had come to redeem them.

But outside of Judea, early Christianity was growing by leaps and bounds. Many of these early Christians were Jews, but many more were Gentiles. These communities were content to live under Roman rule. For them, Rome was not the enemy but a guarantor of stability and economic opportunity. This clashed with the narrative that Jesus had been put to death by the Romans. To resolve this dissonance, the evangelists developed the idea that though it was the Romans who did the killing, their hand had been forced by the Jewish community in Jerusalem.

The principal instrument of this shift is Pilate's decision, as recounted by Mark, "to release a prisoner from them, anyone for whom they asked" (Mark 15:6). Mark says this was Pilate's custom during festivals, but no reference to such an amnesty has been found in any Roman records of the period or in Josephus's (who would have seized on such a show of mercy to extol the benign character of Roman rule). Some scholars, however, have cautioned that a prefect had wide latitude in dispensing justice, so the possibility of an amnesty is not out of the question.

When Pilate gave the crowd a choice between Barabbas, a convicted murderer, and Jesus, "the chief priests stirred up the crowd to have him release Barabbas" (Mark 15:11). Despite Pilate's objections, the crowd shouted that Jesus should be condemned. And so Pilate "handed him over to be crucified." Lest there be any lingering doubt about Pilate's complicity in the matter, Matthew shows the prefect washing his hands before the crowd, saying, "I am innocent of this man's blood" (Matthew 27:24). ■

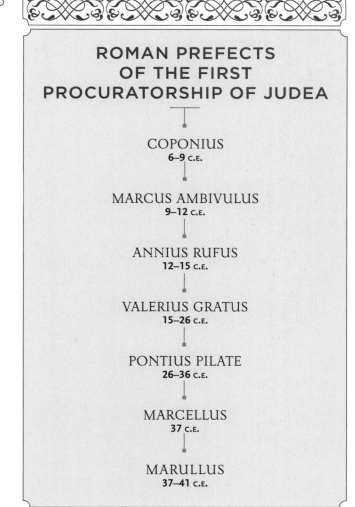

**ROMAN PREFECTS
OF THE FIRST
PROCURATORSHIP OF JUDEA**

COPONIUS
6–9 C.E.

MARCUS AMBIVULUS
9–12 C.E.

ANNIUS RUFUS
12–15 C.E.

VALERIUS GRATUS
15–26 C.E.

PONTIUS PILATE
26–36 C.E.

MARCELLUS
37 C.E.

MARULLUS
37–41 C.E.

OPPOSITE: *A stunning pale green glass goblet from the late first or early second century C.E. with a splayed rim and narrow folded base could have been used by Jerusalem's elite, including the chief priests.*

FOLLOWING PAGES: *The richly detailed "Christ Before Pilate" was painted by Hungarian artist Munkácsy Mihály (1844–1900) and completed in 1881.*

CHAPTER TWENTY-FOUR

DEATH AT GOLGOTHA

Jesus turned to them and said, "Daughters of Jerusalem, do not weep for me, but weep for yourselves and for your children."

LUKE 23:28

Jesus Is Crucified by the Romans

Crucifixion, a process whereby a victim is nailed to a tree or cross and left to die, is a particularly cruel form of execution that was developed by the Persians, perhaps inspired by the Assyrian custom of impaling victims on wooden stakes. Persian King Darius I was known to have executed as many as 3,000 people during a mass execution in Babylon in 519 B.C.E. The Romans adopted the practice as a special form of punishment for any act that challenged Roman sovereignty, including piracy and rebellion. Runaway slaves fit that category as well, because by fleeing their master, they challenged the very economic foundation of the Roman state.

Unlike other forms of execution, such as hanging or beheading, a crucified victim could take several days to die, usually in excruciating pain and invariably in a shameful position: exposed and nude, for all to see. Thus, the procedure served as a perfect deterrent for all those who contemplated similar crimes. Particularly during the late Republican and early Imperial periods, when Roman forces were stretched thin across their newly conquered territories, crucifixion was greatly valued for its preemptive effect. In the wake of the Spartacus revolt of 71 B.C.E., for example, 6,000 slaves were crucified along the Via Appia, Rome's busiest road, at ten-yard intervals; some of these victims survived for two days or more.

Crucifixion was not a simple procedure. It involved some skill on the part of the executioners, particularly with regard to the placement of the nails and the position of the body on the cross. Although Christian

art invariably shows Jesus with nails through both palms, a hand is too soft to sustain the weight of a human body. Instead, the nail was driven through a spot just below the wrist, between the radius and ulna bones of the upper forearm. This required the expertise of a group of specialists, known in Roman military parlance as *immunes*.

Given that the procedure was complex and labor intensive, victims were often crucified during regularly planned group executions. This is shown by the fact that in addition to Jesus, at least two "bandits" were executed as well (Mark 15:27). It may also indicate that the execution had been scheduled in advance. From Pilate's point of view, the concentration of so many Jewish pilgrims in one place was a perfect opportunity to remind everyone who was in charge.

THE SCOURGING

It was not uncommon for a condemned man to receive a thorough flogging before being force-marched to his place of execution. Some authors believe that such physical punishment, whether a scourging or beating, was the usual

ABOVE: *The Church of the Holy Sepulcher in Jerusalem, rebuilt during the 12th-century Crusader period, marks the traditional location of Golgotha where Jesus was crucified.*

OPPOSITE: *A Roman brooch, worn on a sword belt, features the insignia of the Tenth Legion Fretensis, stationed in Antioch, Syria.*

PRECEDING PAGES: *Spanish Baroque artist Diego Rodríguez de Silva y Velázquez (1599–1660), a court painter to King Philip IV, painted "Christ on the Cross" in 1632.*

penalty for anyone who violated the sanctity of the Temple, including Jeremiah (Jeremiah 20:2) and Peter (Acts 5:40). According to Josephus, a man named Jesus, son of Ananias, was arrested during Pentecost of 62 c.e. for unruly behavior in the Temple and flogged for his trouble.

But others suggest that scourging had a more specific function: to weaken the prisoner by inflicting blunt trauma and blood loss so as to hasten his death on the cross—particularly in the Middle East, where daytime temperatures could rise very high and Roman soldiers were relatively thin on the ground.

It was, however, Jesus' misfortune that the soldiers stationed at the Antonia were not Roman legionnaires but auxiliary forces. The creation of standing Roman armies, or "legions," was a recent development, initiated by Emperor Augustus, but these highly trained troops were typically garrisoned in provinces that could afford to pay for them from local taxes. In Jesus' day, the nearest Roman legion was the Tenth Fretensis based in Antioch, headquarters of the Roman governor of Syria and Palestine.

Judea, by contrast, was poor, and its tax yields hardly justified the cost of a full Roman legion. As a result, Pilate had only a few Roman cohorts at his disposal, and these were based at his headquarters in Caesarea. For the remainder, Pilate had to make do with units of so-called auxiliaries, a rather different category of soldiering altogether. Culled from second-class recruits from Syria and other surrounding territories, they were given a minimum of training, inferior equipment, and an odd assortment of clothing and armor. They received less pay, lower quality rations, and a lot less respect than standard legionnaire forces.

This may explain the unusual and sadistic cruelty with which the soldiers in the Antonia set about their task of scourging Jesus. The fact that Jesus was convicted because of his claim of being a "king" further inspired their

Dice of bone and bronze from the Roman period are perhaps similar to the dice that the soldiers rolled to divide the garments of Jesus.

So they took Jesus; and carrying the cross by himself, he went out to what is called The Place of the Skull, which in Hebrew is called Golgotha.

JOHN 19:16-17

savagery. After flogging him thoroughly, they clothed the bleeding figure in a purple cloak, traditionally a mark of royalty, and pushed a crown of thorns on his head. They spat on him and beat him while crying, "Hail, King of the Jews" (Mark 15:16-19). This doesn't sound like a cohort of disciplined Roman soldiers but rather like a rabble of barely trained militia with a deep loathing for the Jewish population.

St. Helen's Chapel in the Church of the Holy Sepulcher marks the place where, according to tradition, Queen Helena found the True Cross in a Roman cistern around 328 C.E.

And then, says Mark, "they led him out to crucify him."

THE ROAD TO GOLGOTHA

Slowly Jesus followed his tormentors out of the Antonia Fortress, stumbling under the weight of the wood he was forced to carry. Since it was a feast day, only a few people were about; most worshippers were going in the opposite direction, toward the Temple. On this day, the second day of unleavened bread, pilgrims from all of the farming regions, including Galilee, were expected to place a sheaf of freshly cut barley on the Temple altar, in homage to God. Most of the people on the street, therefore, were women and servants, carrying pitchers of water from public cisterns and fountains. As the cortège of the condemned passed by, some of them stopped and stared, overwhelmed by pity for the man

A fragment of an anklebone pierced by a Roman nail dramatically illustrates the crucifixion procedure used by Roman forces in the first century c.e.

OPPOSITE: *"Christ Carrying the Cross," using oils on panel, is the work of Spanish Renaissance artist Vicente Masip (1475–1550).*

in tattered clothes, but all stood well away. Contact with the prisoner, whose open wounds were bleeding under the chafing weight of the wood, would contaminate them and render the water they were carrying impure.

The "cross" that Jesus bore was not a true, full-size cross (Mark 15:21). Any apparatus large and strong enough to suspend a man above ground would have been much too heavy for any individual, let alone a man weakened by scourging. More to the point, wood was scarce in Judea and therefore very expensive. As a result, the Romans had equipped their execution zone with a series of permanent upright stakes, or *stipes*. This meant that the condemned would only have to carry the crossbeam, known as a *patibulum*. Such a beam still weighed between 70 and 80 pounds.

Inevitably Jesus stumbled under the weight on his way to the killing ground. The Roman officer in charge probably cursed and kicked the prostrate man under the beam, but Jesus lacked the strength to get up with the wood on his back. Annoyed, the officer looked around and spotted a passerby, a solidly built man who went by the name of Simon of Cyrene. Without further ado, Simon was pressed into service to carry the beam for Jesus (Mark 15:21).

Cyrene was a large Greek city in the Roman province of Cyrenaica, today's Libya, which in the first century boasted a large Jewish population. This would suggest that Simon was a pilgrim who had traveled to Jerusalem for the Passover festival. The Book of Acts also refers to people from Cyrene who had come to attend the Pentecost festival (Acts 2:10). Mark adds that Simon was "the father of Alexander and Rufus," two individuals who are not otherwise identified. Some believe that "Rufus," a Latin name, may be the person to whom Paul extends his greetings in his letter of the Romans, which could have motivated Mark to

THE SCOURGING

A scourging by Roman soldiers usually involved a special instrument known as a *flagrum*. This was a leather whip consisting of several thongs, each equipped with sharp fragments of metal or sheep's bone. Properly applied, a flagrum could shred a prisoner's back to ribbons until only a mass of exposed flesh remained. The prisoner was often tied around a large column to render him immobile for his punishment. There were many such columns in the two courtyards of the Antonia Fortress, the military headquarters Herod built right next to the Temple. The Roman army included many specialists, each known as a *flagrifer,* or whip carrier. They were experienced in wielding the scourge, particularly since flogging was the favored method for punishing wayward soldiers as well. Self-flagellation became a favored custom among the monastic orders of the early Middle Ages in order to imitate Christ's suffering. ∎

An Imperial Gallic helmet of a Roman legionnaire with ear guards and sloping neck guard, found in Judea, is dated to the second century B.C.E.

A Roman city gate, excavated underneath today's Gate of Damascus in Jerusalem, was built with limestone ashlars taken from the Second Temple after its destruction in 70 C.E.

include him in the story (Romans 16:13). According to one Church tradition, Mark was born in Cyrene himself.

THE CRUCIFIXION

Simon willingly took the rough-hewn beam from Jesus and hefted it on his shoulder. Jesus was dragged to his feet, and the procession continued. A short time thereafter, the exhausted victims and their executioners arrived at the place of execution, known as Golgotha in Aramaic, and Calvaria, or Calvary, in Latin. It meant, appropriately, the "place of the skull." Here, the condemned men were subjected to one last indignity: They were stripped, in open defiance of the modesty so prized by Jews. Naked, Jesus was forced to lie down on the ground, while his arms were quickly bound to the patibulum with henna rope. With the prisoner thus immobilized, the immunes could begin their work.

One of them produced a set of iron nails, which he dangled before Jesus' eyes. Roman nails were longer than the average modern nail—some six inches in length—and immensely strong, with a square shaft some three-eighths of an inch

Standing near the cross of Jesus were his mother, and his mother's sister, Mary the wife of Clopas, and Mary Magdalene.

JOHN 19:25

in width. The executioner then pulled a mallet from his bag and carefully positioned his nail above Jesus' left forearm, near the radius, making a tiny prick, just enough to draw blood, to mark the spot. Then the Roman raised his mallet and brought it down on the nail with all his strength, driving it through the median nerve and causing massive damage. The wave of pain, akin to that caused by complex regional pain syndrome, or causalgia, would have been instant and overwhelming. Like any other man, Jesus probably screamed in agony, to the amusement of the Roman *immunes*, who were expecting it. Then the executioner got up, brushed the dirt off his knees, and leisurely made his way to the opposite side, there to repeat the procedure with Jesus' right forearm.

With both of the prisoner's arms nailed to the crossbeam, the soldiers removed the henna rope to ensure that the full weight of the condemned would be brought to bear on the nails. Finally, two burly soldiers picked up the beam with Jesus attached and, using ropes or ladders, raised it over one of the upright stakes, slamming it onto the notch on top. Jesus was now suspended from a cross in the shape of a capital T—known as *tau* cross.

There remained one more task: the feet. One *immunis* turned Jesus' ankles sideways and pushed them into a small wooden block, shaped in the form of a U. This block was affixed to the bottom of the upright stake by driving a long nail through both of Jesus' heels and the block, ending in the wooden post. This position also pressed the legs together and bent them, so that Jesus seemed to be kneeling sideways.

"Christ Carrying the Cross to Golgotha" is a gilded wood sculpture carved by an anonymous Flemish artist around 1400.

A depiction of a crucified Christ in bronze on an enameled cross was made in Limoges around 1220.

With this last step, the crucifixion was finished and the long agony of the victim could begin. Suspended in this posture, hanging by one's forearms, it is very difficult to breathe. To take a breath, the condemned must lift himself up; by lifting himself up, he puts great strain on his nailed arms and feet, thus eliciting fresh waves of pain. The torment of crucifixion is therefore largely self-inflicted. The victim must choose between suffocation or taking a breath by suffering unimaginable pain. The human impulse for survival will force him to choose the latter, and to do so over and over again, minute after minute, hour after hour.

THE DEATH OF JESUS

While Jesus suffered on the cross, the Romans settled on the ground to cast lots over the garments of the condemned. Foreign auxiliaries received a salary of only 225 denarii a year, less deductions for food and arms, so any chance of winning loot was eagerly sought. One of the soldiers posted a sign over

WHERE WAS GOLGOTHA?

The Antonia Fortress was probably located on the spot currently occupied by a madrassa, or Islamic school, in Jerusalem's Old City. Nearby is the convent of the Sisters of Zion, previously believed to be the place where Jesus' flogging took place. Farther down is a fragment of a Roman arch, which tradition held was the place where Pilate showed Jesus to the crowds with the words *Ecce Homo:* "Behold the man" (John 19:5). Professor Jodi Magness, among others, has shown that the arch and pavement were probably built around 135 C.E., when Jerusalem was destroyed and rebuilt as a Roman city named Aelia Capitolina. This is also why it is impossible to reconstruct the route of the Via Dolorosa, the road that Jesus walked to his place of execution;

The so-called Ecce Homo Arch, traditionally associated with the location where Pilate showed Jesus to the crowd, is believed to have been built in the second century C.E.

the layout of Jerusalem in Jesus' day no longer exists, and today's walls run differently. But the location of Golgotha is better documented. Pilgrim accounts indicate that Emperor Hadrian ordered a Venus temple built on the spot, which was promptly torn down by Queen Helena, the mother of the Emperor Constantine, in the fourth century. In its place rose the Church of the Holy Sepulcher, which was destroyed and rebuilt several times. Although other places have been considered, including the Garden Tomb near the Gate of Damascus, few historians today question the identification of the Church of the Holy Sepulcher as the place of Golgotha, which in its current form dates from the 12th century, during the Crusader period. ∎

Jesus' cross, to complete the propaganda aspect of the exercise. This was a common procedure; often a placard was hung around the neck of the condemned, describing his crime. The sign over Jesus' cross read, mockingly, "The King of the Jews" (Mark 15:26). John's Gospel says that the chief priests had suggested a different text: "This man said, I am King of the Jews." But Pilate had overruled them and replied, in his typical oblique fashion, "What I have written I have written" (John 19:21-22).

For five long hours, Jesus struggled on the cross while the sun slowly tracked across the killing field. Each breath he took seared his body with pain, and yet the will to breathe was too strong: It forced him to lift himself up on his ruined arms and his feet, time and time again. Before long, the crickets in the olive trees began their afternoon song, offering a measure of relief from the sobs and moans emerging from the wooden stakes. Then suddenly, Jesus cried out, *Eloi, Eloi, lama sabachthani?*

In his final cry of despair—"My God, My God, why have you forsaken me?"— Jesus invoked the Psalms, as Jews often did in moments of peril (Psalms 22:1). The Apostles, his loyal followers, were nowhere to be seen; many had already fled the city. Only the women remained, among them Mary Magdalene; Mary, "the mother of James the Younger," possibly Jesus' mother; and a woman named Salome (Mark 15:40). John places "the beloved disciple" at the cross as well (John 19:25).

And then Jesus sagged against the nails that held him. He no longer had the strength to force air into his lungs. The young rabbi from Nazareth died of asphyxiation, compounded by shock and loss of blood, shortly after the ninth hour, at approximately 3:10 p.m. ■

"The Crucifixion of Christ" was painted by Renaissance artist Andrea Solario (1460-1524), an associate of Leonardo da Vinci, around 1507.

FOLLOWING PAGES:
"The Crucifixion" is a large panel from circa 1450 by the so-called Dreux Budé Master, believed by some to be Flemish artist André d'Ypres (active 1425/26-1450).

CHAPTER TWENTY-FIVE

THE TOMB

Now there was a garden in the place where he was crucified, and in the garden there was a new tomb in which no one had ever been laid.

JOHN 19:41

Jesus Is Laid to Rest by Joseph of Arimathea

While the Romans generally took little notion of the Jewish Law, there was one *mitzvah,* or commandment, that they could ill ignore. That was the requirement in Deuteronomy that after someone was executed and hung from a tree, "his corpse must not remain all night; you shall bury him that same day, for anyone hung on a tree is under God's curse" (Deuteronomy 21:22-23). To leave the condemned on the cross overnight was bound to provoke the population, and perhaps incite the very rebellion that Pilate tried so strenuously to prevent.

Thus, shortly before sunset, the Roman soldiers got up, took a truncheon or a mallet, and moved from cross to cross to smash the legs of the victims. Once his legs were broken, the prisoner could no longer raise himself to breathe. One by one, those who were still alive struggled, gulped for air, and finally suffocated to death. In his Gospel, John attests to this rather macabre procedure. "But," he writes, "when they came to Jesus and saw that he was already dead, they did not break his legs." Just to make sure, one of the soldiers took a long lance, known as a *pilum,* and pierced Jesus' side, "and at once blood and water came out" (John 19:33-34). This satisfied the soldier, but the passage may have served another purpose as well. By the time John wrote his Gospel, rumors were circulating that Jesus had never actually died and that he was merely in a coma after being taken from the cross. John may have added the story of the spear, which does not appear in the earlier Gospels, in order to refute these rumors. Indeed, John even offers a personal endorsement of

sorts: "He who saw this has testified so that you also may believe. His testimony is true, and he knows that he tells the truth" (John 19:35). At the same time, John's reference to blood and water may also have a symbolic significance, in the sense that Jesus' blood is the drink of eternal life (John 6:54) and that "living water" is the source of the Holy Spirit (John 7:38-39).

JOSEPH OF ARIMATHEA

As soon as the victims were pronounced dead, the crucifixion process was reversed. The nails were driven out of the feet and hands of the condemned, and the crossbeams were removed from the stakes. Much care was taken to ensure that the nails did not bend or break. Many people at the time believed that nails used in executions had magical powers, and the auxiliary soldiers knew that each of these could fetch a hefty price on the open market. The

ABOVE: *The Rotunda of the Church of the Holy Sepulcher in Jerusalem is traditionally identified as the location of the tomb where Jesus was buried.*

OPPOSITE: *The "Pietà" was sculpted between 1498 and 1499 by Renaissance artist Michelangelo da Buonarotti (1475–1564).*

PREVIOUS PAGES: *Renaissance artist Andrea Solario (1460–1524) painted the "Pietà" or "Deposition from the Cross" between 1504 and 1507.*

And so, because it was the Jewish day of Preparation, and the tomb was nearby, they laid Jesus there.

JOHN 19:42

The "Deposition from the Cross" was painted by Cologne-based Master of St. Lawrence (active 1415–1430) between 1425 and 1430.

corpses were then thrown on a cart and made ready for burial in a designated potter's field. As the Mishnah states, condemned men could not be buried in their family plots, only in designated graveyards (Mishnah Sanhedrin 6:5). But then, just as the execution detail prepared to march off, a well-dressed man appeared, followed by an entourage of servants, and sought out the centurion in charge. In his hand, he brandished a special permit, signed by Pontius Pilate himself.

Joseph of Arimathea is an enigmatic figure who does not appear anywhere else in the Gospel story. But as Mark explains, he was "a respected member of the council, who was also himself waiting expectantly for the kingdom of God" (Mark 15:43). This clearly suggests, as we saw earlier, that Joseph was a Pharisee and a member of the Sanhedrin who had much in common with Jesus' teachings. Matthew even calls him "a disciple" (Matthew 27:57). Luke adds that Joseph "had not agreed to their plan and action" (Luke 23:50). Joseph, in other words, had not been aware of the secret hearing at Caiaphas's residence, and when he did find out, it was too late: Jesus was already being crucified. Joseph then undertook the only decent thing left to do: He "went boldly to Pilate," a courageous act indeed, to petition the prefect for Jesus' body. Joseph knew what fate awaited the corpse of a condemned man, and he wanted to spare Jesus this final indignity.

Pilate was surprised when he heard Joseph's request. He wondered aloud if Jesus "was already dead." Experience had taught him that a crucified man could live for a very long time. But when the centurion assured him that Jesus had died on the cross, he "granted the body to Joseph" (Mark 15:45). Perhaps a bribe changed hands, given Pilate's nature; as Matthew tells us, Joseph was a rich man (Matthew 27:57-58).

JOSEPH'S TOMB

Now Joseph faced another challenge. It was late in the afternoon; soon the sun would set and a new day, the Sabbath, would begin. The Law specified that all burial formalities had to be concluded before the start of the Sabbath, lest this holy day be defiled. So Joseph was racing against the clock. He had to move the body of Jesus into a tomb, *any* tomb, and complete the most basic burial rites before sundown.

First, he "took the body and wrapped it in a clean linen cloth" (Matthew 27:59). This cloth could be either a series of cotton strips or a large linen shroud. In 2002, archaeologist Shimon Gibson made a dramatic discovery that confirmed this type of burial. He found a tomb with a body still wrapped in a single burial shroud, blackened with age. As we saw in the case of Caiaphas's ossuary, as soon as a body had decomposed, usually after a year, its bones would be gathered for a second burial in a small stone box. But in this case, the deceased—whom scientists were able to date by radiocarbon methods to 1 to 50 C.E., exactly the time of Jesus—did not receive a secondary burial, and so his shroud was left intact. Gibson theorized that since his tomb was located next to that of the high priest Annas (r. 6–15 C.E.), Caiaphas's father-in-law,

Herod's Family Tomb in Jerusalem (above), in which members of the king's family were buried, still retains the round stone used to close the entrance. Precious perfumed unguents were often kept in delicate glass containers, such as this lusterware flask (below) from the late first century C.E.

he must have been a very prominent priest, which is probably why his body was left undisturbed.

The tomb of this unknown priest was typical of the burial places used in the first century. A single entrance led to a windowless chamber with several niches, or *kokhim,* some of which were large enough to contain a single body. Other alcoves were smaller, just large enough to hold an ossuary containing the bones from secondary burials. What's more, the tomb was a cave, carved out of the rock in the lower Hinnom Valley of Jerusalem.

As Mark writes, Joseph, too, decided to lay the body of Jesus in a tomb "that had been hewn out of the rock" (Mark 15:46). Most likely Joseph owned the tomb and intended it for members of his own family. Matthew confirms that he placed Jesus "in his own tomb, which he had hewn in the rock" (Matthew 27:60). Because the Sabbath was about to begin and Jesus needed to be buried right away, Joseph probably felt that his family tomb should serve as a temporary site until such time after the Sabbath that a more permanent resting place could be found.

THE ANOINTING

Usually the body of a deceased was not only washed prior to burial but also wrapped in fragrant spices so as to cover the odors of decomposition. This was necessary because the relatives of the deceased were expected to visit the tomb for the next three days, to ascertain that its occupant was truly dead and not in a deep coma. A passage in the tractate Semachot of the Babylonian Talmud refers to two occasions on which a man was found alive during this three-day period and

NICODEMUS AND THE JARS OF SPICES

According to Mark, Matthew, and Luke, Jesus was buried in haste, before the women had time to complete the anointing. John, however, argues that the women were able to wrap the body while applying the special perfuming agents and ointments provided by a man named Nicodemus. It was Nicodemus who brought "a mixture of myrrh and aloes, weighing about a hundred pounds"—a fantastic amount, equal to some 75 pounds in our day, which clearly must be a poetic exaggeration (John 19:39). While myrrh was essentially a perfume, applied in powdered form, aloe was an adhesive agent, used to bind the ointments with the linen in which the body was wrapped. Thus, says John, "they took the body of Jesus and wrapped it with the spices in linen cloths, according to the burial customs of the Jews" (John 19:40). ■

Wealthy families built rock-cut tombs in the Kidron Valley, including these Tombs of Zechariah and Benei Hezir, in the belief that this is where the Last Judgment will take place.

The women who had come with him from Galilee followed, and they saw the tomb and how his body was laid.

LUKE 23:55

FOLLOWING PAGES: *The "Pietà of Villeneuve-lès-Avignon" was painted by French Late Medieval artist Enguerrand Quarton (ca 1410–ca 1466) in 1455.*

lived to old age. According to the Midrash Iyyob, a rabbinic commentary on the Book of Job, the soul of the deceased hovered over the body for three days, trying to reenter it, before it agreed to depart. The same three-day interval features prominently in the story of Lazarus, and it would do so again in the story of Jesus.

But by then, Joseph and the women who accompanied him had run out of time. "It was the day of Preparation," says Luke, "and the Sabbath was beginning" (Luke 23:54). There was no time to anoint Jesus' body properly. Regretfully, Joseph ushered the grieving women out of the tomb, while a servant rolled a stone against the door (Mark 15:46). This was meant to prevent anyone, including young children, from stumbling into the cave and coming in contact with the deceased. This is why new burials were also marked with white paint, a sign to all who passed that the tomb contained a fresh body.

The women, including Mary and Mary Magdalene, had no choice but to memorize the location of the tomb and the niche where "his body was laid" and go home to prepare the spices and ointments (Luke 23:56). As soon as the Sabbath was over, they planned to return and complete this last phase of Jesus' burial. ■

Epilogue: The Apostolic Mission Spreads

Three days passed, during which "the soul hovered over the body." By Jewish reckoning, the first day was Friday, the day of execution. The Sabbath was the second day, which ended at sundown on Saturday. And then the sun rose on Sunday, the third day. Back in Bethany, Mary, Salome, and Mary Magdalene were already awake. They dressed quickly, then took the vessels of myrrh and aloe that they had carefully prepared and hoisted them on their shoulders. There was no one to help them. Even now, the men were still in hiding, afraid to show themselves lest they be arrested as well.

But as it happened, the Romans had already forgotten about the rabbi from Galilee. The Passover festival had passed without further incident, and now the pilgrims were getting ready to return to their homes and fields. Pilate was up as well. His tribune had already mustered the cavalry detail that would escort him home. If they moved quickly, they would be able to reach Caesarea by sundown.

As Mary Magdalene and her companions made their way down into the valley, they passed hundreds of pilgrims walking in the opposite direction to Jericho and the villages up north. But Mary had her mind on other things. She was worried that she and the other women would not be able to move the heavy stone from the opening of the grave. "Who will roll away the stone for us from the entrance to the tomb?" she wondered out loud (Mark 16:3). Perhaps they could ask a friendly pilgrim or a servant boy to lend them a hand.

But as Mary approached the tomb, she stopped dead in her tracks. Her hand flew to her mouth. The stone had already been rolled away. And inside was a young man, dressed in a white robe, who told them that "Jesus of Nazareth, who was crucified . . . has been raised; he is not here" (Mark 16:6).

THE RESURRECTION

Jesus had risen from the dead, but Mark's Gospel doesn't describe the actual event or provide any information about what Jesus did *after* his resurrection. It is the "young man, dressed in white," who provides the coda to Mark's story: "Tell his disciples and Peter that he is going ahead of you to Galilee; there you will see him, just as he told you" (Mark 16:7).

The subsequent Gospels developed this void into a new narrative: the story of the risen Jesus. But their reports do not always agree. In some versions,

ABOVE: *Though no longer believed to be a possible location for Jesus' burial, the Garden Tomb is a good example of a Jewish burial chamber from the Second Temple period.*

OPPOSITE: *Italian early Renaissance artist Fra Angelico (ca 1387–1455) painted this panel of "The Resurrection of Christ and the Pious Women at the Sepulcher" around 1442.*

Venetian Renaissance artist Tiziano Vecelli (1490–1576), or Titian, completed "Noli Me Tangere," showing Mary Magdalene and the resurrected Christ, around 1514.

Jesus is a man of flesh and blood who is hungry and eats a piece of broiled fish (Luke 24:42). At other times he is a more ethereal presence who is able to walk through a door (John 20:26-27). In the Gospel of John, Jesus reveals himself to Mary Magdalene, but when she wants to embrace him, he must stop her, telling her "not to hold on to me, because I have not yet ascended to the Father" (John 20:17). In another story told by Luke, two disciples were traveling on the road to Emmaus when they met a stranger who apparently was not aware of the terrible events during Passover. Later that evening, they were reclining at dinner when the stranger took the bread and blessed it. It was only then that their eyes were opened and they recognized Jesus, but he vanished from their presence (Luke 24:13-31).

The purpose of these accounts is to attest that the Apostles were convinced that Jesus had risen from the dead, even though others remained doubtful. Matthew's Gospel confronts this skepticism head-on. In his version of the empty tomb, the chief priests ask Pilate to post guards at Jesus' grave; "otherwise his disciples may go and steal him away, and tell the people, 'he has been raised from the dead' " (Matthew 27:64). Regardless, among the community of followers, the belief was strong. Ultimately this faith in the Resurrection would become the bedrock foundation of Christianity. Paul later wrote to the Corinthians that if Christ had not been raised, then all faith would be in vain (I Corinthians 15:14).

THE APOSTOLIC MISSION

As soon as Jesus ascended into heaven (Luke 24:50), the Apostles were left in disarray. What should they do? Should they spread the teachings of the Kingdom of God, even though their leader, their Messiah, was no longer among them? How could they continue a ministry that had been so closely associated with Jesus' charismatic presence? Should they even stay in Jerusalem, or go back to Galilee? In the end, they decided to return to the room "where they were staying" (Acts 1:1; 13). Here they devoted themselves to meditation and prayer while waiting for some form of divine intervention—for the "promise of the Father," as Jesus had told them (Acts 1:4).

That intervention took place ten days later during the feast of Shavuot ("weeks" in Hebrew, also known as Pentecost, a Greek word meaning "fiftieth," since it occurs seven weeks after Passover, the day after 49 days). Suddenly, their house was filled with "a sound like the rush of a violent wind," while "divided tongues, as of fire appeared among them" (Acts 2:2-3). Now infused with the Holy Spirit, the Apostles broke out of their hiding place and began to preach to the crowds outside.

Thus began the Apostolic mission, the campaign by which the Apostles and their followers would bring the good news of the heavenly Kingdom throughout Judea and, indeed, the Roman world. Peter formulated the purpose of this new mission in three articles of faith. The first one was that Jesus, a man "with deeds of power, wonders and signs," had died on the cross but had risen from the dead. The second was that his resurrection proved that he was indeed the Messiah, the Anointed One, the "Christ" (or Christos in Greek). And third, all who repented their sins and agreed to be baptized in the name of Jesus (the) Christ, would receive the gift of the Holy Spirit (Acts 2:22-39). According to the Book of Acts of the Apostles, as many as 3,000 people agreed to do so on this day alone.

But as we saw previously, the Temple authorities observed the revival of the "Jesus following" with alarm. They had assumed that by killing Jesus, they had also eliminated his movement. In the weeks and months to come, Peter and his fellow Apostles were repeatedly arrested, thrown in prison, and interrogated by Caiaphas and his Sadducee associates. One of their recent converts, a Greek-speaking disciple named Stephen, was denounced to the Sanhedrin for "speaking blasphemous words against Moses and God" and stoned to death (Acts 7:58). The tensions then escalated into an all-out persecution of the

A third-century ampulla, or pilgrim's flask, often used as a souvenir of a Christian pilgrimage, bears the image of St. Menas, an Egyptian saint.

This sestertius with the legend "Judaea Capta" ("Judea Captured") was struck after the Jewish Rebellion in 70 C.E.

Paul may have walked down this colonnaded street in Ephesus, his principal base for two years.

followers of Jesus, and many fled to Cyprus, Phoenicia, and Syria, particularly the city of Antioch on the Orontes.

PAUL OF TARSUS

One of the leaders in charge of this persecution effort was a man named Saul. A highly intelligent and educated Jew from Tarsus in Cilicia (today's southern Turkey), Saul had been present at Stephen's stoning. He then petitioned the priests to let him take his campaign to Damascus, where many Christians had reportedly sought refuge (Acts 9:2).

But on the way to Damascus, something extraordinary happened. Saul experienced an acute change of heart, prompted by a voice that said, "Saul, why do you persecute me?" (Acts 9:4). From that moment on, Saul, now renamed Paul, wholeheartedly devoted himself to spreading the word of Jesus Christ. But his sudden conversion was met with suspicion in Apostolic circles. Many didn't trust him and believed he was simply trying to infiltrate their movement. In response, Paul retreated to his hometown of Tarsus, but was persuaded by a disciple named

Barnabas to join him in Antioch, capital of Roman Syria, to nurture the growth of a Syrian Christian community. It was here, in Antioch, that the term "Christians" (Christianos in Greek) was coined to identify the disciples of Christ (Acts 11:21).

Paul then embarked on the first of three major international campaigns to convert the people of Asia Minor (today's Turkey), as well as Greece and Rome. Along the way, he made an astonishing discovery. He found that while many Jewish communities rejected his message of Jesus as the Messiah, scores of Gentiles were actually quite intrigued. Up to this point, contact with Gentiles had been anathema for most Jews, because non-Jews did not honor the purity laws. But the enthusiasm with which many Gentiles welcomed the words of Jesus could simply not be ignored.

A sixth-century wall painting of martyred saints from Wadi Sarga, Egypt, illustrates the growth of Christianity in North Africa.

Peter had encountered something similar while ministering in Joppa (today's Jaffa). The Apostle had even baptized a Gentile centurion named Cornelius, together with his family (Acts 10:28). But there was an important difference. Peter and the Jerusalem community welcomed only Gentiles who accepted both the Jewish Law and Christian baptism. Paul, however, knew that many Gentiles who were attracted to Christian spirituality had no intention of living as observant Jews as well—including the need to be circumcised and to observe the kosher dietary laws. This raised an important question: Should a convert to Christ also be expected to become Jewish?

For some of the original Apostles, who were mindful of Jesus' strong adherence to Jewish tenets, the answer was an unqualified yes. But Paul disagreed. As he writes in his letter to the Romans, the Jewish Law had been replaced by baptism and faith in Christ. "Real circumcision is a matter of the heart," he writes in his letter to the Romans; "it is spiritual, not literal" (Romans 2:29). While this may not have been Paul's intention, this decision began the dissolution of the early Christian movement from its Jewish roots, laying the foundation for the emergence of Christianity as a religion separate from Judaism.

This head of Constantine I (306–337 c.e.), now at the Capitoline Museum in Rome, once belonged to a colossal statue of the emperor.

OTHER CHRISTIAN MOVEMENTS

Modern research by scholars such as Bart Ehrman and Elaine Pagels has shown that there were actually multiple Christian movements circulating around the Mediterranean, many of which had a very different interpretation of Jesus and his teachings. Since there was no authoritative document that explained the principles of Jesus' doctrine of the Kingdom of God, many of these communities had to rely on oral traditions, which often differed in scope and emphasis. This is why each Gospel sometimes features passages that don't appear in the others. What's more, Paul and the Apostles were not the only ones who were propagating the new faith. There were many others, including soldiers, merchants, and officials, who introduced their families and friends to Christian ideas throughout the empire, without Apostolic guidance.

As a result, different Christian factions began to emerge. One sect believed that deep meditation would ultimately lead to a secret knowledge (*gnosis* in Greek) of God. These Gnostic Christians thought that this was the reason that Jesus spoke in mysterious parables. One such group, the Docetists, believed that Jesus' physical presence had been an illusion and he had always been a divine being. Another group that may have originated in the Jerusalem community, known as the Ebionites, remained faithful to their Jewish roots and believed that Jesus had always been a mortal. The fragmentation of early Christianity was acerbated by the occasional persecution by Roman authorities, as well as the hostile and occasionally violent attitude of the local citizenry.

And yet, despite these considerable obstacles, the Christian ideal continued to spread throughout the Roman Empire, traveling as far as the ancient trade routes of Mesopotamia. Syriac missionaries even carried the Gospel to India, inspired by the Apostle Thomas. By the end of the first century, there were almost 300,000 Christians in Asia Minor alone.

THE FINAL TRIAL

As the Christian movement entered its third century, it experienced its greatest trial. One reason was that Christian worship was very different from pagan ritual. The Christian emphasis on love, regardless of class boundaries, clashed with the norms of a society where classes were rigorously separated. Christians also refused to offer sacrifices to Roman gods or to the reigning emperor. This reinforced the impression that Christianity was a foreign cult, profoundly at odds with Roman interests.

As Rome's power went into decline and the empire suffered numerous barbarian invasions, the hostility toward Christians as an "unpatriotic" sect erupted into open persecution. Emperor Decius (r. 249–251) ordered that all citizens obtain a *libellus,* certified proof of faithful sacrifice to Roman gods, or suffer the punishment of death. During the reign of Emperor Diocletian (r. 284–305), all Christian worship was outlawed. Church leaders were arrested and church buildings destroyed.

And then, in 305, Diocletian decided to retire. This led to a protracted struggle among as many as six claimants to the throne. Six years later, in 312, only two were left standing: Constantine, the son of Constantius I (r. 305–306), and Maxentius, the son of Maximian (r. 284–310). Their armies met at the Milvian Bridge across the river Tiber. On the eve of battle, Constantine had a dream in which he was told to decorate the shields of his soldiers with the monogram of Christ (the Greek letters *chi* and *rho,* the first two letters of the word *Christos*). Another version suggests that Constantine saw a luminescent cross in the sky, blazing with the words *en toutoi nika* ("by this [sign] conquer").

Constantine defeated the army of Maxentius and credited his victory to the God of the Christians. This was the decisive turning point. One year later, Constantine (r. 312–337) issued the Edict of Milan, declaring a policy of religious toleration of all cults, including Christianity. Less than 80 years later, Emperor Theodosius (r. 379–395) issued a decree that outlawed all pagan religions and cults, except Christianity.

In all, it had taken 350 years for the ideas of a rabbi from Nazareth to conquer the world and become the sole religion of the Roman Empire. ■

"The Battle of Ponte Milvio," a fresco in the Vatican Palace, was executed by followers of Raphael (1483–1520) after the artist's death and completed in 1524.

APPENDIX: THE SCRIPTURES

THE FOLLOWING PAGES LIST the books of Hebrew Scripture and their arrangement within the Christian Old Testament, as well as the works of the New Testament, from which this book has cited extensively.

Hebrew Scripture is traditionally organized into three divisions: the Torah, or Law, also known as the Laws of Moses; the Nevi'im, or Prophets; and the Ketuvim, or Writings. In Jesus' lifetime, only the first two divisions were collectively recognized as Scripture. That is why Jesus often refers to the Bible as "the Law and the Prophets" (Luke 16:16). Nevertheless, although the third division was still being formed in the first century C.E., Jesus was most likely familiar with some of these books, specifically the Psalms.

The New Testament literature includes the Book of Acts of the Apostles, which covers the early development of the Christian Church; the Letters or Epistles attributed to Paul; additional Apostolic letters; and the apocalyptic Book of Revelation.

THE HEBREW SCRIPTURES
(TANAKH)

THE LAW *TORAH*	THE PROPHETS *NEVI'IM*	THE WRITINGS *KETUVIM*
Genesis	*Former Prophets:*	Psalms
Exodus	Joshua	Proverbs
Leviticus	Judges	Job
Numbers	Samuel (I and II)	Song of Solomon
Deuteronomy	Kings (I and II)	Ruth
		Lamentations
	Latter Prophets:	Ecclesiastes
	Isaiah	Esther
	Jeremiah	Daniel
	Ezekiel	Ezra-Nehemiah
		Chronicles (I and II)
	Twelve Minor Prophets:	
	Hosea	
	Joel	
	Amos	
	Obadiah	
	Jonah	
	Micah	
	Nahum	
	Habakkuk	
	Zephaniah	
	Haggai	
	Zechariah	
	Malachi	

THE BOOKS OF THE OLD TESTAMENT

Genesis	Isaiah	*Deuterocanonical/ Apocryphal:*
Exodus	Jeremiah	Tobit
Leviticus	Lamentations	Judith
Numbers	Ezekiel	Esther
Deuteronomy	Daniel	The Wisdom of Solomon
Joshua	Hosea	Ecclesiasticus
Judges	Joel	Baruch
Ruth	Amos	Letter of Jeremiah
I Samuel	Obadiah	
II Samuel	Jonah	*Additions to Daniel, including:*
I Kings	Micah	Prayer of Azariah
II Kings	Nahum	Song of Three Jews
I Chronicles	Habakkuk	Susanna
II Chronicles	Zephaniah	Bel and the Dragon
Ezra	Haggai	I Maccabees
Nehemiah	Zechariah	II Maccabees
Esther	Malachi	I Esdras
Job		Prayer of Manasseh
Psalms		Psalm 151
Proverbs		III Maccabees
Ecclesiastes		II Esdras
Song of Solomon		IV Maccabees

THE BOOKS OF THE NEW TESTAMENT

THE GOSPELS	TRADITIONAL ATTRIBUTION	POSSIBLE DATE
Matthew	Matthew (Levi)	75–90 C.E.
Mark	Mark, Peter's interpreter	66–70 C.E.
Luke	Luke, Paul's attendant	75–90 C.E.
John	John (disciple)	85–100 C.E.

ACTS	TRADITIONAL ATTRIBUTION	POSSIBLE DATE
Acts of the Apostles	Luke, Paul's attendant	75–90 C.E.

PAULINE EPISTLES	TRADITIONAL ATTRIBUTION	POSSIBLE DATE
Letter to the Romans	Paul	56–57 C.E.
First Letter to the Corinthians	Paul	54–55 C.E.
Second Letter to the Corinthians	Paul	55–56 C.E.
Letter to the Galatians	Paul	50–56 C.E.
Letter to the Ephesians	Paul (pseudonymous)	80–95 C.E.
Letter to the Philippians	Paul	54–55 C.E.
Letter to the Colossians	Paul	57–61 C.E.
First Letter to the Thessalonians	Paul	50–51 C.E.
Second Letter to the Thessalonians	Paul	50–51 C.E.
First Letter to Timothy	Paul (pseudonymous)	90–110 C.E.
Second Letter to Timothy	Paul (pseudonymous)	90–110 C.E.
Letter to Titus	Paul (pseudonymous)	90–110 C.E.
Letter to Philemon	Paul	54–55 C.E.
Letter to the Hebrews	Paul (pseudonymous)	60–95 C.E.

GENERAL EPISTLES	TRADITIONAL ATTRIBUTION	POSSIBLE DATE
Letter to James	James, brother of Jesus	50–70 C.E.
First Letter of Peter	Peter (pseudonymous)	70–90 C.E.
Second Letter of Peter	Peter (pseudonymous)	80–90 C.E.
First Letter of John	John (disciple)	ca 100 C.E.
Second Letter of John	John (disciple)	ca 100 C.E.
Third Letter of John	John (disciple)	ca 100 C.E.
Letter of Jude	Jude, brother of Jesus	45–65 C.E.

PROPHECY	TRADITIONAL ATTRIBUTION	POSSIBLE DATE
Revelation	John (disciple)	70–100 C.E.

FURTHER READING

JESUS BIOGRAPHY

Aslan, Reza. *Zealot: The Life and Times of Jesus of Nazareth.* Random House, 2013.

Beilby, James K., and Paul R. Eddy. *The Historical Jesus: Five Views.* InterVarsity Press, 2009.

Borg, Marcus J. *Jesus: Uncovering the Life, Teachings, and Relevance of a Religious Revolutionary.* HarperSanFrancisco, 2006.

Charlesworth, James H., ed. *Jesus' Jewishness: Exploring the Place of Jesus in Early Judaism.* Crossroad, 1991.

Chilton, Bruce. *Rabbi Jesus.* Doubleday, 2000.

Crossan, John Dominic. *Jesus: A Revolutionary Biography.* HarperCollins, 1994.

———. *Who Killed Jesus? Exposing the Roots of Anti-Semitism in the Gospel Story of the Death of Jesus.* HarperCollins, 1995.

Crossan, John Dominic, and Jonathan L. Reed. *Excavating Jesus: Beneath the Stones, Behind the Texts.* HarperCollins, 2001.

Ehrman, Bart. *Jesus: Apocalyptic Prophet of the New Millennium.* Oxford University Press, 1999.

Evans, Craig. *Jesus and His World: The Archaeological Evidence.* Westminster John Knox Press, 2012.

Fredriksen, Paula. *Jesus of Nazareth, King of the Jews.* Knopf, 1999.

Gibson, Shimon. *The Final Days of Jesus: The Archaeological Evidence.* HarperOne, 2009.

Horsley, Richard A. *Jesus and Empire: The Kingdom of God and the New World Disorder.* Fortress Press, 2003.

Isbouts, Jean-Pierre. *In the Footsteps of Jesus.* National Geographic Society, 2013.

Levine, Amy-Jill, ed. *Historical Jesus in Context.* Princeton University Press, 2006.

McCane, Byron R. *Roll Back the Stone: Death and Burial in the World of Jesus.* Trinity Press International, 2003.

Meier, John P. *A Marginal Jew: Rethinking the Historical Jesus.* 3 vols. Doubleday, 1994.

Porter, J. R. *Jesus Christ: The Jesus of History, the Christ of Faith.* Barnes and Noble, 1999.

Reed, Jonathan L. *The HarperCollins Visual Guide to the New Testament.* HarperCollins, 2007.

Sanders, E. P. *Jesus and Judaism.* Fortress Press, 1985.

Senior, Donald. *Jesus: A Gospel Portrait.* Paulist Press, 1992.

Stemberger, Günter. *Jewish Contemporaries of Jesus: Pharisees, Sadducees, Essenes.* Fortress Press, 1995.

Theissen, Gerd, and Annete Merz. *The Historical Jesus: A Comprehensive Guide.* Fortress Press, 1997.

Wright, N. T. *Jesus and the Victory of God.* Fortress Press, 1996.

THE NEW TESTAMENT, THE MISHNAH, AND OTHER SOURCES

Chilton, Bruce, and Deirdre J. Good. *Studying the New Testament.* Fortress Press, 2009.

Danby, Herbert. *Tractate Sanhedrin, Mishnah and Tosefta, with Commentary.* Macmillan, 1919.

Humphrey, Hugh M. *From Q to "Secret" Mark: A Composition History of the Earliest Narrative Theology.* T&T Clark, 2006.

Kee, Howard Clark. *The Beginnings of Christianity: An Introduction to the New Testament.* T&T Clark, 2005.

Kloppenborg Verbin, John S. *Excavating Q: The History and Setting of the Sayings Gospel.* T&T Clark, 2000.

Levine, Amy-Jill, and Marc Zvi Brettler. *The Jewish Annotated New Testament.* Oxford University Press, 2011.

Mack, Burton L. *The Lost Gospel: The Book of Q and Christian Origins.* HarperSanFrancisco, 1993.

Moloney, Francis J. *The Gospel of John: Text and Context.* Brill, 2005.

Mullen, J. Patrick. *Dining with Pharisees.* Liturgical Press, 2004.

Neusner, Jacob. *Introduction to Rabbinic Literature.* Doubleday, 1999.

———. *The Mishnah: A New Translation.* Yale University Press, 1988.

Porter, Stanley, ed. *Hearing the Old Testament in the New Testament.* Eerdmans, 2006.

——. *Paul and his Theology*. Brill, 2006.

Resseguie, James L. *Narrative Criticism of the New Testament: An Introduction*. Baker, 2005.

Sanders, E. P. *Jewish Law from Jesus to the Mishnah: Five Studies*. Trinity Press International, 1990.

Schiffman, Lawrence H. *Reclaiming the Dead Sea Scrolls: The History of Judaism, the Background of Christianity, the Lost Library of Qumran*. Doubleday, 1995.

Valantasis, Richard. *The New Q: A Fresh Translation with Commentary*. T&T Clark, 2005.

Whiston, William. *The Complete Works of Josephus*. Kregel, 1981.

CULTURE AND ARCHAEOLOGY OF GALILEE

Arnal, William E. *Jesus and the Village Scribes: Galilean Conflicts and the Setting of Q*. First Fortress Press, 2001.

Chancey, Mark A. *Greco-Roman Culture and the Galilee of Jesus*. Cambridge University Press, 2005.

——. *The Myth of a Gentile Galilee*. Cambridge University Press, 2002.

Finegan, Jack. *The Archaeology of the New Testament*. Princeton University Press, 1992

Goodman, Martin. *State and Society in Roman Galilee, A.D. 132–212*. Rowman and Allanheld, 1983.

Hezser, Catherine. *Jewish Literacy in Roman Palestine*. Mohr Siebeck, 2001.

Horsley, Richard A. *Bandits, Prophets, and Messiahs: Popular Movements in the Time of Jesus*. Trinity Press, 1999.

——. *Galilee: History, Politics, People*. Trinity Press, 1995.

——. *Jesus and the Spiral of Violence: Popular Jewish Resistance in Roman Palestine*. First Fortress Press, 1993.

Reed, Jonathan. *Archaeology and the Galilean Jesus: A Re-Examination of the Evidence*. Trinity Press International, 2002.

Runesson, A., D. D. Binder, and B. Olsson. *The Ancient Synagogue from Its Origins to 200 C.E.: A Source Book*. Brill, 2008.

Zvi, Gal. *Lower Galilee During the Iron Age*. Eisenbrauns, 1992.

ROMAN PALESTINE: ECONOMY AND SOCIETY

Archer, Léonie J. *Her Price Is Beyond Rubies: The Jewish Woman in Graeco-Roman Palestine*. JSOT Press, 1990.

Duncan-Jones, Richard. *Money and Government in the Roman Empire*. Cambridge University Press, 1994.

——. *Structure and Scale in the Roman Economy*. Cambridge University Press, 1990.

Edwards, D. *Religion and Society in Roman Palestine: Old Questions, New Answers*. Routledge, 2004.

Evans, Jane DeRose. *The Coins and the Hellenistic, Roman, and Byzantine Economy of Palestine*. American Schools of Oriental Research, 2006.

Fager, Jeffrey A. *Land Tenure and the Biblical Jubilee: Uncovering Hebrew Ethics Through the Sociology of Knowledge*. Sheffield Academic Press, 1993.

Fiensy, David A. *The Social History of Palestine in the Herodian Period: The Land Is Mine*. Edwin Mellen Press, 1991.

Finley, M. I. *The Ancient Economy*. Hogarth Press, 1985.

Garnsey, Peter. *Cities, Peasants, and Food in Classical Antiquity*. Cambridge University Press, 1998.

——. *Social Status and Legal Privilege in the Roman Empire*. Oxford: Clarendon Press, 1970.

Hamel, Gildas. *Poverty and Charity in Roman Palestine, First Three Centuries C.E.* University of California Press, 1990.

Hanson, K. C., and Douglas E. Oakman. *Palestine in the Time of Jesus: Social Structures and Social Conflicts*. Fortress Press, 1998

Magness, Jodi. *Stone and Dung, Oil and Spit: Jewish Life in the Time of Jesus*. Eerdmans, 2011.

Oakman, Douglas E. *Jesus and the Economic Questions of His Day*. Edwin Mellen Press, 1986.

Pastor, Jack. *Land and Economy in Ancient Palestine*. Routledge, 1997.

Safrai, Ze'ev. *The Economy of Roman Palestine*. Routledge, 1994.

Wallace, Sherman LeRoy. *Taxation in Egypt from Augustus to Diocletian*. Greenwood Press, 1969.

POLITICAL HISTORY OF ROMAN PALESTINE

Elsner, Jas. *Imperial Rome and Christian Triumph*. Oxford University Press, 1998.

Grant, Robert M. *Augustus to Constantine: The Emergence of Christianity in the Roman World*. Harper SanFrancisco, 1970.

Ilan, Tal. *Jewish Women in Greco-Roman Palestine*. Hendrickson, 1996.

Jeffers, James S. *The Greco-Roman World of the New Testament Era: Exploring the Background of Early Christianity*. InterVarsity Press, 1999.

Mommsen, Theodor. *A History of Rome Under the Emperors*. Routledge, 1996.

Netzer, Ehud. *The Architecture of Herod the Great Builder*. Baker, 2006.

Richardson, Peter. *Herod: King of the Jews and Friend of the Romans*. University of South Carolina Press, 1996.

Roller, Duane W. *The Building Program of Herod the Great*. University of California Press, 1998.

Sperber, Daniel. *The City in Roman Palestine*. Oxford University Press, 1998.

Udoh, Fabian E. *To Caesar What Is Caesar's: Tribute, Taxes, and Imperial Administration in Early Roman Palestine (63 B.C.E.–70 C.E.)*. Brown Judaic Studies, 2005.

EARLY CHRISTIANITY

Ehrman, Bart D. *Lost Christianities: The Battles for Scripture and the Faiths We Never Knew*. Oxford University Press, 2003.

Elsner, Jas. *Imperial Rome and Christian Triumph*. Oxford University Press, 1998.

Grant, Robert M. *Augustus to Constantine: The Emergence of Christianity in the Roman World*. New York: Harper & Row, 1970.

Isbouts, Jean-Pierre. *The Story of Christianity: A Chronicle of Christian Civilization from Ancient Rome to Today*. National Geographic Society, 2014.

Jeffers, James S. *The Greco-Roman World of the New Testament Era: Exploring the Background of Early Christianity*. InterVarsity Press, 1999.

Kasser, Rodolphe, Marvin Meyer, and Gregor Wurst. *The Gospel of Judas*. National Geographic Society, 2006.

Kee, Howard Clark. *The Beginnings of Christianity: An Introduction to the New Testament*. T&T Clark, 2005.

Mullin, Robert B. *A Short World History of Christianity*. Westminster John Knox Press, 2008.

Neusner, Jacob. *Judaism When Christianity Began: A Survey of Belief and Practice*. Westminster John Knox Press, 2002.

Pagels, Elaine. *Beyond Belief: The Secret Gospel of Thomas*. Random House, 2003.

———. *The Gnostic Gospels*. New York: Random House, 1979.

Porter, Stanley, ed. *Paul and His Theology*. Brill, 2006.

Robinson, J. M. (gen. ed.). *The Nag Hammadi Library*. E. J. Brill, 1977.

ABOUT THE AUTHOR

DR. JEAN-PIERRE ISBOUTS is a historian and doctoral professor at Fielding Graduate University in Santa Barbara, California. He has published widely on the origins of Judaism, Christianity, and Islam, including the best sellers *The Biblical World*, published by the National Geographic Society in 2007, and *In the Footsteps of Jesus,* published by the National Geographic Society in 2012. His other books include *Young Jesus: Restoring the Lost Years of a Social Activist and Religious Dissident* (Sterling, 2008); *From Moses to Muhammad: The Shared Origins of Judaism, Christianity and Islam* (Pantheon, 2010); *Who's Who in the Bible,* published by the National Geographic Society in 2013; and *The Story of Christianity,* published by the National Geographic Society in 2014. An award-winning filmmaker, Dr. Isbouts has also produced a number of programs, including "Charlton Heston's Voyage Through the Bible" (GoodTimes, 1998), "The Quest for Peace" (Hallmark, 2003), and "Young Jesus" (PBS stations, 2008). He lives in Santa Monica, California, where he and his wife, Cathie, serve as Eucharistic ministers at St. Monica Church. His website is www.jpisbouts.org.

BOARD OF ADVISERS

BRUCE CHILTON, a scholar of early Christianity and Judaism, wrote the first commentary on the Aramaic version of Isaiah *(The Isaiah Targum)* and studies that analyze Jesus in his Judaic context, including the best-selling *Rabbi Jesus.* He has taught in Europe at the Universities of Cambridge, Sheffield, and Münster and in the United States at Yale University and Bard College.

STEVEN FELDMAN works with early-career scholars in helping them transform dissertations into publishable academic books. Previously he served as web editor and director of educational programs for the Biblical Archaeology Society and managing editor of both *Biblical Archaeology Review* and *Bible Review,* published by the Society.

REV. DONALD SENIOR, C.P., is president emeritus and professor of New Testament at Catholic Theological Union in Chicago, the largest Catholic school of theology in the United States. He has published extensively on biblical topics, with numerous books and articles for both scholarly and popular audiences. He has served the last three popes as a member of the international Pontifical Biblical Commission.

ACKNOWLEDGMENTS

This book is the culmination of nearly 20 years of research in the Gospel literature and the figure of Jesus in particular. As both an archaeologist and a historian, I am fascinated by the intersection of culture and faith, of history and hope, in the shaping of these beautiful stories. Once again I owe a deep gratitude to Lisa Thomas, head of National Geographic's Book Division, and Daneen Goodwin, head of the Direct Marketing division, for their ideas about the concept of this book and for their strong and unerring support throughout. In the same breath, I must thank my wonderful editor, Barbara Payne, on this, our fourth book, together. Many thanks also to the superb team for this book, including Sanaa Akkach for her beautiful and sensitive layouts, Matt Propert for his excellent photo research, Carl Mehler for his wonderful maps, and Beverly Miller for her gentle copyedit.

I have profited from the research of many other scholars, whose works are too numerous to mention. In the "Further Reading" section, I have identified works that were of particular value in the writing of this book and that I recommend to readers for further study.

I also owe a debt of gratitude to those who read the manuscript and offered many helpful comments, including Monsignor Lloyd Torgerson at St. Monica Church in Santa Monica; Marian Galanis; Bianca Martino; and Philip Isbouts.

Thanks are also due to my agent, Peter Miller, and his staff at Global Lion Intellectual Property Management. And finally, I must express my deepest gratitude to my wonderful wife, Cathie, who continues to be my patient muse during our many travels through the Middle East, including our most recent journey through Israel, Egypt, Jordan, and Oman, during which I began writing this book.

ILLUSTRATIONS CREDITS

Images from Pantheon Studios, Inc. except as noted below:

Front cover: (desert) science photo/Shutterstock; (figures) Michael Chaloupka/Dreamstime.com; (sky) Roman Tsubin/Shutterstock. Back cover (left to right): Duccio di Buoninsegna (ca 1278–1318)/Duomo, Siena, Italy/Bridgeman Images; Chris Anderson; Courtesy of Gyozo Voros, Hungarian Academy of Arts.

4, Alan Bailey/Getty Images; 11, Torah scroll (wood & parchment), German School, (15th century)/Private Collection/Photo © Zev Radovan/Bridgeman Images; 16, "Announcement to Zechariah," eighth century (fragment of fresco by Benevento School of miniature), apse of Church of Santa Sofia (UNESCO World Heritage List, 2011), Benevento, Campania, Italy, eighth century/De Agostini Picture Library/A. Dagli Orti/Bridgeman Images; 17, Model reconstruction of the Nicanor gate in Jerusalem in 66 A.D. viewed from the Women's Court (photo)/The Israel Museum, Jerusalem, Israel/Holyland Tourism 1992, Ltd./Bridgeman Images; 18, Jerusalem in her Grandeur, engraved by Charles Mottram (1807–1876) 1860 (engraving), Selous, Henry Courtney (1811–1890) (after)/Private Collection/The Stapleton Collection/Bridgeman Images; 19 (UP), Richard Nowitz/National Geographic Creative; 20, Hong Nian Zhang/National Geographic Creative; 21, Window w6 depicting Pharisees in the Synagogue (stained glass), French School, (16th century)/Church of St. Madeleine, Troyes, France/Bridgeman Images; 22-23, Italy, Florence, Santa Maria Novella, Main Chapel or Tornabuoni Chapel, Annunciation of Angel to Zechariah, by Domenico Ghirlandaio (1449–1494), Detail/De Agostini Picture Library/Bardazzi/Bridgeman Images; 25, "The Annunciation" (tempera on panel) (detail of 225657), Lippi, Filippo (ca 1406–1469) (and workshop)/Corsham Court, Wiltshire/Bridgeman Images; 28, "The Annunciation, detail of the Archangel Gabriel, from San Martino della Scala," 1481 (fresco mounted on panel), Botticelli, Sandro (Alessandro di Mariano di Vanni Filipepi) (1444/5–1510)/Galleria degli Uffizi, Florence, Italy/Bridgeman Images; 31, Scala/Art Resource, NY; 32, Richard Nowitz/National Geographic Creative; 33, The Hylle Jewel, in the form of a crowned Lombardic initial M with Annunciation figures, late 14th century (silver-gilt set with rubies, diamond, emerald, and pearls), French School (14th century) (attr. to)/© Courtesy of the Warden and Scholars of New College, Oxford/Bridgeman Images; 34 (UP), Olaf Simon/iStockphoto; 34 (LO), Hanan Isachar/Godong/Corbis; 36-37, "Visitation," from the predella of the Annunciation Alterpiece, ca 1430–1432 (tempera & gold on panel), Angelico, Fra (Guido di Pietro) (ca 1387–1455)/Prado, Madrid, Spain/Bridgeman Images; 39, Scala/Art Resource, NY; 41, Chris Anderson/National Geographic Creative; 42 (UP), Tim UR/Shutterstock; 43, Plaque: "The Journey to Bethlehem," ca 1100–1120 (ivory), Romanesque (12th century)/Cleveland Museum of Art, Ohio, U.S.A./Leonard C. Hanna, Jr. Fund/Bridgeman Images; 46, Medic Image/Getty Images; 47, "Adoration of the Magi," ca 1305 (for detail see 67136), Giotto di Bondone (ca 1266–1337)/Scrovegni (Arena) Chapel, Padua, Italy/Bridgeman Images; 48 (LO), Michael Melford/National Geographic Creative; 49, NASA/JPL-Caltech/STScI; 53, "The Massacre of the Innocents," detail from The Grabow Altarpiece, 1379–1383 (tempera on panel), Master Bertram of Minden (ca 1345–ca 1415)/Hamburger Kunsthalle, Hamburg, Germany/Bridgeman Images; 54, "The Dream of St. Joseph," ca 1535 (oil on panel), Juan de Borgona, (ca 1470–ca 1535)/Museo Catedralicio, Cuenca, Spain/Bridgeman Images; 55, Richard Nowitz/National Geographic Creative; 56, Erich Lessing/Art Resource, NY; 57 (UP), Coins of Herod the Great (metal), Jewish School (first century B.C.)/Private Collection/Photo © Zev Radovan/Bridgeman Images; 57 (LO), Courtesy of Gyozo Voros, Hungarian Academy of Arts; 58 (UP), Erich Lessing/Art Resource, NY; 63, "Circumcision of Jesus," right panel of Champmol Altarpiece, 1393–1399, by Melchior Broederlam (ca 1355–1411), tempera on panel, 167x125 cm/De Agostini Picture Library/G. Dagli Orti Bridgeman Images; 66, "The Presentation in the Temple," from the predella of the Annunciation Altarpiece (tempera and gold on canvas), Angelico, Fra (Guido di Pietro) (ca 1387–1455)/Prado, Madrid, Spain/Bridgeman Images; 67, Grinding wheel, Bethany, Judea (photo)/Bridgeman Images; 69, "St. Joseph, the Carpenter" (oil on canvas), Tour, Georges de la (1593–1652)/Musée des Beaux-Arts et d'Archéologie, Besancon, France/Bridgeman Images; 72, Annie Griffiths; 73 (LO), Anna Kucherova/Shutterstock; 74-75, Erich Lessing/Art Resource, NY; 77, "Christ Disputing With the Scribes," detail from "Episodes From Christ's Passion and Resurrection," reverse surface of The Maestà of Duccio Altarpiece in the Cathedral of Siena, 1308–1311, by Duccio di Buoninsegna (ca 1255–pre-1319), tempera on wood/De Agostini Picture Library/G. Nimatallah/Bridgeman Images; 80 (UP), akg-images/Bible Land Pictures/Z. Radovan; 80 (LO), "Jesus Found in the Temple," illustration for The Life of Christ, ca 1886–1894 (w/c & gouache on paperboard), Tissot, James Jacques Joseph (1836–1902)/Brooklyn Museum of Art, New York, U.S.A./Bridgeman Images; 81, "Jesus' dispute with doctors in Temple," detail of relief decorations on frontal from reliquary of Brescia, ivory, 22x32x25 cm, Italy, fourth century/Museo Civico Cristiano, Brescia, Italy/De Agostini Picture Library/Bridgeman Images; 82, Balage Balogh/Art Resource, NY; 84-85, "Jesus With the Doctors," from a series of Scenes of the New Testament (fresco), Barna da Siena (fl. 1350–55)/Collegiata, San Gimignano, Italy/Bridgeman Images; 87, "The Baptism of Christ," ca 1305 (fresco), Giotto di Bondone (ca 1266–1337)/Scrovegni (Arena) Chapel, Padua, Italy/Bridgeman Images; 90, "John the Baptist" (oil on panel), Ugolino di Nerio, (fl. 1317–1327)/Muzeum Narodowe, Warsaw, Poland/Bridgeman Images; 93 (UP), Olga Popova/Shutterstock; 94, Baptism of Christ, surrounded by the Twelve Apostles (mosaic), Byzantine School, (sixth century)/Baptistry of Ariani, Ravenna, Italy Bridgeman Images; 95, De Agostini/I. Hanan/Getty Images; 97 (UP), Section from the Psalms Scrolls, Qumran cave 11, ca 30–50 (parchment)/The Israel Museum, Jerusalem, Israel/Bridgeman Images; 101, "The Calling of the Apostles Peter and Andrew," 1308/1311 (tempera on panel), Duccio di Buoninsegna, (ca 1278–1318)/National Gallery of Art, Washington DC, U.S.A./Bridgeman Images; 103, Thomas Nebbia/National Geographic Creative; 105, V&A Images, London/Art Resource, NY; 106, Philip Sharp/Alamy; 107 (LO), Olga Popova/Shutterstock; 108 (UP), Roman gold aureus coin showing Emperor Tiberius, A.D. 12–37 (gold), Roman (first century A.D.)/Private Collection/Photo © Neil Holmes/Bridgeman Images; 109, Nicolò Orsi Battaglin/Art Resource, NY; 110, Gianni Dagli Orti/The Art Archive at Art Resource, NY; 112-113, "The Marriage Feast at Cana," ca 1305 (fresco) (for detail see 102732), Giotto di Bondone (ca 1266–1337)/Scrovegni (Arena) Chapel, Padua, Italy/Bridgeman Images; 115, Julian Kumar/Godong/Corbis; 118, "Christ with the Twelve Apostles" (ivory), Byzantine School (sixth century)/Musée des Beaux-Arts, Dijon, France/Bridgeman Images; 119 (UP), Robert Hoetink/Alamy; 121 (UP), Prophet Isaiah (mosaic), right of lunette, south wall of presbytery, Basilica of San Vitale (UNESCO World Heritage List, 1996), Ravenna, Emilia-Romagna, Italy. Detail. Sixth century/De Agostini Picture Library/A. de Gregorio/Bridgeman Images; 122, Nicolò Orsi Battaglini/Art Resource, NY; 123, The Great Isaiah Scroll, columns 28-30, Qumram Cave I, ca 100 B.C. (parchment)/The Israel Museum, Jerusalem, Israel/Shrine of the Book/Photo © The Israel Museum, by Ardon Bar Hama/Bridgeman Images; 125, Erich Lessing/Art Resource, NY; 126-127, Fine Art Images/Heritage Image/age fotostock; 129, Byzantine School/Getty Images; 130, Coffer of the Beatitudes. Spain/Photo © Tarker/Bridgeman Images; 131, Reinhard Marscha/Getty Images; 132, "The Sermon on the Mount," 1442 (fresco), Angelico, Fra (Guido di Pietro) (ca 1387–1455)/Museo di San Marco dell'Angelico, Florence, Italy/Bridgeman Images; 133, Alfredo Dagli Orti/The Art Archive at Art Resource, NY/Art Resource, NY; 135, The Trustees of the British Museum/Art Resource, NY; 136 (UP), Erich Lessing/Art Resource, NY; 137, Erich Lessing/Art Resource, NY; 138, The Maestà, front, 1308–1311 (tempera on panel), Duccio di Buoninsegna, (ca 1278–1318)/Duomo, Siena, Italy/Mondadori Portfolio/Electa/Antonio Quattrone/Bridgeman Images; 143, Alfredo Dagli Orti/Art Resource, NY; 145, Annie Griffiths/National

INDEX

Jesus: An Illustrated Life
Jean-Pierre Isbouts

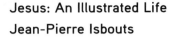

Published by the National Geographic Society
Gary E. Knell, *President and Chief Executive Officer*
John M. Fahey, *Chairman of the Board*
Declan Moore, *Chief Media Officer*
Chris Johns, *Chief Content Officer*

Prepared by the Book Division
Hector Sierra, *Senior Vice President and General Manager*
Lisa Thomas, *Senior Vice President and Editorial Director*
Jonathan Halling, *Creative Director*
Marianne R. Koszorus, *Design Director*
R. Gary Colbert, *Production Director*
Jennifer A. Thornton, *Director of Managing Editorial*
Susan S. Blair, *Director of Photography*
Meredith C. Wilcox, *Director, Administration and Rights Clearance*

Staff for This Book
Barbara Payne, *Editor*
Sanaa Akkach, *Art Director*
Matt Propert, *Photo Editor*
Carl Mehler, *Director of Maps*
Matthew W. Chwastyk, *Cartographer*
Grassroots Graphics, *Design and Production*
Marshall Kiker, *Associate Managing Editor*
Judith Klein, *Senior Production Editor*
Lisa A. Walker, *Production Manager*
Constance Roellig, *Rights Clearance Specialist*
Katie Olsen, *Design Production Specialist*
Nicole Miller, *Design Production Assistant*
Darrick McRae, *Manager, Production Services*
Rebekah Cain, *Imaging Technician*

Your purchase supports our nonprofit work and makes you part of our global community. Thank you for sharing our belief in the power of science, exploration and storytelling to change the world. To activate your member benefits, complete your free membership profile at natgeo.com/joinnow.

The National Geographic Society is one of the world's largest nonprofit scientific and educational organizations. Founded in 1888 to "increase and diffuse geographic knowledge," the member-supported Society works to inspire people to care about the planet. Through its online community, members can get closer to explorers and photographers, connect with other members around the world, and help make a difference. National Geographic reflects the world through its magazines, television programs, films, music and radio, books, DVDs, maps, exhibitions, live events, school publishing programs, interactive media, and merchandise. *National Geographic* magazine, the Society's official journal, published in English and 38 local-language editions, is read by more than 60 million people each month. The National Geographic Channel reaches 440 million households in 171 countries in 38 languages. National Geographic Digital Media receives more than 25 million visitors a month. National Geographic has funded more than 10,000 scientific research, conservation, and exploration projects and supports an education program promoting geography literacy. For more information, visit www.nationalgeographic.com.

For more information, please call 1-800-NGS LINE (647-5463) or write to the following address:

National Geographic Society
1145 17th Street NW
Washington, D.C. 20036-4688 U.S.A.

For information about special discounts for bulk purchases, please contact National Geographic Books Special Sales: ngspecsales@ngs.org

For rights or permissions inquiries, please contact National Geographic Books Subsidiary Rights: ngbookrights@ngs.org

Library of Congress Cataloging-in-Publication Data

Isbouts, Jean-Pierre.
  Jesus : an illustrated life / Jean-Pierre Isbouts. -- 1st [edition].
    pages cm
  Includes bibliographical references and index.
  ISBN 978-1-4262-1568-1 (hardcover : alk. paper) -- ISBN 978-1-4262-1569-8 (hardcover (deluxe edition) : alk. paper)
  1. Jesus Christ--Biography. I. Title.
  BT301.3.I84 2015
  232.9'01--dc23
                                        2015012827

Printed in the United States of America
15/QGT-CML/1